MISFIRE

MISFIRE

Inside
the Downfall
of the NRA

TIM MAK

DUTTON

DUTTON

An imprint of Penguin Random House LLC
penguinrandomhouse.com

LIBRARY OF CONGRESS CATALOGING-IN-PUBLICATION DATA
has been applied for.

ISBN 9781524746452 (hardcover)
ISBN 9781524746476 (ebook)

Printed in the United States of America
1   3   5   7   9   10   8   6   4   2

BOOK DESIGN BY KATY RIEGEL

To David Frum, Danielle Crittenden Frum, and Noah Shachtman—who taught me how to dig

Contents

Author's Note   ix

INTRODUCTION   1

CHAPTER 1   Wayne   7

CHAPTER 2   "Just a Volunteer"   18

CHAPTER 3   The NRA's Fiefdoms   27

CHAPTER 4   The NRA Before Sandy Hook   43

CHAPTER 5   The NRA's Lobbying Animal House   54

CHAPTER 6   Sandy Hook   57

CHAPTER 7   Manchin-Toomey Collapses   67

CHAPTER 8   The Rise of Everytown   82

CHAPTER 9   Wayne's Posse and NRA HQ   93

CHAPTER 10   Maria Butina and the Roots of NRA-Russia   111

CHAPTER 11   The Obama Years   123

CHAPTER 12   Operation Second Pozner   137

CHAPTER 13 Ackerman McQueen Power Grows   149

CHAPTER 14 Moscow Bound   162

CHAPTER 15 Butina's Back Channel   174

CHAPTER 16 The NRA and the 2016 Campaign   180

CHAPTER 17 Butina's Downfall   190

CHAPTER 18 The Start of the End   200

CHAPTER 19 Whistleblowers and an Angry Mother   212

CHAPTER 20 Brewer Replaces Ackerman McQueen   220

CHAPTER 21 The Colonel   230

CHAPTER 22 Wednesday, April 24, 2019   251

CHAPTER 23 The Weekend from Hell   262

CHAPTER 24 Rebellion   271

CHAPTER 25 Lawfare   280

CHAPTER 26 The AG Strikes   288

CHAPTER 27 Bankruptcy   291

Acknowledgments   299
Notes   301
Index   363
About the Author   372

Author's Note

This book is the product of roughly 120 interviews over the course of nearly three years. The vast majority of those interviewed have been employed by the National Rifle Association or its contractors.

I offered many sources anonymity so that they could speak frankly about their experiences and observations—many had concerns that they could face professional consequences or legal risks as a result of the myriad investigations and lawsuits that the NRA is entangled in. These interviews are not marked in the endnotes.

I also relied on thousands of pages of leaked documents that were provided to me by a variety of sources. These include confidential depositions, internal NRA emails, and closely held NRA documents.

Quotes in this book are sometimes reconstructed based on source recollections but more often rely on confidential sworn depositions, which I have obtained and marked in the endnotes. The confidential sworn depositions were taken as part of litigation between the NRA and one of its contractors, Ackerman McQueen, and filed under seal in the U.S. District Court for the Northern District of Texas.

I've made an attempt to reach out to all the major players in this saga. Wayne and Susan LaPierre, whom I tried to contact through the NRA, the NRA's primary law firm, and Wayne's personal lawyer, did not respond to requests to be interviewed. Further, they did not respond to a detailed list of questions posed to them. The NRA did not respond to a list of questions related to this book.

MISFIRE

Introduction

"You're a big boy, right?"

Wayne LaPierre froze. He was the chief executive officer and executive vice president of the National Rifle Association, one of the most powerful political organizations in America. Normally a person in his position, with his influence, wouldn't tolerate being spoken to this way.

Yet in the fall of 2019, everything was falling apart for the NRA. For years, Wayne had feted celebrities and wealthy businesspeople, taken lavish vacations and safaris, clothed himself in designer suits and ties, and enriched his family—largely thanks to his nonprofit organization.

When details of this wanton corruption had burst into the news that spring, Wayne had concocted a false narrative that he and his lawyers thought could exculpate him: his total blindness to the misdeeds he himself had set in motion. He knew nothing about the misconduct within the NRA. He knew nothing about the bills he had authorized. He knew nothing about the contracts he had signed off on. He, the head executive of America's most powerful advocacy group, had been the hapless victim of manipulative friends and conspiratorial foes.

They forced him to buy the clothes on solo trips to a luxurious menswear store on Rodeo Drive in Beverly Hills. Security threats forced him to take the private jets—and his extended family too, even when he was not with them. The NRA's ad agency forced him to shop for a mansion in Dallas with his wife. Business requirements forced him to take trips to the Bahamas, with the use of a private yacht. He had never wanted any of it, and in fact, Wayne's supremely ethical judgment and quick thinking had actually saved the NRA from ruin!

In the process of defending himself, he would leave behind everyone who had brought him there. "If I lose every friend," he defiantly said, "I'm prepared to do it."

His insistence on saving himself—over his cause, his friends, and the organization to which he had devoted his adult life— would be taken poorly by those he had betrayed. It would lead, as these corporate blood disputes so often do, to high-priced lawyers. He was now surrounded by a pack of them, sitting uncomfortably in a boardroom at Schertler & Onorato, a law firm specializing in litigation.

Inside the law firm's imposing concrete-and-granite offices in downtown Washington, D.C., one of these lawyers was mocking him. At the time, among the most outrageous public claims about his misconduct related to some six figures' worth of Italian luxury wear from the Beverly Hills boutique Zegna. Wayne had taken the clothing and charged it to an outside advertising agency. He had been such a common guest at the Beverly Hills store that he had a regular sales rep named Noah. Called to account for this, he blamed the agency, Ackerman McQueen, for forcing him to make the purchases.

"You're a big boy, right?" asked David Schertler, an attorney for Ackerman McQueen, which had for decades been the NRA's symbiotic public relations firm.

"Yes," LaPierre managed.

"You're close to 70?"

"Yes."

"You can make your own decisions about what clothes you need and what clothes you don't need. You've been dressing yourself now for a number of years."

It was a stinging rebuke. And Wayne was keenly aware of his age. At that moment, he might have thought about his own mortality. After all, his father had been diagnosed with Alzheimer's at the age of seventy-five. He could have retired years ago, and NRA insiders believe that he contemplated it seven years prior, just before the shootings at Sandy Hook Elementary School in Newtown, Connecticut, changed the trajectory of his life and the National Rifle Association forever.

In the dark wake of the shootings at Sandy Hook, the NRA made a strategic choice: to double down. It took part in negotiations over the Manchin-Toomey universal background check bill, only to withdraw at the last minute and mobilize NRA supporters against the legislation. In the aftermath, it marched into the conservative culture war. It shifted further to the right, embracing Republicans entirely and abandoning even the pretense of outreach to Democrats. This would work for a time, during the Obama years, but a crash was coming.

The NRA's decline started with its greatest success: the election of President Donald Trump. It had spent tens of millions of dollars to ensure his election over Hillary Clinton but had no plan for what to do after it succeeded. The NRA sells fear: with Barack Obama gone and no imminent threat to fundraise off of, the cash began to dry up.

Meanwhile, its opponents were mobilizing. The failure of gun reform legislation after Sandy Hook had infuriated gun control advocates, who poured new resources and effort into creating a national organization to challenge the NRA. The election of NRA antagonist Letitia James as the attorney general of New York opened up the threat of a wide-ranging investigation. Congressional probes before and after Democrats retook the House of Representatives in 2018 did the same.

Surrounded by the lavish lifestyles and elegant mansions of their wealthy donors and friends, Wayne and his wife, Susan, had for years tapped the NRA for personal gain—and subsequent litigation and an investigation by the New York attorney general would finally shine a light on all that. They had managed to keep their misconduct hidden for years, rationalizing that they should get the perks that their corporate millionaire counterparts received. But what might be merely unethical or unseemly in corporate America can be illegal for a nonprofit organization that is exempt from taxes, like the National Rifle Association. And they couldn't hide from the subpoenas that would soon be coming their way.

This is a story about how, when it all came crashing down, Wayne turned his back on his closest confidants. And carrying a great feeling of personal betrayal, his associates would share their stories: to congressional investigators or the office of the New York attorney general—or to the investigative reporter writing this book.

But the National Rifle Association is more than a collection of Wayne associates. Contrary to popular belief, it is not powerful because of money from the gun industry, which makes up a relatively paltry amount of its contributions. It's powerful because of its millions of passionate dues-paying members. But more important than money, its members act: they light up the switchboards and shout at their senators—as they did when the Manchin-Toomey reform bill hung in the balance, helping to scuttle the modest gun reforms proposed in Congress after that appalling tragedy.

And it's these members that Wayne has most betrayed with his fancy getaways and private jets—the blue-collar workers who scrape together five or ten or fifteen dollars a month to contribute to the group. A predominant reason that Wayne's closest associates decided to turn on their old friend was that he had betrayed these Americans.

Some took these sorts of responsibilities seriously: Oliver North is probably best known for his involvement in the Iran-Contra scandal during the 1980s. Following his departure from the military, he had continued his career as a combat correspondent and a conservative talking head. In 2018 Wayne had recruited him to be the president of the NRA, envisioning North as a figurehead who would raise money and not ask too many questions. Wayne didn't want to be responsible for oversight, but he didn't want anyone else to take the responsibility of oversight either—that would make him look bad.

For decades now, that had been the role of the NRA president: to take the extravagant perks of office, bill expenses to the NRA, and attend a few meetings. But North was not that kind of person. He felt that he had been robbed of the only career he had ever

wanted—to be an officer in the United States Marine Corps—
because of a national scandal. He would not suffer through another one again, or at least not quietly.

Ejected from the presidency by Wayne for asking too many
questions, Ollie North would also one day find himself in a room
filled with lawyers, sitting for his own deposition.

"He was a friend," Ollie told a boardroom of impassive suits. "I
thought."

The fact that I can tell you the stories in this book speaks to
the depths of betrayal felt by some of Wayne's oldest and closest
confidants—and their general view that he has destroyed an institution they all once loved.

CHAPTER 1

Wayne

"Where the fuck is Wayne?"

It's a question that everyone close to Wayne LaPierre has asked from time to time. The answer is usually "I have no idea," followed by another series of profanities. The bookish NRA executive has a habit of disappearing in times of stress. But this question, this Saturday in the late summer of 1998, was different. It was his wedding day, and he was missing at the worst time. Wayne had gotten cold feet.

It was not a problem that could be papered over. Guests had already arrived at the Basilica of Saint Mary in Alexandria, Virginia's Old Town district. With the ceremony delayed, word began to spread throughout the crowd as to the reason why. The priest was prepared to mediate, if only the groom could be found. The bride, Susan, began to cry. The guests, numbering between 100 and 150, casually congregated outside in the warm late-summer air as organ music played over and over.

His closest friends began to fan out to search for him. Wayne had made no secret of his reluctance to get married in the days leading up to the ceremony. He had been married once before and had been separated from his ex-wife for years, but the divorce had been finalized only four months prior to this date.

Wayne's conduct in the time leading up to his wedding with Susan was, to any outside observer, absolutely humiliating. He scurried around, according to a witness, nervously polling anyone he ran into about whether he should go through with it. He asked his staff. He asked a secretary. He asked his friends. To anyone watching, it was clear he was looking for a way out of a wedding that he had felt pressured into by the bride. According to two close friends of Wayne, Susan had sent out the invitations for the wedding without telling him.

When Wayne was finally found on the day of the wedding, he said he didn't want to get married. The best man honored that by placing a single, crisp hundred-dollar bill on the dashboard of his car, a Jeep Wagoneer. With the engine running, Wayne's best man told him they could leave whenever he wanted. The best man later recounted to friends that he offered to drive Wayne away.

But Wayne was ultimately persuaded not to leave by Susan and the priest. Wayne was a remarkably weak-willed man, friends said, and could be counted on to yield to any demand if it was issued strenuously and loudly enough. This in itself might not have been so consequential if he hadn't risen to head what would become a $400-million-a-year firearm advocacy organization.

The guests began to stream back into the church. But it is impossible to hide the disappearance of a groom. Wayne's reluctance had delayed the wedding for close to an hour, and the reputation-conscious Susan would not forget this humiliating blow to her social standing—a concept she valued above all else. Her social standing was largely determined by the people sitting in the pews of that Catholic church. Many of Wayne's invitees were linked to the NRA in some form: Angus McQueen, the gruff head of the NRA's symbiotic advertising and public relations agency, Ackerman McQueen, was there. As was Tony Makris, Wayne's longtime business associate who called him a brother. Oliver North, the Iran-Contra figure and future NRA president, was present. So were Millie Hallow, Wayne's personal assistant; Woody Phillips, the accused (though never charged) embezzler whom Wayne chose to be the NRA's chief financial officer; and Chuck Cooper, who would be the NRA's outside counsel for decades.

Even though he went through the motions during the ceremony, Wayne's nervousness and anxiety seemed to betray his true feelings. As she said her vows, Susan stared deeply and lovingly at her groom, but Wayne looked like he was about to faint. His eyes darted everywhere but to his bride: the audience, the priest, the ceiling, the floor. For the guests who looked on, it was extremely uncomfortable to witness, and not the kind of wedding they would forget.

Wayne's wedding is emblematic of his character. By many accounts, he is a man driven by fear and anxiety over all other forces, and his reaction to these emotions is usually to flee and hide. He had told friends that he didn't want to get married, but if this was the case, he nonetheless permitted the ceremony to go forward because he didn't want to cause trouble. Despite being the head of one of the most controversial organizations in America, he is deeply unsettled by personal conflict. This has been his fundamental flaw, and why he has been prey to so many con men over his decades-long tenure at the National Rifle Association. His friends could only look on in horror as those around him manipulated this simple weakness. His best man did not attend the wedding reception that night.

⋅║⋅

Wayne Robert LaPierre Jr. was born in 1949 in Schenectady, New York, but was raised in Roanoke, Virginia, in a firearm-free household. Raised Catholic, he graduated from Patrick Henry High School and attended the Roman Catholic Siena College, his father's alma mater.

While Vietnam War protests raged on college campuses, Wayne landed an internship with a New York state legislator. He managed to avoid the military draft while in college through a student deferment. He also later received a medical deferment—the same categorization as Donald Trump's—although the exact reason for this is unknown.

Wayne is an awkward egghead type, and it's not hard to imagine that with a few different twists of fate he would have ended up as a college professor teaching political science, rather than rising to become one of the nation's most controversial gun rights advocates. He had a soft spot for children and was employed as a substitute special education teacher in Troy, New York, with poor and developmentally disabled students. In 1973 he started a Ph.D. at Boston University but dropped out to help a Democrat run for the Virginia state legislature; a few years later he received an M.A. in political science from Boston College.

His professorial demeanor is not well suited for leadership of a massive, powerful organization. He is easily bullied and doesn't have the ability to make firm commitments, or to keep his promises once he makes them. Perhaps the best description came from former NRA board member Wayne Anthony Ross, who said that Wayne had the "backbone of a chocolate eclair."

He has no core and has a reputation for never being able to say no, especially to the wrong people, NRA insiders said. He disdains the stresses of controversy—internal intrigue most of all—but by being unable to grow a spine and turn down bad ideas, he ends up causing a substantial portion of the drama inside the NRA described in this book. NRA insiders used to joke that even if you came into Wayne's office with a red nose and big rubber shoes, you could get him to approve an expenditure if you pressured him enough. In other words: if you could get in to see him, you could eventually get him to write a check. Wayne could never deliver critical news, and if it was absolutely necessary to do so, he would designate someone else to do it—then panic later over whether it was the right decision.

If he had not been a professor or an academic, there's a chance that his life could have led him to another passion: confections. He's expressed numerous times to friends that he would like nothing more than to retire and open up an ice-cream shop in New England. His heart was never really that much into gun rights advocacy. In 1995, four years into his role as the top leader at the NRA, he told the *Los Angeles Times* that the job was all-consuming, that he didn't want to live this sort of life, and that he couldn't wait to move to northern Maine to open up his ice-cream shop. "Your life goes by," he mused. A quarter century later, he still holds the top role at the NRA, but ice cream remains in the background: when the New York attorney general's office probed his expenses, investigators found that Wayne spent substantial amounts of money sending friends Graeter's ice cream for Christmas, all on his nonprofit organization's dime.

Originally a Democrat, like a substantial portion of the National Rifle Association's longest-serving staff, Wayne was active with the Roanoke Democrats in college but declined a job offer from the office of Democratic House Speaker Tip O'Neill. Instead, he got a job at the NRA. The NRA building at the time was right across the street from the Democratic National Committee, and so he walked right in and ran into some staff that he knew from his work in politics. They were looking for a Democratic lobbyist, so he signed on right away.

Wayne is a clumsy, meek, spastic man with a weak handshake, those who know him personally say. When he first started at the NRA, he was known for his wrinkled suits and detached gaze. Yet he was repeatedly promoted despite displaying no sense of professional ambition or charisma. After starting as a state-level lobbyist in 1978, he was promoted to head the state-level lobbying department in 1979 and then to direct the NRA's federal lobbying the next year.

It was like pulling teeth to get him to take a promotion, said John Aquilino, the NRA staffer who helped hire Wayne in the 1970s. "I've talked people out of murder, and this was harder," Aquilino said, recalling when he approached Wayne to head up the NRA's federal lobbying department. "Gee, I don't know," Wayne replied. It was only through reverse psychology that Aquilino was able to get him to agree: after Aquilino told Wayne not to worry about the promotion after all, Wayne was a lot more interested in the role.

His contemporaries describe him as a skilled lobbyist and strategic thinker, if a bit odd and absentminded. While a lobbyist on Capitol Hill in the 1980s, he earned the nickname "Shoes" because he wore black Florsheim wing tips, unpolished and noticeably scuffed. He paid no attention to his clothing, wearing nondescript, rumpled pin-striped suits. But he managed to cajole lawmakers, and he became good at it. This was true even though he didn't partake in the Washington, D.C., hobby of drinking alcohol, aside from an occasional sip of champagne. Wayne would sip on soft drinks and buy members of Congress liquor—and was never ostracized for not taking part.

The stories of Wayne's inattentive personality are plentiful. He had a habit of utterly disassociating from the world around him and was allergic to practicality. In the 1990s, Aquilino ran into his former subordinate at Reagan National Airport, near D.C. Wayne was sitting on the floor, his head in his hands, totally overwhelmed. He had lost his itinerary, or he had been insufficiently informed about what it was, and had no idea what he was doing or how to fix the problem.

During that same decade, LaPierre slept in and missed a golf outing with former vice president Dan Quayle—a pretty important meeting for an NRA lobbyist. Wayne's excuse for missing it was not very good: he wasn't aware of the makeup of the golf foursome. "Quayle gets out there and he starts walking around the cart . . . going, 'Where's Wayne?'" LaPierre recalled later in an interview.

In the early 1990s, Wayne's house was burglarized. The local police called NRA headquarters to inform him. Wayne wasn't there at the time, so his staff took a message. When he arrived at the office, he was told to urgently call the police about the burglary at his home. "That's funny," Wayne said. "I was just there. I didn't notice a thing."

One joke told in NRA circles was that you would only be able to make eye contact with him if you lay on the floor while the two of you were talking. In social settings, the same scatterbrained Wayne would emerge. He would almost begin to automate his interactions in crowds: "Hi. I'm Wayne LaPierre," he repeatedly told guests at one function, and continued this even when he came across his longtime associate Chris Cox, the head of the NRA's lobbying arm. They had known each other since the '90s. "Hi. I'm Wayne LaPierre!" Wayne said. Cox responded in consternation, "Wayne, what are you talking about?"

Wayne also has an obsessive personality when it comes to documenting the world around him. He doesn't take notes on any electronic devices but instead always carries four colored Sharpies and yellow legal pads. He scribbles constantly during meetings, using a color-coded system that only he can decipher. The terrible handwriting further obfuscates the meaning of the notes. "It was when he was in conversation and thinking," a Wayne associate said. "I think for him, writing like that . . . that helped him think." The practice grew so cumbersome that Wayne would carry a roller duffel bag, the size of a piece of carry-on luggage, specifically to carry the pads, and pull out different pads depending on the topic.

Wayne has a history of hoarding everything: he would attend political events and leave with a stack of notes, agenda items, and brochures. When Wayne was the head of the NRA's federal lobbying team, Aquilino once emerged into the office's lobby to find a long line of pads and congressional publications lining the floor from the elevator, through the lobby, to the curb. Wayne had rushed to a car and had been oblivious to the fact that he was leaving a trail of documents behind him.

Wayne's note-taking habit led to voluminous stacks of yellow legal pads. He once had an apartment in Arlington, Virginia, that appeared to be largely for his collection: filled with boxes, legal pads, and writing utensils—a collection of all the things he took out of his office and dumped there. It wasn't clear whether he ever lived there, or it was just a place to accumulate mail and papers.

He no longer has that apartment. His garage at his home in Virginia was once stuffed with these pads, filling up to fifteen bins, often organized by year. In a room near his NRA HQ office, yet more yellow pads were stacked up between his desk and the executive bathroom, in a pile approximately four and a half feet tall and six feet wide—yet he had the uncanny ability to find precisely what he was looking for in those messy stacks. The various government investigators looking into his conduct may have been stymied by this cumbersome system.

"It's kind of my own shorthand. It's hard to read if you're not me, but I can read it," Wayne once said when questioned by lawyers. "I used to keep them in my house. . . . They're all with the attorneys now."

He doesn't use computers at all, and doesn't text as a means of communication. Rather than read emails, he would have his staff compile printouts of clippings and messages that might interest him. He was stuck in the analog age.

Wayne would be spotted far more often with his legal pads than with a pistol. He looks at guns through the lens of politics—as a political junkie, not as a lover of firearms. Some gun aficionados love the way it sounds when a rifle's charging handle is released, allowing the bolt carrier to slide forward with a metallic clang. Wayne's not the type to notice that kind of thing. He couldn't care less about the technicalities or features of guns, and when given the choice would far prefer to sit quietly in a gazebo than take aim on an outdoor firing range.

This was obvious from the start. In the early 1980s, after Wayne had already been at the NRA for several years, his boss, the prominent gun rights activist Neal Knox, offered to take him skeet shooting near Damascus, Maryland. Wayne showed up with an embarrassing, poorly maintained single-barreled shotgun, not fit for use. Visible rust coated the outside. The older Knox condescendingly examined the offending firearm, popped the hood of his 1978 Cadillac Seville, and swiped some oil from the dipstick to lubricate the shotgun and improve its general appearance. As a lobbyist at the NRA, Wayne would have been able to get a decent shotgun; he just never cared enough to do it, or to take care of the one he had. He was just not a gun guy, those that know him say.

Stories about his dangerous gun-handling behavior have become NRA lore. An old joke circulated around NRA HQ: "The safest place you could be when Wayne had a gun was between Wayne and the target." Staff described ducking and weaving during a video shoot because Wayne was waving the muzzle of his rifle around carelessly. When an engineer called for a sound check, Wayne swung his rifle around with him, pointing it directly at the engineer. Alarmed at his lack of muzzle awareness, someone hurriedly confiscated his weapon. The anecdote evolved into yet another joke: those who underperformed at work were told they might have to "go hunting with Wayne."

During one hunting trip in Africa, Wayne illustrated his general incompetence with firearms. Video later leaked to *The New Yorker* showed this had cruel consequences. While tracking African bush elephants in 2013, he shot and wounded one of the large mammals, sending it crashing to the ground. "All right." He exhaled nervously. Approaching to close range, he attempted three times to fire a fatal round into the elephant, per his guide's suggestions. He missed the intended target all three times, drawing a chuckle from the guide. Wayne's friend had to step in to deal the final blow. As they surveyed the carcass, the guide said, "I didn't think you were going to shoot, because I was telling you to wait. Maybe you didn't hear me with those earplugs." Wayne replied, "You said 'wait'? Oh, I didn't hear you." Throughout the video, Wayne appeared edgy, tense, and anxious—far from the competent outdoorsman image he had tried to convey to the public.

For all his flaws, he had remarkably few vices aside from ice cream. He didn't smoke, drink, or chase women who were not his wife. When news circulated in 2019 that the NRA had paid for the apartment of a young female intern who worked with him, online gun forums lit up with speculation of a lurid affair. Wayne's not the type. Not only is he not lecherous, but those who interact with him get the sense he doesn't like to touch people at all.

When his associates learned that he was dating Susan, who would become his second wife, the first reaction was one of shock. Many hadn't even been aware that he'd been married before. "He's just asexual—you know, like an amoeba," was how one NRA lobbyist who worked with Wayne described him.

"Holy shit—Wayne knows an attractive girl? I thought he was a eunuch," Aquilino said, describing his reaction at the time. "I never thought of him having normal urges that humans have."

But that "attractive girl" Wayne knew would have an enormous—and thus far undercovered—influence on the trajectory of the National Rifle Association.

CHAPTER 2

"Just a Volunteer"

Susan is as pushy as Wayne is a pushover. At the pinnacle of the National Rifle Association's power, around the inauguration of President Donald Trump, it was *good* to be Susan LaPierre. The NRA had spent over $30 million in support of Trump's candidacy, more than even the leading pro-Trump super PAC. Susan felt that the NRA had been instrumental in getting Trump elected president, and thus not only did Trump owe the NRA, she thought that by extension Trump owed her. She believed then, and has continued to insist for years, that she was up for an appointment by the Trump administration to be ambassador to Slovenia. She got an assignment to the National Park Foundation board instead.

Susan is a well-dressed woman living almost exclusively in a social circle of other wealthy, well-dressed women. Seldom seen in the same outfit twice, she's far more often found attending a gala than going on a safari. She was not known for her love of hunting, although when she did partake she was not above a bit of savagery. *The New Yorker* published leaked video showing her hunting an elephant in Botswana, although the word "execution" might be a better way to describe it. In the clip, a defenseless elephant stood in front of her cluelessly. Susan fired a shot, and the animal instantly collapsed. Susan burst into laughter after killing the animal, exclaiming, "That was amazing . . . wow, my heart is just racing. I feel great!" Grinning, she then sliced off the end of the elephant's tail, held it in the air, and cried out, "Victory!" Susan personally requested that the elephant's body parts be surreptitiously shipped back to the United States, and the animal's front feet were turned into stools for the LaPierres.

Susan tried hard to project authenticity, to share an image of herself as someone who would hunt. She would encourage Wayne's aides to take him on hunting trips, even though Wayne never really cared about any of that. People need to see him doing that stuff, she said. But neither Wayne nor Susan were built for the sport. In her quest for authenticity during the elephant hunt, she engaged in an uncouth spectacle and inadvertently revealed herself as a dilettante. Anyone deeply immersed in the hunting community would have known that her actions in Botswana were, well, not very sporting.

When you speak to individuals within the NRA world about Susan, they commonly respond with a series of unprintable insults. She is described as pretentious, manipulative, unpleasant, a person who grew up to forget her humble roots, according to a dozen sources who knew her personally at different times in her life. When Susan wanted something, she pestered Wayne constantly. She knew his character, once describing her own husband's management style as "no management style at all." Wayne reacts to his wife as he does to all the people he is close to: if she pesters enough, she gets the green light. Around the office, her power was either innately understood or quickly learned: Susan has absolute control over Wayne on the issues she cares about. Staff refer to her as "the boss' wife" or even "the First Lady of the NRA." She luxuriated in that power, that status as Wayne's wife, and would frequently drop this fact in casual conversation. "My husband, Wayne," she'd say over and over again.

Another favorite Susan phrase is "I'm just a volunteer," as if emphasizing how much she'd sacrificed by not taking a salary from the NRA. She is not just the boss's wife but a force within the organization with all the de facto authority of an executive. And she was rewarded with perks that would make a corporate executive blush. The "volunteer" had a full range of staff and consultants working on her communications, according to NRA insiders. They ordered her Christmas gifts, and arranged events for the vanity project Susan organized to draw in women who support the Second Amendment. The "volunteer" had her own personal security. She drove around in her own Mercedes, and when not in the Washington, D.C., region, she would hire a driver and a black car, often a Chevy Suburban.

She was ostensibly the cofounder and cochair of the Women's Leadership Forum, a group of high-dollar donors to the NRA. Her budget came from multiple pots, much of it from the Office of Advancement, which is in charge of high-dollar fundraising. But if she needed more money to fund her extravagant tastes, she would pull from Wayne's budget from the office of the executive vice president, the formal title that he holds. Other times she would get what she wanted by billing Ackerman McQueen and having it send the bill right back to the NRA, the invoices bearing nondescript explanations. Her staff saw these practices up close: an ongoing torrent of bills. For the staff, it was hard to know where Ackerman stopped and the NRA began.

·‖·

Susan Mary Znidorka grew up in a working-class family in Pewaukee, Wisconsin. Private jets, black cars, and lavish dresses were not on the menu. Her parents ran a motel in Waukesha County, first called the Wayside Motel and then later the Blue Mound Court Motel. Susan helped manage the family business, including cleaning rooms. Tragically, her mother died not long after she went off to college at the University of Wisconsin–Madison.

Unlike Wayne, Susan was a natural leader. Assertive and charismatic, she could rally others to her cause, which often involved conservative and Republican politics. In college, she was eager to cast off her humble beginnings, earning the nickname "Gator" because she was always wearing Lacoste, the preppy clothing brand with the prominent green crocodile logo.

She joined the Gamma Phi Beta sorority (where, incidentally, she was sorority sisters with Laurel Clark, an astronaut who would later perish in the space shuttle *Columbia* disaster). Despite it being an extremely liberal school, the prominent conservative was able to leverage her connections in the fraternity and sorority system to create a voting bloc that elected her copresident of the student council. "She was persuasive," recalls her college friend Mike Fritz, and became very popular among those in Greek life.

Records show she did not ultimately earn a degree, but buoyed by successes in politics, she threw herself into campaigns, rising to become the GOP's finance director in Wisconsin. She moved to Washington, D.C., in the 1980s and worked in political fundraising before meeting Wayne through an NRA vendor.

She never looked back, and developed a special disdain for those who knew about her roots, lest they remind her of where she came from. Those who witnessed her behavior said she put on an air of pretentiousness toward those who had less money or came from lower classes—neither of whom she saw as her cultural peers. She became set on impressing individuals in the same social stratosphere as members of the elite Shikar Club, a London hunting club formed in 1909 by alumni of the prestigious boarding school Eton. "If the Safari Club is Yale, Shikar is Skull and Bones," one gun community insider explained. "Susan loved hanging out with the Safari glitterati," said another.

NRA staff could always tell when she was in the office because of the strong smell of her telltale perfume. Over her years as the NRA's First Lady, she spent tens of thousands of dollars on hair and makeup. She tried to keep these expenses hidden, routing them through Ackerman McQueen, but both her staff and the New York attorney general would realize the pattern.

Susan preferred to use Brady Wardlaw, a Nashville, Tennessee, makeup artist whose clients include LeAnn Rimes, Reese Witherspoon, and Taylor Swift, which necessitated plane flights from Nashville and the best luxury hotel suites for her stylists. In 2017, right before the Women's Leadership Forum at the Four Seasons Resort in Las Colinas, Texas, Susan ejected her own staff from their rooms at the hotel so that her hair and makeup artists could each have a suite, plus a separate empty suite where she could have her makeup done—at a cost of nearly a thousand dollars a night for five nights. Between May 2016 and May 2017, the NY AG found that one stylist was paid $16,359 for three events.

The perks didn't end there. The NRA would pay for her personal Christmas, baby shower, and wedding anniversary gifts, and the New York attorney general's investigation later noted that "gifts [paid for by the NRA] were especially common for those affiliated with the Women's Leadership Forum." That same probe found that she raided her husband's consulting budget to pay six-figure salaries to her personal assistant and a communications consultant that did "special projects."

The extravagance rubbed her staff the wrong way. The NRA had created a narrative about being for Middle America, often stoking cultural resentments to do so. Meanwhile Susan was playing off this to go to Lake Como on a private jet, all while treating her staff like dirt, those who witnessed her conduct said. Her staff was absolutely harried by her constant demands and profligate spending—thousands of dollars on everything from flowers to lighting.

"She would always be very political. . . . She'd only speak to you when necessary," said one former NRA staffer who worked in fundraising. "Anyone working on Women's Leadership Forum stuff was very stressed out."

Susan demanded loyalty from staffers but never displayed any to those who worked for her. She would play a game where she gave people affection, then took it away. Staff who tried to get her to like them realized that they would never succeed—because she thought they were beneath her.

That is, unless you could be useful to her. Susan once unexpectedly burst into an aide's apartment while the aide was on maternity leave. The aide had just returned from giving birth at the hospital when Susan made an unannounced visit, according to two people with knowledge of the incident. She forced her way in, and took unflattering photographs of the aide while she was still recovering from childbirth—all so that Susan had photos to share with other Women's Leadership Forum members. It was as if Susan needed the photos for social capital and did not care how she made her aide feel.

Susan has always been a strategic social climber, and Wayne's success as the head of the NRA gave her an opportunity to live the life she had dreamed of. In the 1990s, she worked for Brad O'Leary, the head of one of the NRA's major vendors, and he introduced the two. Wayne never cared for mansions, private jets, or expensive clothing before he met Susan. "He was Mr. Rumpled Suit," said former NRA lobbyist Richard Feldman, who knew him best in the 1980s and '90s. Feldman wrote in his book *Ricochet*: "I hadn't thought of Wayne as notably avaricious. He didn't live ostentatiously; he didn't gamble. I always assumed he wasn't overly interested in money." But Susan has always been remarkably attuned to the finer things in life. Feldman recalled an incident in 2003 when he saw Susan at an event, wearing expensive designer clothes:

> Her haute couture had caused a stifled groundswell of discontent among the traditional conservative higher-ups in [the NRA]. It was one thing to make a killing in a nonprofit, membership-funded organization. But it was another thing altogether to flaunt it.

The anecdote shows just how dramatically attitudes about the display of wealth have changed within the NRA over the past twenty years. Among the women associated with the NRA now, haute couture is the minimum. And Susan has been the driving force behind that change in attitude.

While much of the spotlight has been on Wayne, Susan has

been a primary driver of his actions at the NRA. She's tightly integrated into his work life. If you wanted to reach Wayne, who doesn't use email, you could reach out to Susan and she would get a message to him. The two people with access to the email address that is nominally Wayne's are his assistant and his wife. And when Wayne wanted his chief of staff to have a document quickly, he would have Susan take a photo of it and send it.

To outside observers, their relationship can seem to be more professional than personal. When Wayne had a health scare in 2018, he took a business associate, not his wife, along with him to the Mayo Clinic to confront his medical crisis.

Wayne did not discover money's alluring glow on his own. Susan pushed and prodded him all the way. She wasn't the only one, but she was the only one who lived with him. Both were motivated to keep up with the lifestyles of those around them, and they surrounded themselves with millionaires in the gun-owning community.

Wayne's salary jumped from $200,000 in the mid-1990s to $2.2 million in 2018. Of the more than six hundred nonprofit organizations tracked by CharityWatch, Wayne is the fifth-highest-paid nonprofit leader in the country. If you exclude health care nonprofits, Wayne is the second-highest paid. And that's without counting the perks the LaPierres afforded themselves along the way: from 2013 to 2017, he was reimbursed for $1.2 million in expenses, according to the NY AG.

There are things you see when you hobnob with the rich that, if you want to match them in opulence, are very expensive and, more importantly, possibly illegal if you use nonprofit funds to pay for them. If Wayne had been an executive at General Electric, their expenses might well have been within bounds, if properly filed and reported. But they were using nonprofit funds, which are tax-exempt because the organization is meant to act in the public good—and thus are subject to greater oversight from government bodies. Now both Wayne and Susan are hanging on desperately, hoping that Wayne doesn't go to jail.

CHAPTER 3

The NRA's Fiefdoms

The National Rifle Association lists its headquarters as being in Fairfax, Virginia, where its main offices have resided since its departure from downtown Washington, D.C., in 1993. But the organization's real center of gravity, where gossip was traded and deals were discussed, is twenty miles away. Just two short blocks from the Potomac River in Old Town Alexandria, Virginia, is an Italian restaurant where anyone important in NRA circles dined.

If the NRA is understood as a series of fiefdoms, then the feudal lords meet at Landini Brothers. Opened in 1979, Landini's is a two-floor, family-run restaurant specializing in Tuscan cuisine, a quiet, cozy place with white linens and exposed-brick walls. Its chef, Rigoberto Ramos, has been there since opening day. The menu is in Italian, with English descriptions, and features a $56.95 Filetto di Kebab served over risotto. Of the more than four hundred wines available on the menu, around a dozen are Italian wines exclusively made for Landini Brothers. Bottles can exceed $2,000.

Wayne LaPierre's close friend and Ackerman executive Tony

Makris lived in Old Town and loved Landini's, so Wayne began going there too. Makris had been an NRA member since he was eight years old. Over the years, Makris had advised legendary NRA president Charlton Heston, and came to be a trusted member of Wayne's inner circle as well. Makris was not only an adviser on NRA issues but advised Wayne on personal issues as well: security concerns, health care—even where to eat. Makris has frequented Landini's since the 1980s and had a house account there.

Above the restaurant is an exclusive, members-only cigar bar called CXIIIREX, pronounced One-Thirteen Rex, or Rex's for short. There is a private entrance along King Street, or members could choose to use an elevator inside Landini Brothers that operates only with a key. As refined as Landini's already is, the cigar club is Landini's on steroids—an elevated microcosm of the NRA's elite society of executives and associates. Everything costs more than it does downstairs, and bottle service flows freely. Makris is a big fan of cigars and has donated much of the decor inside the club, including taxidermy from his many hunting trips.

The smoke hangs thick over the club's tables, so much so that spouses would complain that members stunk. So the club features locker rooms so that members could shower and change before they went home. For most of Washington, D.C., smoky back rooms are a part of the antiquated political past. But for the National Rifle Association, they live on in the present. "It was a mirage. Everyone just breathed everyone else's exhaust," quipped one former frequent guest.

Landini's and Rex's were where deals were cooked up: Wayne LaPierre asked a man named Josh Powell to be his chief of staff after a number of meetings in a private room there. NRA CFO

Woody Phillips, top NRA fundraiser Tyler Schropp, and NRA head lobbyist Chris Cox were also frequent visitors. A pattern emerged: Wayne, Susan, Millie, and other NRA bigwigs would take people to dinner at Landini's, then charge it to Makris's account for future ambiguous reimbursement by the NRA back to Ackerman McQueen. These meals would sometimes range into the thousands of dollars. During litigation, an NRA lawyer would suggest that there were more than 200 meals, totaling $140,000 worth of food and drink, charged through Makris's account and back to the NRA for reimbursement in 2016 and 2017.

After the New York attorney general started issuing subpoenas and taking depositions as part of the investigation into the NRA, the centrality of the restaurant to the organization's social and professional life became clear. The way other NRA executives paid for their expensive meals was by having them charged to Ackerman McQueen credit cards, which would then pass these expenses back through to the NRA.

NRA executives slapped down Ackerman-issued American Express cards at Landini's dozens of times: over a five-year span, for example, Schropp rang up 127 charges at this restaurant—all charged to Ackerman McQueen and then billed back to the NRA. "The NRA also directed Ackerman to purchase several memberships to a members-only cigar bar affiliated with the upscale Italian restaurant," the New York AG found.

The expenses at Landini's is just one example of a much larger problem. The New York AG concluded that the millions of dollars in other NRA entertainment and travel expenses were paid for—and obfuscated from view—by routing expenses through Ackerman McQueen. This practice allowed NRA executives to avoid the prying eyes of judgmental accountants, their board, and the general public.

Landini's became such a strategic locale because it was near the offices of Mercury Group, a subsidiary of the NRA's most important vendor, Ackerman McQueen. When Ackerman Mc-Queen moved to the Washington, D.C., region, the company situated itself in Old Town Alexandria, adjacent to the Potomac River. The space included an outdoor area overlooking the river, and a jumbotron for parties. In Old Town, there is the continual, deafening sound of airplanes taking off from nearby Reagan National Airport, an ongoing annoyance for the half-deaf gun lovers in the NRA orbit who want to have conversations on the balcony.

Wayne spent a lot of his time at these offices in Old Town, dropping a small fortune at the Ben & Jerry's across the street. It was a strategic way for him to avoid going into the NRA HQ. He had a habit of disappearing for days at a time: he could be at HQ, or at Mercury Group, or somewhere else entirely. Sometimes even his closest staff would have no idea where he was. By mixing up his locations, he fed the narrative that he was at that *other* locale.

For decades the Old Town neighborhood was where some of the association's most important decisions were made. It was a reflection of how much power Ackerman McQueen, known as Ack-Mac for short, held over the NRA. Tony Makris was there, so Wayne went there. Wayne and Makris went there, so other execs went there. Makris, Schropp, and Cox all lived nearby in Alexandria. The neighborhood became the NRA's de facto mecca.

You could do a whole NRA walking tour around Alexandria. It's where Wayne LaPierre rushed to strategize after the shootings at Sandy Hook. And it's where Makris used to own a gun store, called the Old Town Armory (it's now a place for tarot card readings). When their relationship collapsed, the NRA filed a lawsuit against Ack-Mac at the Alexandria Circuit Court. Russian Maria Butina, who tried to infiltrate the NRA, was held for a time at the Alexandria Detention Center after she was convicted for failing to register as a foreign agent. We'll get to those stories later.

⫴

The mentality within the NRA sphere is zero-sum: if you are winning, someone else is losing. This would of course lead to madness, chaos, and a healthy dose of intrigue.

The NRA is best understood as a series of warring tribes. Ackerman McQueen executive Angus McQueen once took Wayne LaPierre's then chief of staff Josh Powell aside for a heart-to-heart.

"The NRA is like a country full of warlords," McQueen said.

"Well, we're all on the same team, right?" Powell responded, somewhat naively.

"Fuck that, it's every man for himself," McQueen said. "The NRA has been like this forever."

It can be hard to keep track of all the dueling fiefdoms. To understand the various allegiances in the NRA world, it's important to understand the components of the NRA that are in conflict with one another. These include the NRA's General Operations division, the NRA's Institute for Legislative Action (NRA-ILA), and the NRA's board of directors, as well as Ackerman McQueen and Mercury Group.

GENERAL OPERATIONS AND NRA-ILA

Though high-level executive decisions were made in Alexandria, most of the NRA worker bees are based in a massive six-floor structure that employees refer to simply as "the Building," just under twenty miles west of the White House. The complex houses the offices of many executives, whom staff would refer to as "the Royals." The building, as you can imagine, is filled with firearms—it would not be unheard of to see an AR-15 laying out on a desk, and employees commonly walk around with their Glocks displayed in plain sight.

The National Rifle Association is split into divisions such as membership, fundraising (known internally as advancement), and publications. The General Operations division, on the sixth floor, oversees many of the activities traditionally associated with the NRA: hunting promotion, gun safety, and shooting competitions. In 2019, before a series of layoffs due to a financial crisis, the NRA had approximately 550 full-time employees, the bulk of whom worked in this division.

The Institute for Legislative Action is the NRA's lobbying muscle. Many of the NRA's lobbyists work at HQ on the fifth floor, but federal lobbyists work in separate offices on Capitol Hill. Though it is one of the NRA's main engines of political power, the ILA makes up a relatively small percentage of the NRA's staff and budget. In 2016, NRA-ILA had seventy-eight staffers, representing just over 10 percent of the group's employees, and spent around $30 million, also about 10 percent of the NRA's total budget.

This division was led from 2002 to 2019 by Chris Cox, a well-connected and charismatic chief lobbyist whom many in the NRA orbit saw as Wayne LaPierre's heir apparent. Gun control advocates admit privately that Cox is the one they most worried about taking the helm of the NRA. He's one of the few figures in this whole saga who has generally earned the respect of his staff—many of whom appreciate his "first one in, last one out" work ethic and have passionately defended him against any form of criticism. Like Wayne, he started out in Democratic politics, having worked for Democratic representative John Tanner of Tennessee before joining the gun rights group.

ILA has a remarkable amount of autonomy, even though it ostensibly falls under the purview of Wayne LaPierre. Wayne knew to keep his hands off, telling his chief of staff not to interfere with its jurisdiction: "Don't mess with that," he once told Powell. "We don't want to upset Chris."

The reasons are historical and personal: the NRA's chief lobbyists have typically been assertive, dominant personalities; the NRA's bylaws envision a degree of independence for its lobbying arm; and though it is part of the NRA, it raises its own separate funds. The broader NRA pays for ILA's salaries and operating expenses, but the lobbying arm is responsible for fundraising to execute its own advocacy projects.

This independence makes ILA a natural antagonist to other parts of the organization. The division holds the prestige of operating in the area that the NRA most often makes the news for: political power plays on Capitol Hill, at state legislatures, in the courts, and at the White House. So this meant a rivalry with General Operations, whose staff were paid less and did less glamorous work. But that superior position does not satisfy ILA: gun rights advocacy is a core motivating factor for why Americans join the NRA and pay membership dues. And yet, far more money goes to General Operations than to ILA.

Historically, ILA would raise money off political matters—the defense of the Second Amendment—and General Operations would raise money off hunting, gun safety, and its other programs. But over time, leaders at General Operations decided to ditch this detente and to start raising money off legislative fights. As with most political bodies run by ego-driven personalities, tensions skyrocketed as the two different parts of the NRA competed against each other for donor dollars.

ILA's independence also made it the one part of the National Rifle Association that Ackerman McQueen couldn't influence. And as Ackerman McQueen's power as a key NRA vendor grew, Cox objected to the use of this expensive outside firm over the use of in-house staff. Ack-Mac was always seeking to take over ILA's social media accounts, for example—a constant source of conflict. Ack-Mac and Wayne also had a habit of making decisions without informing or consulting the NRA's lobbyists, which of course infuriated them because they were the ones who would have to publicly defend the decisions.

Ackerman McQueen and ILA had diverging goals: Ackerman was in charge of ginning up the base, driving contributions and membership, and raising the NRA's profile. ILA was in charge of easing lawmakers into the NRA's legislative position and making them comfortable voting the way the NRA's lobbyists wanted them to vote. For Ackerman, incitement and controversy was good; for ILA, a little finesse was preferable. These conflicts became especially pronounced after the shootings at Sandy Hook.

Cox's objections to Ackerman McQueen were in the spirit of a long tradition of ILA-Ackerman paranoia and conflict. Given the controversial nature of its work, ILA used to regularly sweep its offices for phone taps and other listening devices. In the early

1990s, the NRA was located in downtown D.C. and Ackerman McQueen owned an adjacent office. During a routine sweep of ILA's offices, a technical consultant found a device that could survey six of its phones. A wire from the device led into the wall, in the direction of Ack-Mac's offices. The lobbyists never blew the whistle, and they never explored conclusively whether Ack-Mac was responsible. It was unclear during this time whether they could win if they started a knife fight with Ackerman. So they adopted anti-bugging countermeasures and acted like nothing had happened. Ackerman McQueen vehemently denies having anything to do with this event, contends it has no capability to do such things, and questions whether this event ever occurred.

BOARD OF DIRECTORS

"If you want to understand the NRA Board, you study the Politburo," quipped Neal Knox. The NRA's board of directors is a seventy-six-seat behemoth, making it unwieldy for oversight or governance of a nonprofit organization. All but one of the NRA's seventy-six directors are elected by NRA members for three-year terms, and the remaining one is elected by attendees of NRA's annual meeting for a one-year term. Though unpaid, board members receive perks including being able to charge expenses to the NRA.

The board has dozens and dozens of committees—thirty-seven standing committees plus a number of additional special committees—but only a small number hold any real power. These include the audit committee, which oversees internal financial

controls and deals with financial conflicts of interest and whistleblower complaints; the officers' compensation committee, which
determines salaries for the NRA's senior leadership; and the nominating committee, which determines who gets to be on the ballot
when members vote on who should be elected to the board of
directors.

"Trying to get the board to agree on anything was like con-
vening the Italian parliament. And as Wayne admitted to me in
confidence, they exercised almost no genuine oversight on the
NRA executive leadership," former LaPierre chief of staff Josh
Powell wrote. Powell had first gotten involved with the NRA's
governance after being tapped by Wayne to become a board
member. "I discovered that the finance committee was more of a
rubber stamp. We weren't really there to question Wayne's expen-
ditures or Chris Cox's lobbying efforts."

The cumbersome size of this enormous board is not the only
problem. The vast majority of the board has no experience in
nonprofit governance, and almost no one elected to the board is
qualified to oversee a nonprofit that brings in hundreds of millions of dollars a year. Instead, board members are often celebrities or conservative figures tapped by Wayne to serve—ensuring
their loyalty to him.

The board's loyalty is further purchased by NRA funds. Although board members are prohibited from receiving payment
for serving on the board, a number are indeed paid handsomely
by the NRA, purportedly for other purposes. Both NRA internal
rules and New York state law require that the board rule in advance
of such transactions that the money is spent in the organization's
best interest.

Actor Tom Selleck and musician Ted Nugent have been members of the board, for example, and both were paid six figures by the NRA—$476,000 to Selleck for a number of antique firearms and $120,000 over two years for Nugent to appear on a television hunting program. These transactions were not approved by the board until over a year later.

That's just the tip of the iceberg. All in all, eighteen members of the NRA's seventy-six-member board—nearly a quarter—were paid in substantial funds in recent years. Many of these payments were in the six figures. This set up an obvious conflict: they were being paid by the NRA while being tasked to oversee the non-profit's finances.

The New York attorney general's investigation revealed that Dave Butz, a former professional football player, had been paid $150,000 a year plus expenses to conduct fundraising work. His contract began in 2002 and was extended in 2016. The NRA was not able to provide investigators with any documentation regarding Butz's actual work. Butz was one of at least five board members who held contracts that the NY AG probe found were entered into against New York law.

Perhaps the most fearsome of all the board members is staunch LaPierre ally and gun lobbyist Marion Hammer, a diminutive woman who prefers blue and pink blazers and sports a bowl haircut. "Nobody that tiny should be that terrifying. You feel like you shouldn't be afraid, and [yet] you are afraid," one former NRA lobbyist said. As she approached the age of eighty, Hammer was given a ten-year consulting contract that paid her $220,000 a year, and Wayne had signed it without the board's knowledge. In the face of such a powerful, assertive person, Wayne had been—as he had been so many other times—cowed into compliance with her demands for higher payments.

When Wayne was asked about this later, and why her contract had not been approved by the board at the time, as the law requires, Wayne acknowledged that he had signed the contract but could not point to a single thing that the contract required her to do in order to earn that money.

"If she just sat there for the next ten years and didn't do anything, you would still be obligated to pay her $220,000 a year?" a lawyer grilled Wayne, according to a confidential deposition.

Wayne could only muster, "She's a workaholic. She really is."

But perhaps the strongest reason why the board remains loyal to Wayne, even after years of reporting on the NRA's financial difficulties and Wayne's centrality to them, is that being an NRA board member is part of their identity. "These people were nobodies. We made them feel special," said one source whose job included interacting with the board. Firearms and the gun rights organization have had such a central place in their lives that taking a stand that would risk their role was not worth it to many members.

ACKERMAN MCQUEEN AND MERCURY GROUP

To understand the firm Ackerman McQueen, you have to understand the man Angus McQueen, who led the organization for thirty-two years. He had some friends and many enemies—but they all agree on two things: first, that he was a ruthless jerk with a violent, uncontrollable temper; and second, that he was absolutely brilliant. "If he chooses to inspire you, he can," one associate said. "If he chooses to destroy you, he can."

Wayne first got to know Angus in 1984, relatively early in his tenure at the National Rifle Association. At this point, Wayne was an NRA lobbyist on Capitol Hill. Angus had been a director and producer for NBC affiliates and later served in the Nixon administration before starting with Ackerman McQueen, the company cofounded by his father.

For years, Wayne and Angus spoke every day, sometimes more than once a day—and Wayne came to call Angus his "Yoda." The nickname came up in litigation between the NRA and Ackerman McQueen when Wayne was asked why he used that term. "I thought that from a branding and imaging and crisis management skill, I thought that he had a certain amount of exceptional, unique, genius quality," Wayne explained. In any time of crisis, Wayne's first call would be to Angus. Wayne would hang on to Angus's every word, scribbling down notes fervently on one of his yellow legal pads.

Angus was also an incorrigible bully. He had a habit of picking on the person he felt was the weakest in the room. Often that was Wayne, even though Wayne was supposed to be the client and Angus the vendor. It astonished Josh Powell how Angus would scream strings of profanity at Wayne. "You're a fucking poodle," Angus once told Wayne. But Wayne never responded in kind; it wasn't in his disposition.

Ackerman McQueen, for its part, denies that Angus ever mistreated staff. While the firm acknowledged he had a strong personality, they also argued that employees stayed for long periods of time and would not do so if he mistreated them.

Angus worked from a corner office on the twenty-first floor of Oklahoma City's Valliance Bank Tower. The company lobby featured an elegant showcase of the firm's advertising work—internally referred to as "the Shrine"—that was nestled between two glass walls over a black marble floor, complemented by a rotating display of exotic floral arrangements.

In the early 2000s, an IT staffer set Angus up with a new laptop, and Angus was having some trouble. Furious, Angus cut every cable—power, mouse, and Ethernet—straight through with scissors. Marching out from his office, he paced fifty feet toward the Shrine and slammed the entire mess down in front of it with a crash. His staff, terrified of his outbursts, left the wreckage to sit there on the marble floor.

Ackerman McQueen started its relationship with the NRA as its advertising firm. At first, there was a casual, quaint, almost familial bond. Angus would bring his family over to an NRA staffer's home for a cookout, and that's where business was conducted. When their business relationship started in 1983, the NRA–Ackerman McQueen contract was $10,000 a month. By 2017, the contract paid Ackerman McQueen $40 million that year. Over his decades-long reign, Angus grew his company from about 25 employees to 250. As the relationship developed, the relationship professionalized. There were more trips, more fancy dinners, more cigars. Ackerman began to make up a larger and larger percentage of the NRA's budget. It increasingly marginalized the in-house NRA staff, who began to wonder why they were always forced to use high-priced Ackerman services for their work.

Its influence grew from advertising to encompass public relations, communications, strategic thinking, research, and crisis management. Later, Ackerman would launch the ill-fated NRATV project. Ackerman dealt with paid media, such as advertising and publications, while its subsidiary Mercury Group primarily dealt with interactions with the press, known as "earned media." It's helpful to think of Ackerman McQueen and Mercury Group as essentially interchangeable, despite technically being distinct entities.

Wayne had a habit of latching on to one adviser and then shutting out the rest. For decades, that adviser was Angus McQueen. If Angus told him to do one thing and all his other friends advised the opposite, he'd likely side with Angus. More than anyone else, Angus shaped the public image of Wayne LaPierre as a Second Amendment warrior. Awkward and meek in his private life, Wayne was a horrendous public speaker. Angus taught him to gesture, to bellow out at key moments, and to lower his voice to a whisper to capture the attention of the room. No one doubted Angus's methods or his success in transforming Wayne's image. But Wayne resisted the whole time, sweating profusely during rehearsal sessions.

"He didn't want to be a public figure," said one person involved in this decades-long transformation. "He didn't want to be the person we manicured out of him. . . . Wayne is above all a timid man who wouldn't walk from one stone to the next if he wasn't certain that it wouldn't pivot on him and make him fall."

Ackerman had a tendency of drawing a line in the sand and then forcing people to take sides. Its goal was to build Wayne's celebrity, to deify him as a political figure. It was Ackerman advisers who advised Wayne to be photographed in a heroic pose so that they could blow up the photo to twenty feet tall and eighteen feet wide and display it at NRA annual meetings. And it was Ackerman who, when Wayne found out that money was nice to have, gave him a way to hide perks from the public.

Ackerman executives had a habit of flaunting their flashy lifestyle: big bonuses, fat expense accounts, sleek cars, and private jets. "Angus wore bespoke suits from London, had the finest dress shoes and a predilection for $250 Charvet ties, which he would toss away after wearing once," recalled Josh Powell. "[Angus] was either driven in a black Suburban or drove his Bentley convertible. He lived well and wasn't afraid to show it." At some point along the way, Wayne and Susan began to imitate Angus's lifestyle. As they observed those glittering charms, they came to act as if they were more important than the cause they claimed to represent.

CHAPTER 4

The NRA Before Sandy Hook

It's a mistake to look at the National Rifle Association as just another single-issue advocacy group. "You would get a far better understanding if you approached us as if you were approaching one of the great religions of the world," former NRA executive vice president J. Warren Cassidy once said.

It's an identity, a way of living, a secular religion. NRA insiders often use religious imagery and terms when they describe the organization. Internally, there's a familiar language of implicit coercion: "Don't go outside the family," higher-ups would say. And the decline of the group over the past few years follows the trajectory of a sect whose leader has taken advantage of his followers for too long, a false prophet preaching the gospel while pocketing the donations.

The NRA is older than the American Red Cross or the Boy Scouts. It was formed in 1871 to improve the marksmanship of American soldiers. At the time, there was a lively debate about whether marksmanship should even be taught. The dominant military tactic of the era was to line up riflemen in rows and have

them fire off volleys of shots toward a wave of approaching enemy troops. Most military experts believed that target practice
would encourage unwelcome individualism in their soldiers. The
NRA's founders disagreed, and the organization was born.

Throughout most of the twentieth century, the NRA was
made up largely of hunters. Its leadership supported regulating
firearms. In 1934, the NRA endorsed legislation that would re-
strict machine gun sales and ban sawed-off shotguns and silencers. That same decade, the NRA contributed to the drafting of a
D.C. law requiring a forty-eight-hour waiting period for the sale
of handguns.

In May 1967, after dozens of Black Panther Party members moved through the California capitol building carrying
firearms—legal under the law at the time—then-governor Ronald Reagan said there was no reason for Californians to be openly
carrying loaded weapons in public. When he signed into law legislation banning open carry in California, the NRA supported
him. After the assassinations of John F. Kennedy and Martin Lu-
ther King Jr., the NRA supported the Gun Control Act of 1968,
which according to one summary "banned the interstate retail
sale of guns, prohibited all sales to juveniles, convicted felons,
and individuals adjudicated as being mentally unsound."

It was in the mid-1970s that the NRA shifted course to become the political powerhouse we know today. Around this time
NRA leadership was considering moving the organization out of
Washington, D.C., to focus on sportsmen and the outdoors, and
even considered taking the word "Rifle" out of the organization's
name. The plan was to build a new recreational facility in New
Mexico and move the headquarters to Colorado.

Gun activists inside the organization strongly rejected this shift and showed up in force to the 1977 NRA annual meeting, held that year in Cincinnati. Armed with walkie-talkies and sporting bright orange hunting caps on the convention hall floor, these rebels submitted motions for eight hours, dragging the meeting on until 3:30 A.M. Those in revolt believed that the NRA establishment had turned off the A/C on that humid evening to get them to disperse. But the determined rebels utilized the hall's vending machine until it ran out of drinks, and kept on submitting changes to the NRA's bylaws. When the dust settled, they succeeded in tossing out most of the existing leadership and putting in its place a much more aggressive regime focused on fighting gun control laws.

The most powerful role in the NRA is that of the executive vice president. This person is the de facto leader of the organization, in charge of the day-to-day management of its divisions. Think of it as a CEO. The president of the NRA, on the other hand, is like a chair of the board—in charge of oversight and broader strategic issues.

During the revolt in Cincinnati, Harlon Carter was elected executive vice president, marking a change in direction for the NRA away from gun safety and toward the elimination of gun restrictions. It was Harlon who decided the NRA needed to do more advertising. A friend recommended an ad agency in Oklahoma City, Ackerman McQueen. Ack-Mac came up with the "I Am the NRA" ad campaign, which showed Americans of all walks of life announcing that they were NRA members, to emphasize the group's diversity.

One day in 1986, Harlon Carter's successor, Ray Arnett, fired the NRA's entire public education division, consisting of seventeen employees, without warning. He hired Ackerman McQueen in its stead. Arnett argued that Ackerman's computerized systems and press contacts were superior. Meanwhile, Arnett had taken a liking to a female NRA staffer named Tracey Attlee. He had promoted her out of the public education division, sparing her from the layoffs, and given her an unauthorized raise of more than $13,000. The NRA board did not like being caught off guard by these developments and fired him shortly thereafter. (Ackerman still retained the NRA's business though, and by 1987 was exclusively running the NRA's advertising and public affairs work.)

J. Warren Cassidy, executive vice president from 1986 to 1991, departed after a female staffer accused him of penalizing those who rejected his advances and rewarding those who submitted to an affair. Embarrassed by the ensuing settlement, worth nearly $1 million in today's dollars, Cassidy stepped down and was replaced by an interim EVP.

Wayne and another NRA lobbyist were two of the leading candidates to replace Cassidy permanently. Wayne initially demurred, saying he wanted to stay in ILA. He tried to recruit someone else to be EVP. Between 1985 and 1991 the NRA's top leader changed three times, and was about to change a fourth. "The board sought peace and harmony above all else," said former NRA lobbyist Richard Feldman. "Wayne was bland."

"They all kept saying, you've been out here for a long time . . . you need to throw your hat in the ring, and we'll all back you," Wayne later recounted.

Despite never aspiring to the role, at forty-one years old, Wayne LaPierre stumbled his way into becoming the executive vice president of America's most powerful gun rights lobbying group.

Under Wayne's leadership, which began in 1991, the NRA embarked on an expensive, all-out effort to expand its brand—and Wayne's own brand too. To pull this off, Wayne spent millions on Ackerman for public relations, on an organization called Associated Television International for broadcast time, and on a group called PM Consulting for a membership drive—all without written contracts.

Wayne was spending money his organization couldn't afford to lose. The NRA had a deficit of $38 million in 1992 and of $22 million in 1993. Donations declined after a Republican majority swept into the House of Representatives following the 1994 elections. An audit was ordered by members of the board, and its findings in 1996 indicated that the NRA had raided $51 million from its long-term investment portfolio and that the total decline in NRA assets under LaPierre totaled more than $85 million. "The NRA . . . is operating technically as a bankrupt organization," the audit stated. The audit also showed that LaPierre's NRA had spent millions in violation of internal policies requiring board approvals on contracts, and millions more had been spent without written contracts in place.

Wayne responded by laying off more than 20 percent of the staff and offering members a discount to purchase a life membership. Wayne's former boss Neal Knox was furious about the mismanagement of the organization and spent a year campaigning internally to sideline or remove LaPierre. "If Wayne is no longer EVP, some of NRA's vendors are going to have to go on a diet," Knox wrote at the time.

In late 1996 the influential Knox demanded that LaPierre fire Ackerman McQueen. LaPierre agreed to reforms but deviously replaced Ackerman McQueen with Mercury Group, which, unknown to the board at the time, was a wholly owned subsidiary of Ackerman McQueen.

Aided by these powerful contractors, LaPierre was able to turn back the tide. LaPierre's friends schemed dutifully. Mercury Group president Tony Makris, along with board member John Milius, invited a Knox ally to meet up. Over drinks, the two deceived the Knox ally to join a fake conspiracy to bribe Wayne into leaving the NRA. Milius then informed Wayne of the bribe scheme, the blame of which fell on the Knox camp. Wayne publicly declared himself shocked that he would be the target of a bribe from the Knox camp (Wayne would run a similar play in 2019, claiming to have been the subject of a bribery and extortion attempt).

Knox, then holding the role of a senior NRA board member, not only proved unable to unseat Wayne but also lost his own position in 1997 when Wayne's camp fielded popular actor Charlton Heston to challenge him. Knox lost by just four votes.

Of the money spent that so infuriated Knox, some large portion went to improving Wayne's image. Wayne and Ackerman McQueen worked together for more than six years on a two-hour weekly radio program called *The Wayne LaPierre Show.* The unconfident LaPierre needed some serious hand-holding, but his close aide Millie Hallow said the weekly sessions were instrumental in improving the gun rights advocate's confidence. "Over the period of six or seven years he needed less and less help . . . when a guest didn't show up, or answering questions that were call-ins, and you had to hold fewer and fewer signs up," she said.

In 1994, Wayne wrote—or rather, approved—a ghostwritten book called *Guns, Crime, and Freedom*, with a foreword by Tom Clancy. Wayne didn't write the book, or really much of anything—he was never certain enough to know what to say. That's where Ackerman McQueen would generally come in.

The idea was to build a cult of celebrity around Wayne, making him known as a leader who would forcefully defend Americans' gun rights. The book was a surprise success, the most popular title to that date in his publisher Regnery's forty-seven-year history. Stephen Miller, who would grow up to become one of Donald Trump's closest aides and the architect of Trump's immigration policy, credits this book with making him a conservative.

Wayne's consultants pumped up his book's sales, propelling it onto *The New York Times* bestseller list by sending postcards to NRA members in every city that they would visit on the book tour. In a whirlwind three-month tour, they checked off nearly a city a day.

The forced socialization of this tour took its toll on the already-discombobulated Wayne. He recounted to friends an incident after a long day of signing books. Insistent on finding a salad bar, he wandered into a Wendy's. While searching for leafy greens, Wayne meandered behind the counter. The staff, alarmed at the gangly, pale intruder standing near the cash register, set off a robbery alarm. Pandemonium ensued: lights flashed, alarms blared, and a heavyset employee working the drive-through grew so agitated that she tried to jump out the window and got stuck.

So while Wayne's consultants were busy trying to boost his image, he was the same anxious, nervous wreck he had always been. After mass shootings, those who have seen him say, Wayne's typical response is to fall into the depths of immense self-pity before fleeing into hiding. He spends not a minute concerned with the tragedy of the event—or even how to address the disaster strategically from a practical crisis-management standpoint. He is instead consumed with his personal safety. "Oh God, poor me, here we go again," he'd tell his colleagues, according to a former friend's recollection. "This is going to be so awful, the hate that is going to come from this."

After the shootings at Columbine High School in 1999, NRA higher-ups had a series of tense strategy sessions. The NRA had an annual meeting coming up, and the stress level was through the roof. When NRA executives and consultants arrived at one especially high-stakes meeting, they spotted wing-tip dress shoes sticking out from behind the floor-to-ceiling drapes. Wayne had gotten so overwhelmed by the situation that he hid behind the curtains, apparently for comfort.

The spending of millions of dollars that drove the NRA into a deficit in the 1990s also had an effect on its membership rolls. New members generated cash, but it was like a sugar high. Membership surged across the 3.5-million-member mark before receding below 3 million—many joined for a year to get an NRA hat, then never renewed. Still, buoyed by strong membership numbers, the NRA's political power grew during this period. In the '90s, a popular political adage stated that the NRA was an acronym for "Never Reelected Again," a warning for those lawmakers who might think to challenge the group.

This power was multiplied by the bipartisan coalition that the NRA was able to cobble together through the 1990s and 2000s. Neal Knox, Chris Cox, and Wayne LaPierre all had been former Democrats. And moderate Democrats urgently needed the backing of the NRA. "I worked harder to help pro-gun Democrats than anyone else," one NRA federal lobbyist at the time recalled.

The NRA's bipartisan coalition was partly based on fear. The National Rifle Association helped defeat a number of prominent Democrats when Republicans took back control of the House in 1994. It was a decision James Baker, once the NRA's top lobbyist, said he came to regret. "It was a huge mistake. There was too much emphasis on one vote in a career and ruining people who opposed us," Baker told *The Washington Post* in 2000. "We need Democratic friends. Our survival depends on the gun issue not becoming a strictly partisan issue."

Wayne's rhetoric caused the loss of at least one Republican friend in 1995. One of his fundraising letters, authored by NRA vendor PM Consulting, referred to Bureau of Alcohol, Tobacco, and Firearms agents as "jack-booted government thugs" and federal agents as "wearing Nazi bucket helmets and black storm trooper uniforms to attack law-abiding citizens." This letter caused George H. W. Bush to publicly resign his membership from the NRA. "Your broadside against Federal agents deeply offends my own sense of decency and honor; and it offends my concept of service to country," Bush wrote in his letter of resignation.

Wayne also rubbed Republican senator Mitch McConnell the wrong way. The NRA had filed a lawsuit challenging the McCain-Feingold campaign finance reforms. McConnell had been a lead critic of those reforms and had planned his own challenge, but now the NRA had stolen his thunder. McConnell phoned Wayne, demanding to be the lead plaintiff on a combined lawsuit and calling Wayne "a piece of shit," among other choice words. (A spokesperson for McConnell acknowledged that the senator "did speak with the NRA and expressed his profound frustration with their strategy," but denied using that specific phrase.) Wayne backed down under the pressure: the landmark Supreme Court case is now known as *McConnell v. Federal Election Commission.*

The gun rights group did not endorse Republican presidential candidates for much of the 1990s and 2000s. While it did endorse Reagan in 1980, it declined to actively support GOP candidates George H. W. Bush, Bob Dole, or George W. Bush (it did support W's reelection). It was only in 2008, with John McCain's candidacy, that the NRA began endorsing GOP presidential candidates reliably. It has endorsed both Republican presidential candidates since.

The NRA's relationship with pro-gun Democrats could be complicated, even when the relationships were good. One NRA lobbyist tells the story of his relationship with Democrat Harry Reid, who served in the Senate for thirty years and was the Senate majority leader from 2007 to 2015. Reid was also a gun owner. The lobbyist said that Reid was always receptive to the NRA's ideas, and had once gone to a Reid fundraiser at the Capitol Hill restaurant Bistro Bis to deliver an NRA political action committee check. He introduced himself as being from the "NRA." "Ah, the National Restaurant Association," Reid responded knowingly. It was a sly joke that touched on the sensitivity of their relationship.

In its early days, the Obama administration was utterly terrified of the NRA and the divisiveness of the gun issue. In the first year of the administration, when then attorney general Eric Holder cited the renewal of the assault weapons ban as a key administration goal, the president's chief of staff, Rahm Emanuel, responded caustically, "Shut the fuck up."

In 2008 there were sixty-seven Democrats with an A rating from the NRA, making up about a quarter of the party's caucus.

By 2018, this number had dwindled to three. If Baker is right about the power of a bipartisan coalition, then the NRA's broader power declined dramatically over that decade. Part of this was due to political polarization unrelated to the gun issue, but the lion's share of the explanation had to do with a shooting at a school in Connecticut named Sandy Hook Elementary.

CHAPTER 5

The NRA's Lobbying
Animal House

Abra Belke didn't fit the stereotype of a high-powered gun lobby-ist. A cosmopolitan woman with a flair for fashion, her website had 150,000 daily readers, including a core of devoted followers from the D.C. in-scene. She was a tastemaker for women in po-litical Washington: the professional type As you see jogging out by the reflecting pool near dawn, pacing loudly through Capitol hallways in the morning, taking coffee meetings at Cups in the Russell Senate Office Building all afternoon, followed by drinks with friend-colleagues at Sonoma in the evening.

And today, August 7, 2011, she was starting a new job as a fed-eral lobbyist for the National Rifle Association. She marched down First Street, past the Republican haunt known as the Capitol Hill Club, and came to NRA-ILA offices on the House side of the Capi-tol. After five years on the Hill as a legislative aide, she was excited to get her own office for the first time—and to start twisting arms.

Then reality set in. The public has an idea of the National Ri-fle Association as a cutthroat operation. NRA-ILA is powerful but less glamorous than one would expect. Around the time Abra joined the organization, the NRA lobbyists were located in a space above the popular Capitol Hill bar Bullfeathers. Thus, Abra arrived to the smell of day-old canola oil, hamburgers, and alley trash. The office she was assigned did not present itself much better. The previous staffer had been there for years and had neglected to clean up on the way out: bits of almonds, M&M's, and trail mix lay everywhere.

She later learned that every spring the NRA brought in an exterminator to spray for flies. More alarmingly, the place was rat-infested. An uncomfortable, mold-lined hallway shot off into small cubbyhole offices meant for lobbyists of the nation's most powerful lobbying group. The NRA's higher-ups had meant this location to be an interim space but had ended up staying for years.

Seeking to let in some fresh air, Abra opened the window, only to find that the wind would blow leaves inside. She also found four to five inches of standing water pooling outside the window, and black mold growing on the windowsill. She was forced to go to a nearby CVS to buy Clorox wipes, glass cleaner, and bleach. The bureaucracy was not much better. She had imagined a triumphant entry into a new job. Instead she sat at her desk, smelling like bleach, with no working phone, no computer password, and no email account.

How can we be held hostage by the people at IT? she thought.

A fifth-generation NRA lifetime member, she was initially excited to work for the gun rights group. She proudly retains the NRA membership certificates formerly held by her grandfather and father. She was bubbling with new ideas, with the kind of enthusiasm you really get only when you first start at a new organization and don't know what the unspoken, unwritten rules are. As one of the few female lobbyists on staff, Abra wanted to reach out to female lawmakers. She imagined them arranging to go shooting together, or at least getting to know one another. But she quickly ran into a brick wall. Anything relating to women and the NRA was Susan LaPierre's domain, and unbeknownst to Abra, she had wandered into a no-go area. She called Susan's office with the idea, but got a chilly, dismissive reaction from one of Susan's aides. Undeterred, Abra emailed Susan directly. Susan couldn't be bothered with responding directly—she may have viewed Abra as just another lowly staffer, the hired help. Instead, Susan reached out to Abra's boss. Abra was called into her boss's office for a stern warning—not the type you want to get when you're new on the job. "Don't bring it up again," she was told. She had been at the NRA all of a week and a half.

Being an NRA lobbyist in the era immediately before Sandy Hook was at least enjoyable when you were out of the office. And you were out of the office a lot, because if gun issues were not on the legislative agenda, that meant a ton of time for golfing, schmoozing, dining out, and drinking—all in the name of professional networking, of course.

Anyone who has worked on Capitol Hill knows how incestuous that scene can be. The NRA's lobbying team fell in line with that stereotype, and its lobbyists cultivated a hard-partying afterwork culture. One NRA lobbyist developed a reputation for getting too drunk and exposing himself in public at bars, according to five individuals who worked with him. "It would be like working in a frat house. . . . We did a lot of hard work, we played hard too," another lobbyist of this era said, adding euphemistically, "There was a lot of dating each other."

CHAPTER 6

Sandy Hook

Abra was in Kansas City, on her way to attend her grandmother's funeral, when she first heard about the shootings in Newtown, Connecticut. She woke up that morning in a Residence Inn, walked by the breakfast area near the lobby, and saw one of the first news reports. On December 14, 2012, a shooter entered Sandy Hook Elementary School with a rifle and two handguns. In the course of eleven minutes he killed twenty-six people: twenty children between the ages of six and seven, as well as six adults.

Mass grief roiled the country in the hours and days after the shooting. No one could hear about the tragedy without being deeply affected. Stories spread of adults trying desperately to save children and dying in the effort, of panicked students shot at point-blank range.

There was the audio of children recounting their evacuation, being told by police to hold one another's hands and close their eyes so they wouldn't have the images of dead bodies seared into their young consciousness. The imagery of dead children splayed on the ground. The one child who was spared, found in shock but covered in blood from head to toe. The story of a child found still faintly breathing, and of a desperate first responder crying out for help. The violence and the gore and the pain of it was all too much.

The nation was shook by the shooting of young children so close to Christmas, and the NRA was no exception. Several NRA staffers described being overwhelmed by the information that came out in the days after the shooting. "It was the most horrific thing. I cried for days," said one former NRA lobbyist. Another person said that even now, years later, he sometimes wakes up thinking about the tragedy or that week, which he describes as the toughest week of his career.

Some of this outpouring of national grief turned to anger, and a large part of that anger was directed toward the NRA. The shooter and his mother had taken NRA safety courses, which is how many gun enthusiasts come into contact with the group. But the NRA's reputation among non-shooters was its political power, and many Americans blamed the NRA for standing in the way of gun legislation that could reduce violence.

From an organizational standpoint, the official word was silence. No talking points, no message, just silence in the face of the NRA's biggest existential threat in decades. The order came down from higher-ups: the NRA's social media was to go dark, effective immediately, cutting off all outgoing posts. Staffers were assigned rotating two-hour shifts, 24/7, to police the group's Facebook page and remove the photos of dead babies that angry people kept posting.

As Abra spent the morbid weekend after Sandy Hook mourning her grandmother's death in Kansas, she reflected on the deaths of those children as well. She checked her phone frequently, as a distraction from the realities of the world she was experiencing. Over the weekend she didn't get a single message about what the NRA's response would be to the shootings.

It absolutely baffled her. The National Rifle Association had become a main target of national ire, and for all the crisis management and PR people it paid, the group had not even put out an empathetic word. It had in fact not said anything at all. She didn't get any notices from the NRA until that Sunday, when she received an email telling her not to go into the office on Monday, given the number of death threats that the organization was receiving. She already knew; her brother was watching the television when a story came on that someone had just threatened NRA headquarters.

Abra soon found that she herself became a target when her popular blog transformed into a forum for the public's anger toward the NRA. She had started *Capitol Hill Style* in 2008, when she was working for a lawmaker. She had initially run the blog under the pseudonym Belle, but someone had put together that the author was in fact a gun rights lobbyist for the NRA. Her blog was suddenly flooded with angry comments from Americans incensed about her employer.

On the day of the shooting, Abra had published a post like she did every Friday, titled "Happy Hour." It was usually about a cocktail recipe, but this time, ahead of the coming holidays, it was about hot chocolate.

"How is it being a lobbyist for the National Rifle Association now? Hope you can sleep easy paying for your DFW shoes and Ann Taylor suits," read one comment. Another added, "I stopped by today to see if she had taken a break from her snotty, snobby posts over meaningless superficialities for a moment to reflect on what she does for a living. What a surprise—not a word. Vile."

Many more pledged never to read her fashion blog again. "Anyone whose 'dream job' is to be a lobbyist for the NRA is no one I want to associate with," read one such comment. Read another: "How could you write this post and not think about 20 kindergartners who will never drink a cup of hot cocoa again? This will be my last visit to your site."

Abra's hands were tied—she couldn't publicly address the shooting without angering her employer. The exodus from her apolitical style website started that day, and most readers never returned. Her readership was halved from two million page views per month to less than one million page views a month in the weeks after the shooting. It has never recovered.

She was also the recipient of even more menacing messages. Someone had posted the first six digits to NRA-ILA's phone numbers, and angry NRA opponents were randomly dialing numbers and leaving vitriolic messages. Security warned NRA staff not to answer with their names but instead to just say hello so they wouldn't be personally identified. Her voice mail was full of violent messages every morning.

During this period the NRA received scores of death threats a day. Twice, her office on Capitol Hill was evacuated because of a bomb threat. A security officer warned that if they left the NRA offices above Bullfeathers during an evacuation, they should stay within the Capitol Hill security perimeter—the threats could be a ruse for a sniper to pick the NRA staff off with rifles.

Abra remembers thinking about how profoundly her world had changed when NRA security staff moved a package scanner into the copy room. Following the shooting, she received a package, and inside were children's clothes—she remembers to this day that they were sizes 5 and 6. The clothes in the box were covered in what later was found to be animal blood.

Abra was hardly alone. NRA head lobbyist Chris Cox also got suspicious mail at his house, and he had to post 24/7 armed security there in response to some of the threats.

Cox told Abra that Wayne was preparing something, a speech that would be measured and reasoned. Abra didn't know at the time who was putting it together—certainly not the lobbyists who would have to make the case for whatever proposal Wayne landed on. The lobbyists at ILA, Abra among them, were left totally in the dark for what would happen next.

⋅╫⋅

In the days after the Sandy Hook shooting, Wayne had engaged in his regular course of self-pity. Rather than confer directly with his lobbyists or huddle at NRA HQ, he rushed down to the Mercury Group offices in Old Town Alexandria. There, in a conference room, he would strategize with Ackerman McQueen over how to respond. His crisis management specialists agreed: he had to say something before the holidays. A substantial part of the nation was crying out for the dismantlement of the organization. The NRA could not let this massacre go unaddressed.

They dithered for seven days, after which the NRA rolled out its response via remarks at the Willard InterContinental. NRA president David Keene introduced Wayne, prefaced by the warning that they would not be taking any questions.

Following the shootings at Columbine in 1999, Wayne had given a speech in which he had laid out the NRA's position: "First, we believe in absolutely gun-free, zero-tolerance, totally safe schools. That means no guns in America's schools. Period," he said at an NRA annual meeting—to applause. Wayne also added that there could be a "rare exception" for police or security guards.

Wayne's speech thirteen years later would strike a markedly different tone. He called for armed guards in "every single school in this nation" and argued that if there had been an armed guard on-site, lives would have been saved. "Will you at least admit it's possible that twenty-six little kids—that twenty-six innocent lives might have been spared that day?" he said.

Wayne also uttered a memorable line that would shape the NRA's messaging for years: "The only thing that stops a bad guy with a gun is a good guy with a gun," he declared. "Would you rather have your 911 call bring a good guy with a gun from a mile away or from a minute away?"

He tried to shift the focus away from the tool used for the massacre: "Since when did 'gun' automatically become a bad word?" he asked. He blamed the Obama administration: "[We] do know that this president zeroed out school emergency planning grants in last year's budget and scrapped Secure Our Schools policing grants in next year's budget," he said. He blamed the media for being ignorant about the technicalities of firearms while "demoniz[ing] gun owners." He blamed the lack of a national database of mentally ill Americans. He blamed violent video games, movies, and music.

He anticipated how the press would frame his speech: "Now, I can imagine the headlines, the shocking headlines you'll print tomorrow. 'More guns,' you'll claim, 'are the NRA's answer to everything,'" he predicted.

LaPierre, who has always had a problem expressing most emotions other than fear, was unable to match the emotional tenor of the country. He didn't understand the tone he had to strike in order to manage the crisis his organization faced. Wayne just didn't have that kind of empathy—too much of his time after mass shootings was occupied with thinking about what the shooting meant for him personally, a close associate said. So as a result, much of his speech was cultural criticism, media scapegoating, and buck-passing.

Wayne has a deep anxiety about public speaking, and the strain of the moment took its toll. During the speech, covered live on cable TV, he repeatedly stumbled and stuttered. When interrupted by protesters during his remarks, he stared off awkwardly.

By the end of the speech it appeared that he had almost disassociated from reality: he looked to his right while introducing the next speaker, former representative Asa Hutchinson—the problem was that Hutchinson was on his left. Then he exited the stage in the wrong direction, having to awkwardly double back behind Hutchinson. The whole time he had avoided Hutchinson's gaze. He did not stand behind the former congressman during those remarks, as is customary during these sorts of remarks, to show unity. Wayne gave his speech—the absolute minimum—and left as soon as possible.

Two days later, Wayne appeared on *Meet the Press* and associated himself with fanaticism. "If it's crazy to call for putting police and armed security [guards] in our schools to protect our children, then call me crazy," he said.

It was all too much for Wayne to handle. He needed a break: three days after the press conference, he and Susan took a vacation to the Bahamas. The cost for their private-jet flights to Eleuthera, a Bahamian locale known for its pink sand beaches, was almost $70,000.

⠀⠀ ⫶|⫶

Chris Cox, the organization's top lobbyist, was noticeably absent from the press conference. Instead, he was watching the speech from NRA headquarters in Fairfax. He had wanted the NRA to take a more proactive approach to the crisis, to get talking points to key allies on Capitol Hill. He wanted Wayne to take a measured tone: to defend the lawful access to firearms and emphasize mental health. The massacre struck a personal note for him: Cox had a three-year-old child in preschool at the time. Incidentally, he was at his son's preschool the morning the first reports came in about Sandy Hook.

Cox's view was conveyed in a letter ultimately sent to lawmakers weeks later, on January 3, 2013, as they began arriving for the new Congress. Preaching "safe and responsible gun ownership," Cox wrote that every family was focused on preventing a tragedy like Sandy Hook from ever happening again. While objecting to gun control legislation, Cox stressed "a new and hard look at the bureaucratic nightmare that is our mental health system." He spent four paragraphs on mental health, three rejecting gun bans, and just two touching on school security.

But in the days after the Sandy Hook shootings, Cox had been overruled by Wayne and his advisers at Ackerman McQueen. They had allowed a total vacuum to exist for the week following the shooting, and Cox had been completely marginalized in whatever conversations were happening: Wayne and Ack-Mac were not taking input. This was highly abnormal for something this important. And it wasn't just that the NRA lobbyists didn't know the esoteric details; they weren't remotely prepared for the questions that lawmakers were sure to have for them after the press conference. As Wayne had approached the podium at the Willard to give the NRA's response to the shooting, Cox, sitting in front of a big-screen television in Fairfax, didn't know what the organization's executive vice president would say.

The speech droned on, and the normally composed Cox began to cuss out loud. "Fuck this shit," Cox said. He couldn't believe this was the message they were going with: more guns in schools.

"This is a disaster," Cox said, rising from his chair. "I can't even watch this."

He stormed out of the room before Wayne had completed his speech.

Wayne LaPierre had gone completely rogue from his lobbying team, and then given this stumbling, out-of-touch speech that now his team would need to defend. Protesters would target Cox personally in the coming months, spraying his house with fake blood and demonstrating in front of his wife's interior design business.

·⑾·

Abra watched the speech from Montana, where she was visiting her family. Sitting on her brother's couch, she was absolutely shocked by the tone of Wayne's remarks. The emails began to roll in: Members of Congress and their staff were emailing her angrily, telling her not to come to their offices. "How can you support this?" one email asked.

Calling for more firearms in schools after a massacre in an elementary school was so tone-deaf and incendiary, she thought, *I'm going to have to quit my job.*

The Newtown massacre radicalized the National Rifle Association in a number of ways. It gave Wayne, already terrified about his personal security after mass-shooting events, a sense that he and the organization were vulnerable and exposed. It also scared the millions of members who belonged to the NRA, instilling a fear that their rights might be more fragile than they had originally thought. This also prompted growth: the group claims that one hundred thousand new members joined immediately after the shooting. One million new members signed up in the six months after the massacre, as the group offered discounts for fresh recruits and gun control advocates sought reforms.

This alarm from his members gave Wayne an additional impetus to hold a hard-line view, all the better to capitalize, perhaps even profit, off their fear. And Wayne was surrounded by staff and contractors who themselves had been radicalized by the events.

The death threats in the wake of Sandy Hook gave the NRA headquarters a siege atmosphere—it pushed some employees to take even more extreme views than they had before the shootings. This was especially pronounced among the more public-facing sides at NRA HQ, such as the grassroots and membership divisions. They were the ones taking the calls from Americans furious about the NRA's stance after the killing of innocent children.

Abra spent the days around Christmas thinking that she was going to resign and that she couldn't possibly follow Wayne's messaging. But her immediate superior talked her down, convincing her to stay on board into the new year. Congress would soon be considering a series of new gun legislation, and the NRA needed all hands on deck.

CHAPTER 7

Manchin-Toomey Collapses

Just past 4 A.M. on April 4, 2013, Susan LaPierre answered a phone call. A 911 operator was on the line. *Is everything okay?* the voice on the line asked. *The police are outside.* Susan wasn't aware that anything had happened.

Ten minutes earlier, an anonymous individual had contacted Fairfax County police. Stating that he was Wayne LaPierre, he said that he had shot his wife. "If police come in and try to attack me," the caller said, "I will shoot. I do not want to go to jail and I will not be taken alive." The individual said that his wife had just died in his arms, that he had "many guns—my rifle and pistol." He added that he had barricaded himself inside and was willing to kill as many people as he could. The report had come in as an online call, with no associated IP address.

The 911 operator had been able to reach Susan just as police were converging on their home. Wayne soon took the phone from his wife. They were told to turn on all the lights and open the door. Susan refused to go. She didn't believe that the voice on the phone was actually a 911 operator. "Don't go outside," she told Wayne. "You don't know who that is. They're going to kill you."

Wayne kept telling the operator, "I'll call you back. I'll call you back." This went on for five to ten minutes. The standoff ended when Wayne heard radio chatter in the background on the 911 operator's end of the line.

"Okay, I'm coming out with my hands in the air," Wayne told the operator. They emerged from the house, no doubt bleary-eyed and in shock, Wayne in a white shirt and black gym pants, Susan in a gray shirt and pants. They were greeted by more than a dozen officers, all running toward them with their guns drawn, screaming, "Get down!"

They had been swatted, a dangerous prank whereby an anonymous caller contacts law enforcement and pretends to have committed an act of violence. The report then sends armed police sprinting toward the location of the target, where no emergency is occurring.

The already terrified Wayne was further marred by this incident, which would linger in his mind for years. After the Sandy Hook shooting, Wayne was "MIA for months," according to his former chief of staff Josh Powell. "Afraid for his life and the political blowback he suffered for the speech . . . he went low-profile for almost a year."

It was one of the most consequential years in the history of the NRA. Less than two weeks after the swatting incident, the Senate would vote on the Manchin-Toomey gun legislation.

⫸

After Abra Belke returned to Capitol Hill in the new year, the NRA's top federal gun lobbyists all huddled together to share the state of play. The NRA had already scored an own goal. An ad produced by Ackerman McQueen for the NRA had targeted President Obama's daughters: "Are the president's kids more important than yours?" the narrator asked. "Then why is he skeptical about putting armed security in our schools when his kids are protected by armed guards at their school? . . . He's just another elitist hypocrite." NRA HQ had released the spot without telling their lobbyists about it first.

The ad, and the personal nature of it, did not go over well even among the NRA's allies on Capitol Hill. Abra was woken up by a phone call at 5:30 A.M. after it began airing and was shocked to hear a U.S. senator on the line angrily shouting, "Why would you do this?" The lawmaker was Senator Mary Landrieu, a Democrat from a red state, talking about how she had just been put in an impossible situation by the NRA. The next person to call was Senator Marco Rubio, who said he wanted her to understand just how seriously he was taking this. The ad had gone after the president's children, and members of Congress were furious. Every NRA lobbyist got calls of this type in the days that followed.

Even the press-averse NRA lobbyist James Baker felt compelled to publicly distance himself from the ad, telling *Reuters* that it had been "ill-advised." The ad was another example of the tension between Ackerman McQueen and ILA—while the lobbyists were on the Hill trying to make deals, Ack-Mac and Wayne were cooking up this divisive advertisement. Good for the base, bad for legislation.

The national trauma of Newtown had led to a new push to consider gun laws. There had been some talk about reinstating the assault weapons ban, an idea that a White House task force led by Joe Biden recommended. But this was a nonstarter in the Senate: when it eventually came up for a vote, it was defeated

40–60, with more than a dozen Democrats crossing the aisle to join with every Republican (save one) to bury the proposal.

Democratic senator Joe Manchin of West Virginia learned about the massacre at Sandy Hook the day he returned from a hunting trip, and decided he had to do something about it. Nothing in politics had ever impacted him emotionally the way that shooting did. He was well liked by the NRA's lobbyists, who, even when they did not agree with him, respected that he was taking a political risk on gun legislation. West Virginia, after all, is a state where 58.5 percent of households own firearms.

Nationally, the concept of universal background checks was extremely popular. In early 2013, more than 90 percent of Americans were in support of universal background checks. Polling also suggested that the idea was popular among NRA members, 74 percent of whom supported the idea. In fact, in the aftermath of Sandy Hook, a pollster commissioned internally by the NRA to look at the popularity of various legislative options was explicitly told not to ask about universal background checks.

Background checks would not have stopped the massacre at Sandy Hook. The shooter had used firearms obtained legally by his mother. But a prohibition on assault weapons and limitations on high-capacity magazines were political nonstarters, thanks in part to NRA opposition. So when it came to ideas that could reduce gun violence in America, expanding background checks was the only viable legislative option for Manchin to pursue in the spring of 2013.

Manchin had originally started working on gun reform legislation with Republican senator Tom Coburn of Oklahoma. The NRA was not concerned about either of them—they had both received A ratings from the gun rights group. But Coburn just wasn't comfortable with expanding background checks. Coburn never said no, and his aides kept pitching ideas, but it eventually became clear to Manchin's staff that Coburn wasn't going to get to yes. So Manchin was left searching for another Republican who could carry the mantle.

On Valentine's Day 2013, Manchin was on a flight with Republican senator Pat Toomey of Pennsylvania, and their neighboring-state camaraderie sparked an amicable conversation. The next month, on March 18, Manchin and Toomey ran into each other at Washington D.C.'s Union Station, where Manchin pitched the idea of collaborating on gun legislation.

"Why wouldn't I be the lead on this?" Toomey asked his staff. The Republican had been deeply moved by his meetings with victims of gun violence. He had never thought that background checks were a limitation on Second Amendment rights and had actually voted for an expansion of background checks when he was in the House. A fiscal hawk from a moderate state, Toomey had reason to nod to suburban voters in Pennsylvania by championing middle-of-the-road gun legislation. And he had the political capital to do it: Toomey, like Manchin, also had an A rating from the NRA. By Easter—March 31—Manchin and Toomey were working on the text of a gun reform bill.

The next two and a half weeks were a blur of activity as staffers from both offices combined to iron out the details over sandwiches from Taylor Gourmet, a D.C. chain founded by two Pennsylvanians. Momentum was on their side: legislative aides were working close to twenty-four hours a day, stopping home only to shower and take short naps.

·⫶⫶·

As early as Manchin's first legislative drafts with Coburn, the National Rifle Association had been involved in the negotiations. In the flurry of exchanges, the NRA had suggested insertions that would be good for gun owners. Many of these lived on in the Manchin-Toomey drafts.

The view of the NRA's top lobbyists at the time was that background checks were not the hill to die on. In the wake of a national tragedy like Sandy Hook, there was room to score a few wins for the gun community while allowing the gun control folks to let off a little steam with a win of their own. At first, a release valve in the form of Manchin-Toomey was fine with them.

Head lobbyist Chris Cox was personally involved in the ensuing negotiations, attending several in-person meetings in March. The NRA's lawyers were involved in careful readings of the texts.

But at the time, NRA-ILA lobbyists were careful to be coy. They were managing risk: they were trying to get a good bill in case it had the support to pass, but also not committing to backing it. All throughout, they were just a moment from retreat. At no point did they make any pledges that they would support the legislation, even if they hinted that they might be willing to be hands-off in the final reckoning.

The NRA continually took part in negotiations, taking meetings and providing technical legal assistance for the wording of the bill. One of the NRA's key advantages in the gun debate is that the issue can be highly technical; offices are always coming to them for help getting the details right. The NRA made several technical recommendations for the crafting of the background check language—and did not hint to Republicans or Democrats involved in the process that they were resistant to it. Certainly NRA lobbyists had never framed background checks as some sort of affront to gun rights.

After all, background check legislation in the decade prior had the NRA's support. Wayne LaPierre had personally supported expanded background checks after Columbine: "We think it's reasonable to provide mandatory instant background checks for every sale at every gun show. No loopholes anywhere, for anyone," Wayne had told Congress in 1999.

Toomey aides were in charge of bringing hesitant Republicans on board. They had a list of ten Republicans they thought were persuadable. Those on the list had one common ask: "The NRA has to give us cover to support this," GOP Senate offices would say. Staffers involved in crafting the legislation could sense that the NRA was having an internal discussion in which they were open to supporting the bill, and Toomey's office felt that the NRA would eventually support it. Congressional staff have considerable experience in endless rounds of hopeless negotiations for bills that end up going nowhere. But this one felt different: as the bill neared its unveiling, there was serious optimism that it would come together and ultimately pass.

Manchin was responsible for keeping the Democratic caucus together. He also had a home-state issue: he started traveling to gun stores in West Virginia to pitch voters on his bill at the retail level. He did not get a warm reception. Voters may have trusted Joe Manchin, but they didn't trust President Obama, who was supportive of the bill.

This frenetic period was a high point for bipartisanship. Unbeknownst to the public, gun control groups and gun rights groups were secretly negotiating with one another behind the scenes. John Feinblatt, a close confidant of then New York City mayor Michael Bloomberg and a key architect of the gun control group Mayors Against Illegal Guns, was having private conversations with Alan Gottlieb, who headed up the Second Amendment Foundation. Both were trying to shape the legislation in a way that both sides could support it. Gottlieb managed to get a concession from Bloomberg's camp: Mayors Against Illegal Guns would not oppose the pro-gun sweeteners in the bill. Hopes were high by April.

On April 5, 2013, news of the draft legislation being hammered out by Manchin and Toomey found its way to the press. Lawmakers returned to Washington the next week, and on April 10 the details of the legislation were formally announced to the public.

The result was the Manchin-Toomey bill, formally known as the Public Safety and Second Amendment Rights Protection Act. Altogether, it was not a particularly ambitious piece of gun legislation. The bill expanded background checks—already mandatory for most purchases of firearms—to cover all sales at gun shows or by online vendors. However, this would not apply to sales among family or friends. The bill also proposed improving the existing background check system and establishing a national commission on mass violence.

The NRA's top lobbyists, including Chris Cox, had managed to shape a significant portion of the bill. The draft had been negotiated and written with the purpose of bringing on gun rights activists, and it included so-called Second Amendment enhancements—essentially deal sweeteners that these activists had wanted for years. These included allowing interstate handgun sales, shortening the amount of time a seller would have to wait for a response from the background check system, protecting hunters who legally transport firearms to the state they are hunting in, and explicitly prohibiting a national gun registry.

The lobbying on all sides was intense. A number of gun show owners, normally faithful NRA allies, were encouraged by the sweeteners in the bill and urged its passage. Many other Second Amendment activists were staunchly opposed. An NRA lobbyist at the time could expect to receive a new email arguing for or against the bill every ten seconds for twelve hours of the day. A torrent of emails came flowing in as they stared at their in-boxes in utter helplessness.

Both left and right had their problems with the process. That the NRA was a party to the negotiations came as unwelcome news to Democrats. Senator Chuck Schumer, who later cosponsored the bill, said he wasn't interested in negotiating with the National Rifle Association. He also did not view the NRA as a good-faith negotiator. "I am not here to work for the NRA. I am here to cut their throat!" he said in one particularly intense exchange during a meeting among Democratic senators.

Schumer didn't have to worry long. The National Rifle Association was facing immense pressure from its right flank to withdraw. As early as March 23, 2013, *Politico* had reported on rumors that the NRA and Manchin were engaged in secret talks over background checks. Two days later, the National Association for Gun Rights sent out a bulletin to its members: "I've warned you from the beginning that our gravest danger was an inside-Washington driven deal," wrote NAGR executive Dudley Brown. He added that the deal was a "Manchin-NRA compromise bill." The Gun Owners of America followed suit a week later, urging its members to contact the NRA to voice their opinion. Neither of these groups had even a tenth of the NRA's membership, or the NRA's political power, but they threatened to chip away at the NRA's reputation.

The NRA had a number of options: it could support the background check legislation it had helped craft; it could stay neutral and not "score" the vote in its closely watched annual legislative scorecard; or it could mobilize its membership against the legislation. As the vote neared and hopes for the NRA's support became dimmer, Toomey's office reached out to the NRA's lobbyists: "Can you just not score it?"

But the pressure from the right had helped seal the deal. In early April, the NRA had stopped negotiating with Manchin's office. Abra, who had been supportive of the legislation, came into the office one morning and was told to tell all offices she had been in contact with that the NRA was opposed to the bill. A week before the vote, NRA-ILA announced that "expanding background checks at gun shows will not prevent the next shooting, will not solve violent crime and will not keep our kids safe in schools."

Then two days before the Senate took up the bill, the NRA declared that it would score the vote in its annual assessments of senators, signaling that lawmakers who supported Manchin-Toomey would face political blowback from the gun rights group. Even the proposal's architects knew that it was over. Manchin called NRA lobbyist James Baker. "Jim, why'd you change?" Manchin asked. He never got a straight answer.

Some make the mistake of thinking that the NRA's power

comes from political contributions or money from the gun industry. After ILA lobbyists had made up their mind to oppose the bill, they flashed their real power: their mailing lists and ability to mobilize. Marshaled to action, thousands of ardent Second Amendment supporters flooded Capitol Hill phone lines and crowded email accounts. Terrified lawmakers, concerned about their reelection bids, fell into line. Toomey had a list of ten Republicans he hoped to win over: ultimately, he was able to convince only three. Meanwhile, four Democratic senators from purple states joined Republicans to oppose the bill.

Even Gottlieb and his Second Amendment Foundation, which had secretly negotiated with Michael Bloomberg's camp, did not ultimately support the bill. Gottlieb had publicly come out in favor of the bill but pulled his support on the day of the vote, putting out a statement arguing that his support had been contingent on getting a vote on a separate gun amendment unrelated to Manchin-Toomey. "This is not a reflection against Senators Joe Manchin or Pat Toomey, who are staunch Second Amendment advocates, and I want to thank them for all of their efforts to include as many protections for our gun rights as possible," Gottlieb said at the time.

Because of Senate rules, the bill needed a supermajority of sixty votes to be considered for passage. With Vice President Joe Biden presiding over the chamber, Manchin-Toomey failed on April 17, 2013: 54 votes for to 46 opposed. In the Senate gallery, watching in dismay, were shooting victims as well as relatives of those killed at Sandy Hook Elementary School.

Despite Democrats holding the Senate, despite the NRA once having been supportive of the idea of expanded background checks, despite the murders and the tragedy, despite the vast majority of Americans being supportive of the idea, the compromise bill failed.

I can't believe we can't get it done, Abra thought. *What does it hurt to have background checks? We already have a situation where 80 percent of gun sales include checks.*

Little loyalty was displayed by the NRA after Manchin-Toomey failed. Democratic senator Mark Pryor of Arkansas, who stuck with the NRA's final edict, was not rewarded for his *no* vote. In 2014 the NRA endorsed Pryor's opponent, Senator Tom Cotton.

NRA lobbyists who had participated in crafting Manchin-Toomey had not even given those offices a heads-up that they would be opposing the legislation. And now, again without warning, they were targeting both Manchin and Toomey as if they were anti-gun zealots. Manchin was subsequently targeted by the NRA, which spent $100,000 in ads criticizing him. The NRA also revoked Manchin's A rating—when he ran for reelection, they gave him a D. Toomey's A rating was also revoked: he received a C the next time he was graded. The knife in the back leaves a bitter feeling in those Senate offices to this day.

Cox viewed his maneuvers during this time period as part of how politics is done. From his point of view, he engaged with Congress because it was his job, and he withdrew because the NRA made a decision that expanded background checks were unacceptable. "You can negotiate in good faith, and at the end of those negotiations not be in agreement. When elected officials want to craft legislation that would impact the NRA, it was my job to have that conversation," Cox said. "They wanted an agreement, but there never was one."

Two weeks after the collapse of Manchin-Toomey, Abra walked

into the ILA office above Bullfeathers and put in her resignation. In the years that followed, the things that she was most concerned about came to pass: the NRA became a driver of the conservative culture war; was driven further to the right by its interest in fundraising from its base; and alienated gun owners who care only about the right to safely and responsibly bear arms.

By the time she left NRA-ILA, Abra suffered from anxiety attacks and acid reflux due to the stress of her job and the constant violent threats. It was among the most difficult times in her life. One moment she reflected on later was when a concerned coworker approached her and asked her to stop drinking during the day to manage the stress.

She's never managed to shake her association with the NRA, which she views as a set of scarlet letters. Her unrelated fashion and style projects frequently run up against this problem: often the mere fact that she worked for the NRA years ago will be enough to end the prospect of a collaboration. She recalls that after she held an event at women's clothing company M.M.LaFleur in 2017, someone left an online comment asking why the company couldn't have found someone better for an event than a former NRA lobbyist.

"There's something we've lost in our society," she said. "You can be affiliated with one group and you are chronically guilty for the rest of your life." Meanwhile, she's unable to work on firearms issues—after speaking out publicly against Wayne LaPierre, she was told by an industry insider that the NRA had sought to blacklist her. She says that she still supports the NRA's stated mission of helping people use firearms safely and responsibly, but she adds, "That's not Wayne's mission."

·||·

Wayne hadn't been the one to stall Manchin-Toomey. The members of the NRA who jammed up phone lines on Capitol Hill and threatened their lawmakers with defeat were the ones who accomplished that. In fact, it was remarkable how little influence Wayne had, despite being the head of the NRA. He had declared in congressional testimony in January that expanded background checks would create "an unworkable universal federal nightmare bureaucracy." The NRA's lobbyists were still negotiating on background check legislation into early April. It just wasn't Wayne's fiefdom.

The NRA, its consultants at Ackerman McQueen, and ILA had avoided the gun group's most critical threat in decades, and no new gun legislation was signed into law. For all his peccadillos, his flaws, his anxieties, and his weirdness, Wayne had somehow managed to glide along and come out on top. Again.

The whole process had unnerved Wayne, however. Following Sandy Hook and his subsequent swatting experience, Wayne began taking extravagant security precautions. From the time of the shootings onward, his schedule would not be written down and the details of his travels would be shared with very few people. Prior to Sandy Hook, Wayne took mostly commercial flights. But using security as the reason, he now began flying on private jets. This would evolve over time to the need for private jets for virtually all circumstances, and for family members even when he was not along for the ride.

Manchin-Toomey was a key turning point for the NRA. The month after that bill stalled in the Senate, NRA president Jim Porter indicated that the debates over gun rules in America were not just "a battle over gun rights" but instead a broader "culture war." Wayne viewed this as a transition from leading a gun group to leading "a freedom organization." This signaled the NRA's departure from being a single-issue organization that focused on gun issues to its transformation into a group that was about a broader ideological identity. The pretense of working with Democrats was gone. From Sandy Hook onward, it became increasingly difficult for Dems to work with the NRA, and vice versa.

The episode also managed to add to the mythology of the NRA, suggesting that its power was beyond question. Outwardly this appeared to be the nadir for the NRA's opponents: even the killing of innocent schoolchildren was not enough to summon the political will for so much as milquetoast legislation on gun control. But the outrage and frustration that this moment brought would lead to a rebirth of the American gun control movement.

At the time, the American political landscape favored the NRA: only a very small number of people were dedicated to the cause of gun control, and gun rights activists made up the lion's share of people who really cared about the issue. The danger would be if suburban moms in the vast, unengaged middle began to make this a cause.

"The NRA is going to be in real trouble with the general population if soccer moms take up the gun control mantle," explained a former NRA strategist. "We needed to do something to convince the major middle not to take up this cause."

But after the failure of Manchin-Toomey, the soccer moms were *pissed*.

CHAPTER 8

The Rise of Everytown

Shannon Watts was running through sun salutation A, a series of yoga poses, when she decided to quit. She had signed up for lessons on how to become a yoga teacher. It did not suit her, and right in the middle of her training session she decided to walk out of the class. She was extremely agitated that morning and couldn't focus on the serenity that class was demanding. She may have been too type A to become a relaxed, calming yoga teacher anyway.

What *was* on her mind were the images she had seen the day before. A longtime professional in corporate communications, she had years ago become a stay-at-home mom. She had been folding laundry in her bedroom in Zionsville, Indiana, when a breaking-news alert came on the television. There had been a shooting in Newtown, Connecticut, a place she had never heard of before. She spent the rest of the day watching as children were evacuated from the school into the woods and as parents arrived on the scene looking terrified.

What must it feel like to be a family member of a victim? she thought. She—like NRA staff members did, like gun control group members did, like many other Americans did—cried for much of the rest of that day.

She rolled up her yoga mat and drove home. What, if anything, could she do to process this national tragedy? She had wrongly predicted that Congress would pass gun reform legislation after the shooting of their colleague Representative Gabby Giffords in 2011. In the wake of another tragedy, she was angry. She had not worked in politics since she had been just out of college, when she had a low-level job in the Missouri state legislature. She hadn't researched gun laws or the prevalence of gun violence. She just wanted to put her energy *somewhere*.

She clicked through her MacBook Air on a table in her suburban kitchen. She scrolled through a number of groups—D.C. think tanks, advocacy organizations led mostly by men, nothing she could identify with on a gut level. She was looking for something like Mothers Against Drunk Driving, but for the gun control issue.

It was 2012, mind you, and she had just learned how to make a Facebook page. With about seventy-five friends in her social media network and nothing to lose, she started an ambitious-sounding group: "One Million Moms for Gun Control," she tapped out on her keyboard.

"Change will require action by angry Americans outside of Washington, D.C. Join us—we will need strength in numbers against a resourceful, powerful and intransigent gun lobby," Shannon wrote, asking like-minded people to join her for a demonstration in America's capital. "I started this page because, as a mom, I can no longer sit on the sidelines."

Her husband was a little hesitant about her doing this. But in the ensuing hours, the group went viral. She had filled a niche that grieving and angry moms in America had been desperate to fill. Drawing on a background in communications, she paid to put out a press release on PR Newswire, which is how a lot of moms found her Facebook page: by googling "moms" and "gun control." By the time they went to sleep that evening, her husband chimed in again. "This is going to be a big deal," he admitted.

The name took some tweaking. One of her daughters, who is gay, said that One Million Moms was a Christian fundamentalist group that opposes LGBT rights. *Okay.* "Gun control" sounded like a phrase founded on the NRA's terms, offered another adviser. *All right.* So they landed on this: Moms Demand Action for Gun Sense in America.

From just a few dozen friends, the idea shot out into cyberspace and went viral. Within weeks, the Facebook group had morphed into an organization that was actually holding real-world gatherings. Moms Demand Action organized a rally in Washington, D.C.—one of its first in-person events—by late January. Shannon was petrified. She was so terrified of public speaking that as she approached the stage, she was shaking so hard she couldn't even hold her cup of coffee.

Not long after, Shannon's group got a phone call. It was a White House aide: Would they consider organizing to support this new legislative effort that was coming out? It was the bill that would later be known as Manchin-Toomey.

◃╟▹

John Feinblatt's story begins years before Sandy Hook, when he was working as a criminal justice coordinator for New York City mayor Michael Bloomberg, focused on the issue of gun violence in the city. A buttoned-up, professional type, John is a man of data and hard numbers. In 2005 he showed the mayor statistics revealing that 90 percent of firearms found at crime scenes had come from out of state. "I always knew this was a problem," John told the mayor. "I never knew the *extent* of the problem." If they were to stop this flow of guns into New York, they would need a national approach to firearms policy.

For most of the 2000s, the gun control movement was listless and poorly funded. Some, including former president Bill Clinton, felt that the NRA had been the reason why Al Gore had been narrowly defeated in 2000. And the Democratic Party's loss of the House of Representatives in 1994 had similarly been blamed on the passage of the Federal Assault Weapons Ban. When the ban expired in 2004, it was not renewed. In 2006 Democrats regained control of Congress, this was in part due to candidates in moderate districts who had received A ratings from the NRA. Many Republicans and Democrats felt that gun control was an untouchable issue. In any case, there was no strong gun control lobbying group to press them to feel otherwise. The leading gun control group at the time, the Brady Campaign to Prevent Gun Violence, was struggling for resources and forced to lay off staff to stay afloat.

John and Mayor Bloomberg felt there needed to be a new middle ground in the gun debate. They wanted to shift the discussion from taking firearms away from people and toward preventing violent offenders and criminals from getting access to them. They didn't want to talk about "gun control"—they wanted to talk about "illegal guns" and how to keep them out of the hands of criminals. Banning certain kinds of firearms polled poorly in comparison with expanding background checks to cover all gun show sales, for example.

In the bullpen at city hall, on an elevated platform that was being used as a conference room, John huddled with his boss, Mayor Bloomberg, and the then mayor of Boston, Tom Menino, and came up with the idea of a group of mayors that could tackle this problem.

Soon, fifteen mayors convened at the New York mayor's residence to see if they could come up with some consensus on gun reform. Spontaneously, Bloomberg decided to seize the moment. Without much preparation, he decided to announce the formation of a new group that afternoon, with him and Menino as co-chairs. "I think I'm going to say we're going to have two hundred and fifty mayors over the next three or four months," Bloomberg told his aide. John, who knew that *he* would be the one who would have to make that happen, began to protest that this might be too ambitious—especially since they were making this goal on the fly. The next thing John heard was Bloomberg approaching the microphones to announce the project—and the number of mayors they'd aim to bring on board.

On many metrics the first few years were a slog. By the time of Sandy Hook, the gun control movement was still on its back heel. The National Rifle Association was extremely powerful, and no comprehensive gun control legislation had been passed at the federal level in years. Mayors Against Illegal Guns had some small victories under its belt: In 2009 the Senate voted down an amendment that would have allowed Americans to carry concealed firearms across state lines. And in 2012 Bloomberg backed seven candidates against NRA-supported lawmakers—Bloomberg's bets won four of the seven seats.

John happened to be in the White House on December 14,

2012, when the news from Sandy Hook shocked the nation. He had been discussing immigration policy with Cecilia Muñoz, who headed up the Obama White House's Domestic Policy Council at the time, when a White House aide told them about the shooting. John, like Chris Cox on the other side of the issue, had children around the same age as those who had been murdered. He rushed back to New York City immediately.

Bloomberg's initial response was to hold Obama's feet to the fire. He excoriated the president for not acting more aggressively: Obama hadn't enforced existing gun laws and hadn't suggested legislation to curb gun violence, the mayor said on NBC's *Meet the Press*. "At least he's got to try. That's his job," Bloomberg said. "This should be his number one agenda. He is the president of the United States. And if he does nothing during his second term, something like 48,000 Americans will be killed with illegal guns. That is roughly the number of Americans killed in the whole Vietnam War."

Bloomberg also tried to downplay the idea that the NRA was some sort of powerhouse. "The NRA's number one objective this time was to defeat Barack Obama for a second term," he told NBC host David Gregory. "Last time I checked the election results, he won, and he won comfortably. This myth that the NRA can destroy political careers is just not true."

During those hectic weeks of negotiations over gun legislation in 2012 and 2013, John was in Washington, D.C., constantly to shape the federal response. He met with everyone: gun control advocates and gun rights advocates, Democrats and Republicans. While some on the left were pushing for an assault weapons ban, John was pressing for the expansion of background checks.

·ılı·

Shannon Watts's first few months of organizing were guided more by instinct than expertise. It was like a start-up had blossomed overnight at her kitchen table. In February 2013, as they were mobilizing to support gun reform legislation, Moms Demand volunteers thought about writing valentines to senators, encouraging them to support the nascent effort post–Sandy Hook. When they discovered that Senate office buildings would not allow visitors to bring in boxes, they had to surreptitiously stuff valentines wherever they could find room—inside their coats, hats, and purses—to get past security.

Shannon had raised some money but was not in the same league as the NRA. While the gun rights group brought in $347 million in 2013, she had been able to raise about $100,000. It was a lot for her, but it wasn't enough to make a serious challenge to the NRA's preeminence. Not many people were interested in giving large chunks of change to a woman operating from her kitchen table who had no background in advocacy—at least not yet.

Meanwhile, the harassment began. *Had I known what awaited me, would I have been brave enough to start that Facebook page? I don't know,* she thought later. Almost immediately she started getting death threats and, because she's a woman, threats of sexual violence. Within the first two weeks of her starting that Facebook page, her home address had been shared online, and she called the police when a pickup drove past her house very slowly, as if casing the place out.

"I suggest you contact a lawyer," the responding police officer said. "Oh, and by the way, this is what you get when you mess with the Second Amendment."

But all of it would be worth it when Manchin-Toomey would pass, and there would be something concrete to show for all the anguish, organizing, and anxiety—or so she believed. Shannon was in the Senate gallery watching the day the bill failed. A political newcomer, someone had to lean over and explain that the bill would not proceed because, even though it received majority support, sixty votes were required in order to prevent a filibuster. She sat there helplessly as Patricia Maisch, the hero who had wrestled a gun magazine from a shooter in Tucson, interrupted the staid, quiet Senate floor with a piercing, "Shame on you!" before being removed by a security guard.

Our organization is over, Shannon thought to herself while leaving Capitol Hill that day. *Maybe the country wasn't ready for this. We came here, we failed, and now we just go back to our normal lives.* She thought her volunteers, dejected, would leave in droves.

"We were crestfallen," John Feinblatt says, thinking back on the failure of Manchin-Toomey. "But not shocked." Even now, he vividly recalls the various meetings he had with the "maybes" on the bill as the legislation was being considered. He ticks through the ones he thought he could flip—for example, Mark Pryor, whose state of Arkansas John had extensively polled; and Mark Begich, who as mayor of Anchorage had been an early member of Mayors Against Illegal Guns but who as a senator had turned on the issue of firearms. Both those Democrats eventually voted no on the bill.

Reflecting on it now, Shannon thinks that if Manchin-Toomey

had passed, it would have actually taken the wind out of the sails of her budding organization. "All the NRA had to do is come to the middle on this issue and agree there should be a background check," she says now. But they had not.

·⫴·

Shannon's volunteers didn't leave in droves. And rather than move on to another cause, Michael Bloomberg doubled down, pledging tens of millions more dollars to the effort.

After the failure of Manchin-Toomey, John approached the mayor and said, "I can imagine you must be thinking, 'Is this just something we can't achieve?'" Bloomberg said that he wasn't even considering walking away from the issue but that they needed to change their strategy.

First, they needed to build a grassroots movement. Shannon's group had the motivated volunteers but lacked the resources to keep going. "I didn't realize how much it would cost and how much it would take," Shannon recalls. In 2014, Mayors Against Illegal Guns and Moms Demand Action joined to create Everytown for Gun Safety. Bloomberg offered $50 million to get the group off the ground.

Second, they needed to change their focus. With deeply held cultural issues like guns, the most effective way to achieve change, they thought, was to start locally. The newly formed organization decided to adopt the NRA playbook, pivoting to a focus on state capitals, where the NRA had been virtually unchallenged for decades. "Congress is not where it begins; it's where it ends," Shannon said.

The National Rifle Association's core legislative strategy had for decades included dominating state legislatures to amend state constitutions and pass pro-gun measures. "A lot of people in Washington, especially in the media, picture Capitol Hill lobbyists when they think about the National Rifle Association," former NRA lobbyist Richard Feldman recalls his boss once telling him. "That's a mistake. It's in the statehouses from Annapolis to Sacramento, from Boston to Baton Rouge, where a lot of gun laws and most administrative regulations are made, where our members' fight is won or lost."

Everytown was explicitly set up to mimic the NRA's tactics and as a direct counterweight to the gun group. "The NRA should be afraid," Shannon said when the new group started. In 2014, six states where Everytown lobbied passed legislation to make it harder for those convicted of domestic violence to purchase or retain their firearms, and more than twelve seats in six other states were won or retained by lawmakers who supported gun control measures.

To date, Michael Bloomberg has contributed $270 million to gun control efforts in America. Everytown now claims that more than six million people have joined the movement since it launched. By 2018, the gun control movement outspent the NRA in the congressional midterms.

The soccer moms—or moms in general—weren't neutral anymore.

·||·

Elsewhere, the push to start an investigation into the National Rifle Association was off the ground. Marcus Owens was likely the first to comprehensively wade through the Byzantine paperwork that nonprofits are required to file both federally and across many of the states they do business in. Owens had one thing going for him: while he is now a lawyer for the firm Loeb & Loeb, he had once been the director of the IRS division overseeing tax-exempt organizations like the NRA.

A secretive and anonymous group had hired Owens to look through the NRA's filings, and Owens had found quite a number of irregularities. The disclosures and prior litigation hinted that the NRA had for more than two decades enriched friends and relatives of Wayne LaPierre and his wife, Susan. Unwritten contracts were used to avoid internal rules that contracts be disclosed to the board. Noncompetitive contracts were used to benefit friends. Contradictions between varying disclosures suggested that the NRA had lied about the payments it made to lobbyists and on campaigns.

Owens began drafting a letter to the then attorney general of New York, Eric Schneiderman. Dated September 15, 2015, it began:

"I am writing on behalf of my client, of a group of individuals that wish to remain anonymous. The members of the group include individuals who support the fundamental concept behind the Second Amendment to the U.S. Constitution, but who have grave concerns about the behavior of the leadership of the National Rifle Association of America."

CHAPTER 9

Wayne's Posse and NRA HQ

Most of the staff at the National Rifle Association headquarters were totally blind to the grift that was happening above them in the executive offices. They had signed up to work for a nonprofit and were treated like, well, they worked at a nonprofit.

There were two tiers at the NRA: the executives who had the ability to march into Wayne's office and browbeat him into a sweetheart deal—and everyone else. And while Wayne is paid more than almost any other nonprofit CEO in America, the rank and file was being asked to take wages well below what they'd fetch almost anywhere else.

Steve Hoback, who worked on the NRA's training programs for three years, started at $28,000 a year, with his salary rising to $32,000 per year. The logic for many staffers at NRA HQ was that they were employed for a cause and were expected to take a lower salary to do meaningful work. "When I first got there, it was like a dream come true for me," Hoback said. "I'm a super loyal guy if I believe in the product." But he was constantly frustrated over the salaries he heard Wayne and the other executives were earning while he struggled to make ends meet in the Washington, D.C., metro area, one of the more expensive regions in the country. "We were horribly underpaid," he said. He voiced his concern internally about a six-figure executive bonus that he had heard about. Then he quit. His next employer offered more than double his NRA salary.

"If you work there, you keep your head down and your mouth shut. Or you don't work there," said Vanessa Ross, who once headed up the organization's disabled shooting services division. Ross got along with her higher-ups until she questioned budget cuts to her programs, which were part of a long-term endowment. "There was a culture of fear. The moment you poked your head up and started asking questions, that's when I felt everything turn—then it was like I was the pariah," she recalled. She was dismissed not long after.

This was a recurring theme for staff at NRA headquarters in Fairfax, a toxic mix of paranoia, expectations of blind loyalty, and poor salaries. "It's an extremely intimidating place. They're always looking out for who might hurt them in some way," said Aaron Davis, who worked there for years as a fundraiser. "They're secretive at the top, and people at the bottom were not making a lot of money. Fundraising people made some money, but not much compared to a typical DC nonprofit. I'm guessing about ten thousand dollars less than they would at a comparable position elsewhere."

Staffer after staffer after staffer reported being worked to the bone for low salaries, with constant promises of "being taken care of" at some future date that would never arrive. This was a frequent problem: since wages were low, raises rare, and bonuses nonexistent, turnover was high. And of course working for the

NRA had other ramifications—once you had those three letters on your résumé, you immediately made yourself less appealing to hiring managers in a broad portion of the job market, given the controversial nature of the organization.

It wasn't always obvious how much management made compared with how much their staff did. There was no transparency in salaries, and those who asked questions or raised objections were swiftly marginalized. There were always whispers of extravagant meals and private jets, but for the most part they were rumors discussed over brown bag lunches. Small indecencies did leak out to staff from time to time—such as cronyism or a revolving door between the NRA and the gun industry, but they were minor fouls compared with the millions of dollars that were being wasted on a yearly basis, hidden away from public view.

While Wayne stayed at the Ritz and traveled by private jet, underlings had to follow the actual rules set out by the NRA. Travel was always coach, and lodging was at Hampton Inns or an equivalent. "Persons traveling on NRA business have the duty to exercise care and avoid impropriety, or even the appearance of impropriety in any travel expense," the internal travel guidelines read. Employees were expected to take cabs or public transit rather than rent cars when traveling if that was more cost-effective. These frugal directives were simply ignored by the NRA higher-ups.

◦||◦

It was one thing to be on staff at NRA HQ but another thing entirely to be a woman on staff at NRA HQ. Multiple women who worked there reported a clubby, male-dominated culture revolving around smoking cigars. The men in leadership were rarely invested in the professional growth of their female subordinates. While some male junior staffers were invited to cigar meetings with the boys, women were never allowed to join—whether at the cigar club above Landini's or elsewhere.

Women were told to wear pantyhose and forbidden from showing their shoulders—rules that, to the female employees, were obviously set out by men with antiquated views. "There was a very patronizing attitude at the NRA—'be a nice little girl' type of thing," Ross said. "You had to fight for every advancement." The dress code for men was strict—a suit and tie—but they were allowed to wear tactical pants from time to time. Women were generally not given that kind of discretion.

Women often found they were offered even less in salary than their male counterparts. "If you were a sensitive female who didn't like sex jokes and cussing, you wouldn't enjoy [working there]," said one employee who worked at HQ for years. "There was a lot of catcalling. A lot of the building was older gentlemen. . . . Fuck yes, it was a misogynistic place to work."

The situation was different at the highest levels of the organization. Wayne was the worst kind of manager: one who was unable to make decisions on the fly, easily intimidated by subordinates, and unable to dismiss underperformers when the time came for it.

Close observers said he cultivated the confusion, and was conscious of the strategy. Testifying in a later case, former close friend and adviser Tony Makris said that Wayne had referred to his management style as "management by chaos . . . he said if you kept each of his advisers, sources, managers—whatever you want to call them—at odds with each other, then you would maintain control." Makris said that Wayne would frequently instruct his subordinates not to share information with other senior officials or outside advisers, causing a state of division and disorder. "He frequently would instruct me, or instruct Angus, or other Ackerman employees to not provide information to the Treasurer's office, to Josh Powell, to the attorney Bill Brewer, to Chris Cox—and he said . . . 'only give this information to me,'" Makris said.

On one occasion, Wayne had decided to fire Kyle Weaver, the director of General Operations. But the night before the announcement was to be made, Wayne called up his chief of staff, filled with dread and agitation. "You made me do this!" Wayne told Josh Powell. The status of the firing hung unresolved until the last moment. "It was a microcosm of thirty-five years of decision-making under Wayne—he was unable to let anyone go, he hated confrontation, and he was scared to death of catching heat from the board for making tough decisions," Powell would later recall.

Wayne's weak will led to a lot of sweetheart deals for those who worked senior NRA jobs and then left or were dismissed. The golden parachutes given to departing executives were notorious. Senior staff leaving the organization were often provided lucrative contracts that paid out enormous sums—then expected to do little or no work. It was a means of self-preservation from a fearful CEO: Wayne protected himself from challenges and unhappy departures by throwing money at every possible threat, often combined with NDAs. The New York attorney general found that on repeated occasions Wayne had the NRA pay former employees millions of dollars without appropriate approval from his board.

Longtime staffer Wayne Sheets retired from the NRA in 2008 but retained a contract for fundraising worth $30,000 per month—which was due regardless of whether he actually worked. The consulting agreement also included a "Variable Success Fee" that required a minimum of $125,000 annually, regardless of Sheets's success in fundraising, the New York AG found. Sheets also received expense reimbursements as part of his contract—and took advantage of that. In 2016, for example, he submitted $148,314 worth of expenses to the NRA, including monthly truck leases, his home internet bills, and the costs of international hunting excursions.

Weaver, the General Operations director Wayne had been so twitchy about firing, was eased out the door with a $150,000 lump sum in 2016. He continued to be paid for more than two years at a rate of $60,000 a month. A final lump-sum payment of $240,000 was made in January 2019—bringing his total compensation after being fired to $1.8 million. While it was framed as a consulting agreement, it was more like an NDA wrapped in a consulting agreement: "Confidentiality and Non-Disparagement are among the important terms of this Agreement," the language stated. Asked later by the NY AG whether Weaver performed services for the money, Wayne replied, "I don't know whether he did or didn't." The agreement never spelled out what consulting work was entailed by the payments, and the NY AG found that Weaver did no actual consulting work under the agreement.

The habit of awarding these sweetheart deals goes way back to the 1990s. After Wayne dismissed the NRA's top lobbyist, Tanya Metaksa, in 1998, ILA staffers were stunned to discover a year later that she was still getting a full salary and benefits—a deal that Wayne had secretly negotiated. The NRA's lobbyists had to threaten hell to get the payments to stop.

Wayne himself was no exception to this rule: he had in place what the New York attorney general termed a "poison pill contract" that would guarantee employment even if he was removed from his position, and "NRA income for life."

⫿⫿

Wayne also had a tendency of attracting people with bad intentions and worse backgrounds. And they were drawn to him too, perhaps sensing his weak character and malleability.

MILLIE HALLOW

His closest personal aide—official title, Managing Director, Operations Outreach—is Millie Hallow. She's also a felon, which is ironic because felons cannot generally own firearms.

Millie has been an indispensable presence in Wayne's office due to her longevity at the NRA. Born Mildred Bautista in 1946, she attended classes at UCLA and UC Davis but never got a degree. Over her career she developed deep ties to conservative D.C., in part due to her late husband, Ralph Hallow, a legendary reporter for the conservative *Washington Times*.

Originally she was hired as Wayne's "special assistant," and over the last quarter century her salary has increased to a quarter million dollars per year. She started by writing correspondence for Wayne, then helped him with his radio show, *The Wayne*

LaPierre Show. Her closeness to Wayne made her one of the ulti-mate gatekeepers at the NRA: she served as a key link between Wayne and his sometimes-unruly seventy-six-member board of directors, as a point of outreach to conservative organizations, and sometimes as an intermediary between Wayne and Chris Cox. She had a "utility infielder role," was how senior NRA staffer John Frazer described her.

When plucked for Wayne's staff, she was a music teacher at St. Pius X Catholic school in Maryland. She had no formal teach-er's training but had volunteered to help the original music teacher with classes. When the music teacher had a nervous breakdown, Millie stepped in and started teaching music for grades one through eight.

She first joined Wayne's staff after helping with his book tour in the summer of 1994. Conservative public relations specialist and author Craig Shirley helped get Millie the job as Wayne's aide after that tour. When she finished her music teaching contract, she joined Wayne's staff, despite being unqualified for the job and hav-ing no background in gun issues. Her salary more than doubled.

The job offer from Wayne was all she needed. Nowadays she can't remember if they had done a background check on her at the time, but if they had conducted one, they would have found out that she had pleaded guilty to a felony in 1984: the theft of $23,691 (nearly $60,000 in 2021 dollars) when she was the execu-tive director of the D.C. Commission on the Arts and Humani-ties. Her method of embezzlement involved writing checks to people who did not exist or who were not owed money. She then forged their endorsements over the course of about eighteen months in 1982 and 1983. She also created an unauthorized bank account to disburse the funds. An investigation found that Millie had resigned her prior post in Ann Arbor, Michigan, after it was realized that she had falsified her résumé.

Millie had been allowed to resign from the D.C. Commission on the Arts and Humanities and released a statement to the press at the time: "I have done wrong. I have misused public funds and betrayed the public trust," she said. "I feel regret and sadness about my sins, particularly to the many people, friends and associates who have placed their faith in me." She was ordered to pay back the funds, received a suspended prison sentence of up to five years, and was put on probation for three years.

"We did a lot of entertaining that was probably beyond our means . . . food and beverages," she testified more recently. "It was an awful and humiliating time."

Her felony charge would not have been hard to find if anyone at the NRA had done a cursory look: her case was repeatedly covered in *The Washington Post* because she had been a public employee and was one of the D.C. mayor's advisers on cultural issues. Nor was it secret to everyone: in 2021, the president of the NRA said that she had known about Millie's felony charge for more than a decade.

Like Wayne, Millie is a survivor. No one could quite figure out why she had managed to hang on for so long at the NRA in such an important role, despite repeated episodes of malfeasance later outlined by the New York attorney general's investigation and future testimony during litigation. In the 2000s Millie was found to have used NRA funds for her personal purchases: mostly for personal clothing and travel. An internal investigation by the NRA yielded no consequence other than the confiscation of her credit card. She said in one deposition she's not sure how much of it she was asked to pay back.

Despite this brazen breach of trust, she still had access to other corporate credit cards, including that of the chief financial officer, and she still had the ability to authorize up to $240,000 a year for business travel expenses and events. Following her misconduct, Wayne failed to rein her in. Instead he appointed a junior staffer at the NRA, who did not have authority over Millie, to approve her expenses.

As confidential depositions and the New York AG's investigation show, Millie would abuse this lax oversight, often using it to benefit herself, her husband, and her son. In 2012 Millie billed the NRA for $18,000 linked to her son's wedding in Elk River, Minnesota. She played the pious, innocent mother of the groom: in an email to Wayne, Susan, and Chris Cox, Millie described her son's happy wedding with a subject line that is an apparent reference to a biblical psalm. Meanwhile, she was trying to obfuscate the bills: after the wedding she wrote to another of Wayne's aides, asking her to remove references to Elk River from the invoices that were submitted to the NRA. She later testified that she had no memory of Wayne or anyone else at the NRA authorizing the gun group to pay for a portion of her son's wedding expenses. Both her son, Ian Walters, and her daughter-in-law, Carin Walters, now work at the American Conservative Union, where Millie is the vice chairman of the affiliated ACU Foundation.

Wayne would later confront Millie about the wedding expenses, saying he heard a rumor about her using NRA funds for her son's wedding. She looked Wayne straight in the eye and denied it: "That's completely untrue," Millie said.

At the NRA, Millie also regularly used nonprofit funds to pay for chauffeured black cars, and often did so for her family members as well: she charged $1,100 in one day to ferry her husband around, for example; and she also spent almost $1,300 to shuttle her son from New York to D.C. Over just two weeks, she charged the NRA for $100,000 in expenses so that two cars could be available for an August 2018 fundraising trip in France. Wayne "was very generous about my use of the car service," she later acknowledged. Her son was also hired to be a soundstage manager at the NRA annual meeting, and to perform music at an NRA event.

All told, the NRA's general counsel later testified, Millie diverted $40,000 from the NRA for personal, non-business reasons. She was forced to pay it all back in the fall of 2020—eight years after the expenses for her son's wedding had been covered by the NRA.

When the National Rifle Association later got involved in a questionable trip to Russia (much more on that later), Millie had a central role. She decided to reimburse thousands of dollars for the trip to Moscow and cited Wayne's authority to do so: "Wayne approved these special projects," she wrote in an email. After investigations were launched into the trip, Millie testified that she had done so unilaterally and that Wayne had specifically directed her not to spend NRA funds on a trip to Moscow.

In inconsistent sworn testimony from the same deposition, Millie told lawyers in a deposition that Wayne had specifically told her he didn't want to pay for the Moscow trip; but when confronted with a copy of her email that she had cited Wayne's authority to approve those expenses, she said she could not remember whether she had asked him for approval. She blames her medical condition for her lack of clarity, telling lawyers subsequently that she was in chemotherapy and radiation at the time to address cancer. "I'm still on oral chemo to this day—both in work and personal some things just get fogged in my brain," she testified.

In the NRA's version of events, Millie Hallow, a longtime and loyal Wayne LaPierre aide, acted alone and without authorization to approve thousands of dollars' worth of expenses for the Moscow trip. A more straightforward version of events is that Hallow said that Wayne approved them because he approved them.

Somehow, despite the repeated misconduct and the apparent false approval of expenses in the name of her boss, Millie was never punished or dismissed. She was not suspended or docked pay. In most companies, this would be a fireable offense. At the NRA, she received no punishment and continued to make her $250,000 salary without interruption.

When Wayne was later asked by lawyers, he claimed not to have known about Millie's felony theft charge until the summer of 2019, and when he found out he took no action to ask the lawyers at the NRA to check on it. He testified in the fall of 2019 that he had no idea how she paid for her son's wedding or whether she uses NRA funds for personal expenses—and had no concerns that she might be embezzling money from his organization. Despite being her direct superior, Wayne was totally checked out—he didn't know what was happening in his own office, and otherwise didn't care to know.

WOODY PHILLIPS

Woody Phillips was hired as treasurer and CFO early in Wayne's tenure as the head of the NRA. It's not known whether Wayne was aware, but upon arrival at the NRA, Woody had just been fired from a consulting firm called Wyatt Company for allegedly embezzling at least $1 million. Woody had been the CFO for the employee-benefits consulting firm in D.C. when Mary Hughes, the accounts payable manager at the firm, discovered the problem.

In 1991 Hughes received a phone call from a vendor asking about an outstanding debt of $45,000. After looking at her records, she said they showed the debt had been paid—but the vendor hadn't received the funds. After looking closer, Hughes observed that Woody had made multiple payments to an account that he controlled, all while ostensibly paying a Wyatt vendor through fraudulent invoices. She confronted Woody, and his first response was, "Mary, who else knows about this?" Woody was fired without fanfare, and the firm did not pursue charges, as it feared it could lose business if it came out. If it had pursued charges, the amount in question could have warranted felony charges. Soon thereafter, Wayne hired Woody to be in charge of the NRA's finances.

Woody was also wearing two hats: for a time while he was the CFO at the NRA, he was also the CFO at Memberdrive, a key vendor for the NRA at the time, and where Wayne's wife, Susan, worked as an executive.

Together, Wayne and Woody oversaw millions of dollars in National Rifle Association funds. When the New York Attorney General's Office launched its complaint to dissolve the NRA in 2020, both were named in the complaint.

Woody remained as the NRA's CFO and treasurer for twenty-six years and handled many of its important vendors. Many contractors got a steal of a deal from the NRA because Woody didn't care about getting overcharged. Woody "appeared completely absent," observed Wayne's former chief of staff Josh Powell. "The attitude among the senior execs was, 'Hey if we break even, and the cause is just—fighting for Second Amendment rights—we're doing okay.'"

Woody handled the budget with Ackerman McQueen and was a critical conduit for the NRA's relationship with its most important vendor. "At LaPierre's direction, Phillips . . . instituted a practice whereby millions of dollars in entertainment and travel expenses incurred by NRA executives were billed to the NRA as disbursements by [Ackerman McQueen]," wrote the New York Attorney General's Office in its complaint charging Wayne, Woody, and the NRA. "This practice evaded both the NRA's own accounting and Board-established expense reimbursement process, and IRS requirements for proper expense reimbursement."

This was hardly the only sweetheart deal Woody oversaw. In 2014 Woody and Wayne approved a contract with an information technology company called HomeTelos. What Phillips did not disclose to the NRA board at the time was that he had a "personal relationship" with the chair and founder of the company, a woman named Nancy Richards. Only after the NRA had paid HomeTelos close to $1.4 million did the NRA board's audit committee retroactively approve the contract, while noting that Woody should have disclosed the relationship.

Woody and Wayne, along with Wayne's chief of staff Powell, would frequently intimidate staff in the NRA's financial services division, the NY AG found. Woody set up a system that included having junior staff approve the expenses of more senior staff they did not have authority over. One person in the division would later report that she was concerned she could be dismissed simply for asking where missing expense receipts were; others said they were told to process payments against NRA policy because Woody, Wayne, or Powell said it was appropriate. Several of Woody's staff would blow the whistle on this kind of misconduct in the summer of 2018.

Woody Phillips left the NRA in 2018, seeking to retire—and Wayne, though he tried, couldn't convince him to stay. It was bad news for Wayne and Ackerman McQueen, who both lost a key ally. But Woody managed to get a good deal for himself on the way out: while still at the NRA, he arranged a contract that would pay him $360,000 a year for five years for consulting with the senior staff. But when the New York attorney general came to investigate, the treasurer who replaced Woody testified that Woody had never consulted with him—and the NY AG found no evidence that Woody had provided any services for the NRA.

GAYLE STANFORD

Gayle Stanford had originally done some travel scheduling for Angus McQueen, and first began to work with Wayne on his travel during his 1994 book tour. Charlton Heston had been a client, and he had eventually introduced her to Wayne. By the 2020s, she was in her late seventies and was mostly retired.

Gayle isn't registered as a travel agent, contrary to the law in California, where she resides. Even as she was acting as a travel contractor for the NRA, Gayle got caught up in another business that allegedly defrauded small businesses in Texas. The Texas attorney general alleged in a 2009 lawsuit that Gayle and a business partner reached out to companies asking owners to pay $125 to file documents with the state. The filings weren't compulsory, and the money went to Gayle's companies, the lawsuit claimed. She settled the case while denying the allegations. Her husband,

Peter Stanford, is a felon who pleaded guilty in 1990 to charges of participating in an investment fraud scheme.

Despite the fact that the NRA used a company called MacNair for its internal travel bookings, there was a separate system used for Wayne's travel. Following the Newtown shootings, Wayne stopped flying commercial and started flying exclusively on chartered jets booked through Gayle's operation.

Wayne claimed it was for security reasons, but there's little evidence of how using a third-party vendor to book travel would help with that. The head of the NRA fundraising division later testified in court that he wasn't aware of any written policy requiring Wayne to travel by chartered plane, and Gayle said she was never provided a policy that said this either. Gayle also testified that she had never had a discussion with Wayne about confidentiality. It's hard to imagine the threat level remained so high that the NRA's donors should be forced to pay millions to ferry him around by private jet for almost every trip.

The excuse that private jets were necessary for security reasons was further undercut by his approval of numerous flights where he was not present as a passenger, including a flight for his niece and her husband from Dallas to North Platte, Nebraska, in August 2016 ($11,435); a July 2017 flight for his niece and his niece's daughter from Dallas to Orlando ($26,995); and an October 2016 flight for Susan from Madison, Wisconsin, to Kearney, Nebraska ($8,800). A private jet stopped in Nebraska again in January 2017, at a cost of $15,000, to pick up Susan's niece's husband. These are just a few examples that the New York attorney general ultimately discovered—many of them involving flights to Nebraska and his niece. The NRA's then-treasurer told investigators he could not think of any business reason for staff to fly to

North Platte, Nebraska—incidentally near where Wayne's niece lives.

Wayne luxuriated in private travel. According to those who knew him best, he was most comfortable when he was traveling by private jet, imitating the lives of the superrich. "Flying with Wayne always seemed to be a time when we could speak freely, and where I saw the most authentic version of Wayne," his former chief of staff said.

Gayle absolutely cleaned up with Wayne's business. She had an amazing deal and no other clients. In 2014, she was making $15,000 per month in flat fees just to be retained as a travel consultant—that's not counting the actual cost of airfare, black cars, or hotel rooms. This rose to $19,000 per month in 2015—a total of more than $228,000 per year just to be on standby to book travel for Wayne. From then until 2019 Gayle's companies were paid $26,500 per month, or $318,000 per year. On top of these absurd billings, Gayle would add 10 percent to the bills from air charter services when she sent invoices to the NRA. The money was all paid out without a contract and without authorization from the board, in violation of the NRA's own rules.

In addition to the payments Gayle's companies received from the NRA directly, she received an additional $4,000 per month from Ackerman McQueen between 2013 and 2018. The New York AG found that Woody and Wayne had directed Ackerman to pay her this fee and then funnel it back as an expense to the NRA.

The NRA paid Gayle's companies more than $13.5 million between August 2014 and January 2020. In just six months in 2019, the gun group paid her more than $1 million for her services.

In 2020, after being put under investigation by the New York attorney general, the NRA conducted a competitive bidding process for these travel services. The NRA accepted Gayle's bid, which came in much lower than had been previously paid out to her: $7,000 per month, or about a quarter of what she had been paid the year before.

NRA accountants were told to pay bills from Gayle's companies, Inventive Incentives and Insurance Services (also known as II & IS) and GS2 Enterprises, without the usual required expense documentation. Wayne's obsession with security was used to justify secrecy and obfuscation of his records from other NRA staff. He did not want them to know where, when, or how he traveled. His travel documentation was kept in Woody's office, and more elaborate documentation, such as airplane tail numbers, were held by Gayle alone in her Woodland Hills, California, home, where she operates her businesses.

CHAPTER 10

Maria Butina and the Roots of NRA-Russia

In December 2016 I sat across the table from a man who had been a reporting source in the past. It was early in the morning, I hadn't had coffee yet—and I was annoyed. I had a call with my editor at *The Daily Beast* later that morning, and I was fresh out of new reporting ideas.

We were in the cozy confines of the Tabard Inn, the oldest continuously operating hotel in Washington, D.C.—and, unknown to me at that point, a favorite of NRA operatives when its headquarters had been nearby on Rhode Island Avenue, pre-1993. As we awaited our breakfast at a table in the middle of the dining room, my source's eyes darted back and forth across the room, searching for anyone who might be listening in to our conversation. I dismissed his paranoia as an overreaction.

Here's the thing about investigative reporting: you get a lot of trash leads and reach a lot of dead ends before you find a worthy tip. And of those worthy tips, only a small portion become worthwhile stories. Good reporters hone their instincts to minimize trash leads and allow their eyes to glaze over when sources begin ranting about things you know will never cross the finish line—because they are unprovable or uninteresting or both.

A longtime, trusted, and reliable source was going on what I thought was one such rant. He was positive a woman named Maria Butina was a Russian spy. She was sleeping with a Republican Party operative I had never heard of named Paul Erickson, he claimed. And they had infiltrated the National Rifle Association. I didn't know what to make of this tip, and to be honest, I considered the whole thing a wild conspiracy theory. I left that breakfast puzzled. I still didn't have any ideas to bring to my editor. And this tale wasn't going to do.

But my first instinct was so very wrong. The source was one of at least two sources I knew who would later become a source for the FBI. The second source who went to the FBI met with me once at a hotel restaurant in Rosslyn, Virginia—coincidentally just a block away from where Deep Throat met with Bob Woodward in *All the President's Men*.

At the time, a story linking Russia and the National Rifle Association seemed too outrageous to be true. It would turn out to be a tale that I would spend years reporting on, generating story after story, and ultimately the idea for this book. With the backing of a high-ranking Russian-government official named Alexander Torshin, Butina infiltrated the NRA in order to promote Russian interests. She was looking for an unofficial channel of diplomacy that would fly under the radar and not raise suspicion. She was looking to accumulate power.

Along her journey, NRA officials willfully facilitated and funded Butina and Torshin's activities. Those who were explicitly told that Butina's efforts were being undertaken on behalf of the Russian government looked the other way, communications obtained by multiple congressional investigations show.

Some NRA officials did this because they saw there was money to be made in Russia; others were smitten by the Russian redhead's charm and good looks; others just learned not to think too hard about the whole thing.

A bipartisan report by the Senate Intelligence Committee, led by Republicans, found that Butina and Torshin were "engaged in a multi-year influence campaign and intelligence-gathering effort targeting the NRA . . . for the benefit of the Russian government." It also concluded that the Kremlin and Russian Ministry of Foreign Affairs were aware of their actions and "almost certainly" approved them, adding that Butina's work in the United States was "indicative of work for the Russian intelligence services." A Senate Finance Committee investigation into the NRA, written by the panel's Democrats after an eighteen-month investigation, concluded that the NRA had been a "foreign asset" to Butina as she committed a crime (the committee's Republicans called the report "innuendo" that "repeatedly attempts to paint a picture that does not exist").

In the end, Butina and Erickson would go to prison for felonies. Butina's mentor, Alexander Torshin, an NRA life member and Russian government official, would be sanctioned by the U.S. government and banned from entering America. And an NRA president named Pete Brownell would step down in part because of the ensuing scandal, forcing a succession that would ultimately imperil the National Rifle Association and Wayne LaPierre.

·|||·

The story of how a Russian agent named Maria Butina infiltrated the National Rifle Association starts with a man who Russian organized crime types called "the godfather." A member of Putin's United Russia party, Alexander Torshin is a short, rotund man with a chubby face, the kind that reflects a thousand heavy meals in the company of oligarchs, government officials, and the foreign investors who stripped the country raw after the dissolution of the Soviet Union.

As a Russian senator, Torshin was an ally to Vladimir Putin. He was selected to run the parliamentary investigation into the 2004 terrorist siege in Beslan, as well as to help organize a spy swap between the United States and Russia in 2010. As a legislator, he served on Russia's National Anti-Terrorism Committee, a panel that counts among its membership a number of high-ranking national security officials.

He was close to the FSB, an acronym for the Russian internal security service—it awarded him a medal in 2016. He was also linked to the Russian mob, the Taganskaya in Moscow, members of which were intercepted by Spanish authorities referring to Torshin as "the boss" and "godfather." A three-year Spanish government investigation concluded that Torshin had taught members of the Taganskaya crime syndicate how to launder their money through properties and bank accounts in Spain. Spanish prosecutors sought to arrest Torshin in 2013, but Torshin canceled a trip to the country after apparently having been tipped off about their intentions. Torshin told the Spanish newspaper *El Pais* that

Spanish law enforcement has "never brought any charges . . . nor have they made any inquiries" with him, and that he "has never owned real estate or business in Spain."

Long fascinated with firearms, Torshin was friends of General Mikhail Kalashnikov, inventor of the infamous AK-47 rifle. Torshin became a member of the National Rifle Association in 2010 and was an evangelist for gun ownership—that same year he published a Russian pamphlet promoting the concept.

Torshin had always seen himself as something of an America whisperer. Long before his involvement with the NRA, Torshin had been crisscrossing the United States looking to network with American political figures—his earliest known visit was in 2004. He sought a meeting with Alaska governor Sarah Palin in 2009, for example, but had to settle for the lieutenant governor.

But he never got a foothold in American political circles until he linked up with the NRA over a mutual interest in guns. Torshin was introduced to the senior levels of NRA leadership by a man named Kline Preston, a Putin apologist who lives in Tennessee and studied in Soviet Leningrad in the 1980s. Preston made the introduction between Torshin and then-NRA president David Keene in 2011. (Keene did not respond to questions related to this book.)

David Keene is a Washington creature who was friends and contemporaries with Paul Manafort and Roger Stone, two Republican political consultants later convicted of crimes during the Trump era. Though Keene was never charged or convicted of a crime, he operated in the same swamps of political power around the nation's capital and, at least to some, carried the same sort of political greasiness. "There was a strain of a criminal class

going through the Republican Party around the same genera-
tion," said Craig Shirley, Keene's former business partner. "Nixon-
Agnew was their early proving grounds."

Keene spent decades as a D.C. lobbyist, with lucrative ties
to both the conservative establishment and the conservative
grassroots, made possible by his chairmanship of the American
Conservative Union for twenty-seven years. A huckster in conservative's clothing, Keene was always ready to adjust his views
for the right price. My favorite story about his pay-to-play mentality took place early in the Obama era. For between $2 and
$3 million, the ACU told FedEx in 2009, the conservative group
would provide a "grassroots" lobbying package that included
Keene op-eds in support of its position in a fierce legislative dis-
pute. After FedEx declined, Keene backed its rival, UPS, and sav-
aged FedEx in an open letter. The corrupt quid pro quo offer was
incompetently executed: it was put in writing in a letter to FedEx,
which promptly leaked it to the press and exposed Keene's naked
money grab.

A longtime Republican political operative, Keene has somehow always managed to walk away from a scandal unscathed.
"There were a lot of spoiled relations left in his wake," Shirley
said. "[But] he was able to leapfrog bad relationships and land on
his feet repeatedly."

Not so for other members of his family. In 2003 his son David
M. Keene was sentenced to ten years in prison for firing a gun at
a car on the George Washington Memorial Parkway just outside
the District of Columbia. The shot, fired during an apparent
road-rage incident, narrowly missed the other driver's head. In
addition, Keene's ex-wife, Diana Carr, was discovered embezzling up to $400,000 from the American Conservative Union

while he was chairman and she was acting as its bookkeeper. The scheme was discovered in May 2010, and Carr was sentenced to one year in jail.

Shortly after his ex-wife's misconduct was publicly revealed, Keene left the ACU and became the president of the National Rifle Association, holding that position from 2011 to 2013. The role is typically a symbolic one: presiding over the NRA board of directors and living high off the gun group's dime. Don't ask too many questions. Cash in on the title. Don't get in Wayne's way. Keene pulled the job off brilliantly.

Torshin met Keene at the 2011 National Rifle Association annual meeting. Torshin had purchased a lifetime membership in the NRA, listing the email of a Russian diplomat and Preston's phone number on the form. After his first encounter with Torshin, Keene wrote him a handwritten message. "Just a brief note to let you know just how much I enjoyed meeting in Pittsburgh during the NRA annual meeting," Keene said. "If there is anything any of us can do to help you in your endeavors . . . please don't hesitate to let us know." As it turned out, there was.

Torshin attended the NRA annual meeting in 2012 as a VIP guest of Keene's, then went to Tennessee to watch voting as an international election observer. The Russian politician was not shy about how his relationships with the NRA had helped him get access. "The NRA card, to me as an observer from Russia, opened access to any [polling] station," Torshin bragged brazenly at the time. Keene opened other doors, asking Torshin to address the NRA's legislative affairs committee, for example. Their relationship would deepen over time—Torshin attended every NRA annual meeting from 2012 to 2016, and would soon be bringing his friend Maria along.

Maria Butina had a meteoric rise. To her credit, she was incredibly smart—and she dreamed big. She also took advantage of her good looks for social advantage. She flirted with everyone, male and female—"I felt like she was hitting on me the whole time," said one woman who was the recipient of this attention. "She kind of purrs when she talks to you." In no time at all, her life changed: within years of her first-ever plane ride, she would become a well-connected Russian agent accustomed to rides in private jets.

Butina's charm was supplemented by thoughtful gifts that showed careful study of the recipients. One gun rights activist visiting Moscow in 2013 was presented with exotic fabric, which indicated Butina's knowledge that the activist was a needlepoint enthusiast. When Torshin and Butina met up with then NRA president Allan Cors years later, they brought along a Russian book about tanks—Cors's favorite topic.

Washington, D.C., where she would end up, is a long way from home. Butina had come from a humble family from the very center of the Asian continent—where Siberia, the Asian steppes, and Mongolia collide. Specifically, she grew up in Barnaul, a small town in western Siberia, thousands of miles away from Moscow. It can be bleak: average temperatures are below freezing five months of the year. The daughter of a retired furniture maker and an electrical engineer, she had nothing handed to her. As a point of comparison, her sister works in advertising and has a side hustle selling e-cigarettes at the airport. Maria was an exceptional student and excelled especially in English. Her ease with people led her into politics, and she studied the subject at Altai State University.

She was quickly spotted as a woman of great ambition. "She was . . . very focused on achieving a target. I can say she is a person who definitely knows what she wants," said Elena Sochivko, who knew her in high school and then studied with her in the same department in college. To most, Butina conveyed a personality that was well meaning, sweet, and caring—and she spent years genuinely and eagerly promoting gun rights.

Butina moved to Moscow at the age of twenty-two and began expanding her social circles by reaching out to people online. She had learned how to hunt with a rifle as a child, and she swiftly organized a gun rights organization in her nation's capital. The name she chose was the Right to Bear Arms, a nod to the Second Amendment. She instantly drew attention—the controversial nature of the topic and her natural sex appeal helped. At one point, Russian *GQ* profiled her, complete with a photoshoot in which she provocatively handles firearms.

During her first year in Moscow she met Alexander Torshin, who already had some experience with the NRA. Butina and Torshin sought to expand the gun rights movement in Russia—all the more odd considering that Putin personally had expressed his opposition: "I am deeply convinced that the free flow of firearms will bring a great harm and represents a great danger for us," the then Russian prime minister said in 2011.

Their efforts continued nonetheless. Through her public advocacy, she was able to convince two Russian funders to back her: Konstantin Nikolaev, a Russian billionaire who has funded businesses linked to the Russian military and FSB; and Igor Zaytsev, whom she described as the owner of jewelry stores in the Moscow region.

Private gun ownership is severely restricted in Russia, but

despite the controversial nature of the topic, she was able to register her group, work with the Russian legislature, and grow the organization to some ten thousand members. It certainly helped that her supporters included Torshin, Nikolaev, and Dmitry Rogozin, at that time a Putin deputy whose portfolio included the defense industry.

By 2013, Butina was organizing an international gun rights conference and asked Torshin for ideas—Torshin gave Butina the contact information for his friend David Keene, who was at the time the outgoing president of the National Rifle Association. She invited Keene to Moscow, and he accepted, bringing his friend Paul Erickson along for the trip. Keene went to the conference as an NRA official, and the NRA paid for his trip. The NRA hired Erickson, a longtime Republican Party operative, to staff Keene during the duration of the travel, despite the fact that Erickson did not speak Russian and it was uncertain whether he had ever been to Russia before. A more important credential was that Erickson and Keene had been friends for years.

Butina's conference in Moscow was a well-attended and extravagant affair, with more than three hundred participants from all over the globe in attendance to discuss gun rights. The conference even featured a fashion show showing off different ways to carry a gun concealed, where models sported garter belts that also worked as holsters. "There are no peoples that are more alike than Americans and Russians. . . . We value the same kinds of things," Keene said in remarks he gave at the conference, stressing the relationship he had developed with Torshin over several years. "We need to work together."

Keene pulled strings for the conference, not only attending and giving a speech but also tapping former United Nations ambassador (and future Trump national security adviser) John Bolton to provide videotaped remarks. As president of the NRA, Keene had appointed Bolton to the gun group's international affairs subcommittee in 2011, but their relationship goes back way further than that: Bolton had been Keene's intern when Keene worked for Vice President Spiro Agnew.

"Were the Russian national government to grant a broader right to bear arms to its people, it would be creating a partnership with its citizens that would better allow for the protection of mothers, children and families without in any way compromising the integrity of the Russian state," Bolton told the assembled audience at Butina's conference. "That is my wish and my advice to your great people."

Butina's conference set the stage for everything that would come after, and established her two most important relationships in America: with Keene, the NRA board member and former NRA president; and Erickson, who was well connected in NRA and Republican circles. Erickson and Butina remained in contact after meeting in Moscow, and they began dating the following year.

Erickson, a fraudster and shameless suck-up, had spent decades working in politics. Close with Millie Hallow and an attendee at her son's wedding, Erickson had been the national political director for Pat Buchanan. He was also something of a dweeb. During the 1992 presidential campaign, Erickson had gotten into a fistfight with a Clinton staffer. It was not his finest moment: while throwing a punch, he stumbled on ice and broke his own nose.

Erickson represented an eclectic clientele over the years and served as a media adviser to John Wayne Bobbitt, a man who was made famous when his wife cut off his penis and threw it into a field (good friend and now disgraced lobbyist Jack Abramoff played a role in the introduction). He has also been a lobbyist who advocated on behalf of Zairean president Mobutu Sese Seko (Paul Manafort and Roger Stone's old lobbying firm also represented the dictator in the past). When Erickson was eventually arrested and jailed, it was for defrauding investors over a years-long scam.

"Erickson felt oily," said former Keene business associate Craig Shirley. "In Washington, with all that money, power, and celebrity, you're going to attract your fair share of dirtbags. He was one of the dirtier dirtbags."

Butina had been rejected for a U.S. visa in years prior. But following the 2013 Moscow meeting, she had new friends. Erickson and Butina came up with the idea of using a visit with the NRA as a way to get a visa to the United States. With an invite to the 2014 National Rifle Association annual meeting, Keene's guidance on how to handle the visa interview, and a phone call from Keene to the office of House Foreign Affairs Committee chairman Ed Royce, Butina was able to overcome those visa problems that had prevented her from entering the United States in the past, the Senate Intelligence Committee found.

With this, a whole new world of prospects opened for Butina. In the fall of 2014 she began discussing with Erickson other ways she could enter the United States and stay for longer periods of time—including a work visa. None of her prospects would have been realized, no connections made, without the active help of the National Rifle Association, which helped fund her political activities, introduced her to influential contacts, and actively organized her itineraries. But at this time, the NRA had reason to feel invincible. They were bringing in a ton of cash as they fundraised off worries about President Barack Obama.

CHAPTER 11

The Obama Years

When Susan LaPierre cofounded the NRA Women's Leadership Forum (WLF) in 2006, its stated mission was to fundraise by connecting women who are passionate about gun rights. In truth, it was less about guns and more about a showcase for status, and for judging those who did not quite measure up. The most elite members were part of what was called the WLF's executive committee. Below that, members were segregated by how much each had given to the gun rights group, indicated by the different brooches worn. The sapphire brooch indicated a gift of at least $50,000; emerald meant at least $100,000; ruby meant a contribution of at least half a million dollars; and the coveted diamond brooch showed that a member and her spouse had contributed at least one million dollars to the National Rifle Association. There was a competitiveness about the brooches. "You wear it like a shield," said one donor.

The organization was centered on events that flaunted wealth. Members would gather for tea at the Salamander Resort, a posh country getaway just outside the capital, for example. One attendee recalled being struck by the scene of WLF members writing $50,000 checks, many of them spending money earned by someone else.

High-dollar donors were extravagantly wined and dined by Susan and her aides, but the joke was on them. It was *their* donated money being spent. "It was a delicious con," said one NRA insider. And the jealousy was immense: those taken out for dinner by NRA bigwigs were told to keep it a secret, lest other WLF members hear about it and get jealous about the meal with Susan. There were favored groups and those seeking favor. There were those who wore the chicest clothing, and those who were not sufficiently trendy. There were those who had money, and then those who had *money*.

In her time at the NRA, Susan had transformed the group from one that was almost embarrassed by ostentatious shows of wealth to one that was fueled and driven by it. Susan aspired to attract women for whom $200 bottles of wine and celebrity hairdressers were the norm. Find a group of ten NRA members anywhere in America, and most of them would prefer to wear boots, jeans, and plaid shirts. Many WLF members wouldn't be caught dead wearing anything but haute couture, or flying in anything other than a private jet. Susan set the tone: she was rarely seen in the same outfit twice, her entry into a room signaled by her signature perfume.

It was all about cliques and standing. Every year women would gather together at the NRA annual meeting for lunch and an auction. Donors compared brooches, compared the guests at their table—even, *How close is your table to Susan's table? How close is your table to the front?* The live auction reinforced the Susan cult: one of the items up for bidding was the "crown table" at the very front of the room. If you won the auction, you and your ten closest friends could be served champagne at that table, joined by Susan, at the next year's luncheon. In 2019 this reward went for $25,000, according to a witness.

There was a sort of secrecy among members of the club—frequent allusions to being part of a family, though the loyalty went only one way. Women in the organization were expected to stay in line: fealty to Susan—and Wayne, by association—was demanded and explicitly requested from its members. Those who were associated with the WLF and later departed would compare it to, among other things, an abusive relationship—one in which you could rationalize a situation while you were in it, but it became repulsive once you put a little distance in between.

Retribution for questioning Susan was harsh. A former member of the WLF's executive committee found out the hard way when she had a few drinks during an NRA annual meeting and questioned whether the NRA needed new leadership. In the gossipy insider world of the Women's Leadership Forum, she was snitched on immediately. The member was iced out overnight, with senior staff making frantic calls to remove her from her position on the executive committee. Others who questioned Susan would meet a similar fate: social ostracism from the rarefied groups of the NRA's most wealthy and powerful women.

Fundraising was especially hard given Susan's approach to this aspect of the NRA. The amount she would spend was breathtaking, according to those familiar with her actions at the time. No matter that she was representing a nonprofit—everything had to be of the finest quality: the bistro lights, the tablecloths, the flowers, the live music. Susan operated as if the Second Amendment would be protected with the purchase of overpriced hydrangeas.

But whatever Susan wants, Susan gets. That applied even when the organization she was leading—which ostensibly exists to raise money—hemorrhaged cash year after year.

In 2015 the country music group Rascal Flatts was hired to perform at the WLF annual meeting, at a cost of hundreds of thousands of dollars. The music choice alone erased much of the funds the event was supposed to raise. Told how much the band was, Susan said, "Well, this is how much they're charging us."

As with much of the spending inside the NRA, even staff working with the Women's Leadership Forum couldn't make heads or tails of the bills and invoices. A series of consultants, some of whom were never seen in the office, were put on the payroll to cater to Susan's whims. This included hiring her own niece. Not that working for Susan was some sort of special privilege—those who worked with her reported being overworked, talked down to, and being stressed out more than staff in any other department of the National Rifle Association.

Money for the Women's Leadership Forum came from multiple pots within the organization, preventing too many individuals from forming an accurate figure of Susan's spending. Consultants who worked for Susan on fundraising were billed to Wayne's office, for example. Other expenses would be charged to the Office of Advancement, the fundraising department. When Susan ran out of money, she would hassle Wayne or other staff until they found the cash from another pot. Those who had issues with Susan's expense reports would face the question: Well, do you want to be the one to tell Susan she can't do this? A culture of fear prevailed.

Susan, like Wayne, would engage in the practice of sending bills to Ackerman McQueen—bills that Ackerman would then charge back to the NRA. The New York attorney general's investigation would later find that, for example, the NRA used its arrangement with Ackerman McQueen to pay expenses for Youth for Tomorrow, a nonprofit totally unrelated to the NRA, except that Susan was then serving as president of its board of trustees. In what may be just a portion of the NRA-related money that made its way to Susan's charity, the NRA Foundation sent at least $180,000 to Youth for Tomorrow. (The foundation may also have run afoul of regulators by not properly disclosing these contributions.)

She was using money donated to the NRA to help unrelated charities—and personally benefiting from the social clout. In fact, there was what some in the NRA universe referred to as an "annual shakedown": Susan would demand money for her charity of choice and demand those from the NRA, Ackerman McQueen, and other vendors contribute to it. This of course put the NRA's staff and vendors in a bind: *Who are you to refuse Wayne's spouse?* On Capitol Hill, a well-worn piece of wisdom among congressional aides is that the one person you want to keep at least as happy as the senator is the senator's spouse. That described vendor feelings toward Susan perfectly.

All in all, contributing to the secret funneling of money to Youth for Tomorrow is among the least harmful things Susan could have done: gun control advocates may even think it's a good thing that Susan was sending NRA funds to a charity that helps children in crisis, rather than spending it on gun rights advocacy. But it reveals two things about Susan's mindset: her leveraging of Wayne's power to get money where she wanted and the feeling that she could act with impunity.

As with those on Wayne's side of the organization, those

affiliated with Susan's domain could expect to receive extravagant gifts merely for being associated with her—expensed to the NRA, of course. Insiders say that most of the time the Women's Leadership Forum spent more money than it brought in.

The Obama era represented a time of prosperity for the National Rifle Association. Susan's fiefdom aside, the organization's coffers swelled as those Americans worried about gun restrictions rushed to contribute to the NRA, and this time of plenty encouraged corruption. While warning darkly about the dangers of Washington's elites, Wayne and Susan spent NRA cash on travel, luxuries, and generous salaries for the well connected.

Despite running a nonprofit that depended on the goodwill of its members, the NRA's leadership traveled in the utmost style. Once when Josh Powell booked a room at a Sheraton hotel in Dallas, Wayne told him, "We all stay at the Ritz. Move your room." Powell now recalls, "I quickly discovered that everything the executives at the NRA did was first class. . . . There seemed to be a sense of entitlement when it came to travel and hotels."

Over the Obama years, Wayne and Susan charged Ackerman McQueen close to a quarter million dollars for trips to places like Lake Como, Italy; Budapest, Hungary; Eleuthera, Bahamas; Palm Beach, Florida; and Reno, Nevada, according to a leaked memo. And he did all that without providing receipts or documentation for why those charges were legitimate business expenses. The credit card charges lay out an opulent trip to Hungary and Lake Como in late 2014: meals at indulgent restaurants like Godunov, Costes, and Onyx; and accommodations at the Four Seasons in

Budapest and at the five-star CastaDiva Resort in Como, Italy. Their hired car in Italy and Hungary cost more than $18,000, more than even the chartered jet to Budapest, which was $17,550.

Wayne claimed that the hefty price tag of the trip to Hungary was justified because he visited a museum in Budapest to talk about a loan of firearms to the NRA museum. His trip to Italy, he said, was to produce a short documentary about the Berettas, the wealthy Italian family behind the firearm company. He and Susan "went over a couple days early to get on the same time zone," Wayne told the lawyers who would later question him about it. The price of Wayne and Susan's experience in Italy over about a week cost nearly $50,000, not including the cost of producing the documentary.

Later, when confronted about the charges that had been placed on an American Express card in his name, Wayne claimed not to know whether he had been issued a card. "I don't know," he said. "I have no idea. . . . I had so much harassment going on. . . . I don't know whether it was in my name or not, to tell you the truth." Wayne claimed at the time of his trip to Italy in 2014, "Everything we had was being hacked. Our credit cards were being hacked." This was classic Wayne: playing the victim while also claiming ignorance. Who was paying for thousands of dollars' worth of luxury experiences he was enjoying? He didn't know, and he didn't seek to know.

The NRA's insistence on the finer things didn't end at their travel accommodations. Leaked documents, published during a season of NRA infighting, show that between 2004 and 2017, Wayne spent nearly $275,000 at the Italian luxury menswear store Zegna on Rodeo Drive in Beverly Hills, including $39,000 in a single day in 2015. Purchases were directly billed from the store to Ackerman McQueen. The clothing was then shipped to Wayne's address. He claimed never to have known how much the suits, shirts, and ties cost. "I never saw the bills," Wayne said repeatedly in a deposition. It was blissful ignorance.

Wayne later justified the purchases by saying that he was "the primary brand spokesperson" for the National Rifle Association: "We thought it was perfectly appropriate, given all the TV interviews, media appearances, speeches, and everything I do." But that excuse ignores the reality that Wayne, terrified of being on television or being challenged in media appearances, rarely does interviews. The public record shows that he very infrequently consents to open, unscripted questioning.

The leaked documents also detail housing expenses for a woman named Megan Allen. When the news emerged that an intern's housing had been secretly paid for and routed through Ackerman McQueen, a suspicious instinct might lead you to imagine that some sort of romantic affair occurred. But the story is less scandalous than meets the eye. It's more of a story about how Wayne spent thousands of NRA dollars on a family friend.

A few months after Sandy Hook, Wayne and Susan's home was struck by lightning, causing one of the circuits to begin to smoke. So they called the fire department, and the fire chief of Great Falls, Virginia, who arrived happened to have also responded when Wayne had been swatted. They became friendly, and the chief told Wayne that his daughter was a college student, an NRA member, and looking for an internship. Wayne saw to it that the twenty-year-old college student not only got an internship—part of it with Ackerman, part of it with the NRA— but a luxury apartment and a full-time job afterward as well.

Under questioning in a deposition, Wayne said that this internship "came so late" that they had to find her housing because university housing was not available. He also said that her family lived ninety or one hundred miles outside D.C., and so the NRA was obligated to find her housing. Megan Allen was put up in an apartment at a cost of $4,500 per month, for a total of $13,804.84 over less than three months in the summer of 2016. The one thing that doesn't quite sit right with Wayne's explanation is that according to current public listings, even the largest apartment at this complex does not cost that much (some inside the organization have speculated that she was also paid a partial salary through this invoicing). In any case, the expense was wildly more extravagant than what an intern would normally have been provided with.

The idea that Wayne would have an affair is laughable to those who know him well. "There is no relationship," Wayne said under oath. "There never was a relationship." While there are lecherous men associated with the NRA, Wayne is not one of them. He is much more likely to want to take a nap by himself than to sleep with an intern. Susan is now also Allen's boss; Allen was eventually given a permanent job with Susan's Women's Leadership Forum.

Susan LaPierre also hired her niece Colleen Sterner for a role at the Women's Leadership Forum, at about $70,000 per year. Susan is close with Colleen and Colleen's daughter. NRA resources were frequently used to hail private jets to pick up or drop off the Sterners. The New York attorney general would discover at least eight occasions on which private jets were used for the Sterners' travel, most of which did not involve Wayne traveling with them. From May 2015 to April 2019, the NRA spent more than $1 million on private jets in which Wayne was not a passenger.

Colleen was, as an NRA employee, expected to file her own expenses—but Wayne had it done for her, avoiding any pesky lower-level staffers who might be keen to provide oversight. The New York AG found that over a two-year period, Wayne had expensed more than $38,000 in lodging and airfare for his niece, including eight nights at the Dallas Four Seasons, at $1,350 a night.

The New York attorney general's investigation found that Wayne and his relatives chartered flights between the Bahamas and the United States at least eight times since 2015. And on most of these adventures, Wayne made layovers in Nebraska to accommodate Colleen and her family. These flights wound up costing the NRA over half a million dollars.

One of Wayne's excuses for his trips to the Bahamas was that he was visiting a man named David McKenzie. McKenzie is a Hollywood producer who was the principal stakeholder in four NRA vendors that have collectively been paid some $100 million by the National Rifle Association for things like fundraising, printing, mailing, and PR services.

Wayne and McKenzie are close, and Wayne took chartered planes to California to visit him at least twenty times between 2013 and 2016. Wayne typically booked five-star lodging on Sunset Boulevard. McKenzie has also treated Wayne: When Wayne and his family attend these "retreats" in the Bahamas, McKenzie often pays for his stays at the Atlantis resort on Paradise Island. And in the summer, McKenzie has lent him a 108-foot yacht called *Illusions*, which includes four staterooms, a sixteen-foot jet boat, and two Jet Skis.

Wayne's use of the yacht contravenes NRA policy, which is to disclose any gifts received from people who have a business relationship with the NRA. "In his testimony . . . LaPierre said that the reason he failed to disclose the use of the yacht was for security reasons and because he considered the yacht to have been used for a legitimate business purpose," the New York attorney general reported.

In later court proceedings, Wayne went even further about his need for an annual trip on a yacht to feel safe. From 2013 to 2018 he visited the yacht every summer. "I was basically under presidential threat without presidential security," he said. "I remember getting there going, 'Thank God I'm safe, nobody can get me here.'"

He claimed he needed to go to the Bahamas on a yacht as a "security retreat" but did not explain how being in a foreign country surrounded by unvetted staff would make him more safe. Or how free food would make him more safe. Or why he needed his niece Colleen there. He didn't disclose his trips to the Bahamas "because it was a security issue and it was private," he stammered.

Challenged on his trips to Europe, or to the Super Bowl, or the Bahamas, Wayne painted himself as the real victim of the situation. "With those responsibilities that I've had to undertake, there has come a lot of tremendous burdens that I've had to deal with, and I've dealt with them," Wayne said during a deposition. "And I haven't whined about them, but they've been extraordinary and unique."

Wayne's inability to constrain his own impulses extended to his management style. He was grossly outmaneuvered by the vendors that the National Rifle Association paid. One of the prime examples of this is InfoCision, the company the NRA uses for telemarketing and handling incoming calls from its members.

InfoCision is headed by the Taylor family, which between 1996 and 2010 contributed more than $330,000 to various Republican causes, then suddenly stopped doing so. The telemarketing company is heavily reliant on the NRA for its business: over the past few years, the gun rights group has made up more of InfoCision's nonprofit business than all its other clients combined.

InfoCision has a sweetheart deal, according to public filings and required financial disclosures. Its extraordinary contract with the NRA includes a provision: if InfoCision acquires a new member or reactivates a lapsed donor for the gun rights group, it gets to keep 100 percent of the over-the-phone credit card payments ostensibly made to the NRA. The company gets paid twice: first, to fundraise; and second, with a cut of the amount fundraised. The result of the contract is that InfoCision is paid significantly more than it actually brings in.

From 2008 to 2018, InfoCision raised $113.5 million for the NRA. Of that, it kept a cut of $64.3 million, or 56.6 percent—sort of like a commission. On top of that, the NRA paid InfoCision a whopping $210 million over that same time period for its services. The bottom line is that the NRA paid over $200 million so that it could raise less than $50 million.

The NRA's annual spending on the vendor has been increasing. In its most recent filing with the IRS, for the year 2018, the NRA said that InfoCision was its second-largest contractor, which it directly paid $25.7 million.

Regulatory filings by InfoCision also reveal how the NRA fundraised during the Obama era. NRA-approved fundraising scripts were filed with the state of Alaska in 2012 and give a window into the messaging. The telemarketer would ideally open a conversation with a prospective donor with a shout-out: "I'm calling today for our Executive Vice President, Wayne LaPierre. Wayne asked me to call our most loyal supporters like you."

The potential donor would then be asked which of a list of concerns would be most alarming: a U.N. agreement to "force gun registration," Hillary Clinton supposedly seeking a gun treaty at the U.N., or the Obama administration "endorsing new gun bans." The telemarketer was instructed to ask for money after hearing the prospective NRA donor vent.

If the phone call recipient asked about what percentage of their contribution would go to the NRA, the telemarketer was apparently instructed to lie—while the contract with the NRA dictates that InfoCision gets a percentage of the contribution, the telemarketer's script says that InfoCision gets a fixed fee regardless of contributions.

If the potential donor agreed to give, InfoCision then would shamelessly upsell by asking them to "support our troops" by sponsoring an NRA membership for a military service member, for $25 more. "It's a great way to say THANKS to those that deserve it most!" It's unclear whether money was actually segregated for this purpose.

The NRA's telemarketing strategy and its deal with InfoCision add up to a terribly inefficient way to raise money. Often half of each dollar raised gets paid to the vendor. But it is an effective way to increase the National Rifle Association's claimed membership count.

Meanwhile, during the Obama years, the National Rifle Association drifted from its core mission. And as the NRA diverged from its stated aims, Wayne just kept racking up the big bucks. During the Obama era, his salary rose from around $970,000 to $1.4 million. By the end of the Obama administration, in 2017, eight NRA executives were paid more annually than the CEO of the American Red Cross, a nonprofit with ten times the revenue of the gun group.

But salary was just one way that Wayne personally benefited from the NRA. From 2013 to 2017, he was paid back more than $1.2 million in expenses, the New York attorney general found. And he used parts of that to build goodwill among staff, donors, and personal friends: using $65,000 for gifts on the NRA's dime.

Security was also paid for by the NRA, eclipsing the base amount of his salary. Always paranoid about his safety, Wayne's budget set aside several million dollars each year for this purpose, with a security team that protected him at home and on the go. The NRA's director of security obtained an armored vehicle for Wayne, the New York Attorney General's Office found, without going through the proper procedure or notifying the organization's purchasing division.

Golf was also covered. The New York AG investigation found that he had spent more than a hundred thousand dollars between 2009 and 2017 on membership fees for a golf club near the nation's capital. Wayne had a trick for getting hundreds of thousands of dollars in expenses approved: not only was he the boss, but until 2019 he had assigned a low-level employee in ILA the responsibility of approving his expenses. High-level expenses had a tendency to get approved without many questions. Like expenses related to Russia.

CHAPTER 12

Operation Second Pozner

As Maria Butina's operation began to unravel, dubious tales were told about what she was doing and what the NRA's role was.

The NRA said that Wayne had explicitly opposed developing connections with the Russians and, most importantly, that interactions with Butina were made by NRA-linked people but not with the blessing of the NRA itself. These interactions were not official NRA actions, his spokespeople argued, but made by officials in their private capacities.

Butina's argument—and defense during her subsequent trial— was that she was just an innocent, hopeful Russian citizen interested in bolstering relations with the United States who was simply caught in a situation way over her head and who had made a minor regulatory filing error.

Keep these arguments in mind as these chapters proceed, and how the facts gathered and documents obtained by the Senate Intelligence Committee, the Senate Finance Committee, and federal law enforcement undercut them all.

⫿

Alexander Torshin was in for a big promotion. He had served in the Russian legislature from 2001 to 2015 and was now being appointed as the deputy governor of the Central Bank of the Russian Federation. He was not an expert in banking (other than his alleged involvement in money laundering), and one person who spoke to him about the subject was left wondering how he ever got such a role, given his poor grasp of the topic.

Still, Butina excitedly emailed David Keene, who, along with his wife, Donna, had become mentors to her. Butina wrote an email dripping with secrecy, saying that Torshin's appointment was "the result of a 'big game' in which [Torshin] has a very important role," but which she could explain to Keene "only in person." She asked Keene to extend a formal invitation to the 2015 NRA annual meeting. Keene obliged, and cc'd trusted Wayne aide Millie Hallow with the request.

In another email Butina told Keene that Torshin's appointment was due to "private conversations" directly with Vladimir Putin, which "greatly improved" Torshin's stature in Russia—and that Torshin had directed her to expand her ties with the Republican Party.

Butina formalized her proposal in a Russian document, presumably for potential Russian backers, which she hastily translated to English through Google Translate and sent to Paul Erickson to review in March 2015. It bore the subject line "The Second Pozner," a reference to Vladimir Pozner, who first worked in the disinformation department of the KGB and later became a leading American apologist for the Soviets during the Cold War.

The email would later be obtained by the FBI and the Senate Intelligence Committee.

The plan, which she titled "Project Description: Diplomacy," was to use her relationships within the NRA to build an informal channel of diplomatic relations with Russia. Noting how much influence the NRA had in the GOP, she highlighted her and Torshin's ties with the gun group's leadership and said that while the GOP traditionally had been hostile to Russia, her work could be an opportunity to change that.

Arguing that she was the best-positioned informal Russian point of contact with Republican Party leaders, she made the case that she should be a conduit with the American press and the leadership of the GOP. "The groundwork for reliable contact in negotiating with the future US administration can be said to have been laid," Butina wrote. She sought $125,000 to attend "all upcoming major conferences" of the Republican Party, as well as a mandate to meet with Russian diplomats and business representatives to determine where their interests lay. The proposal was meant to be a plan to serve as an agent for the Russian government, prosecutors would later argue.

Butina was right to say that the groundwork had been laid for her future work. The NRA had helped her do that by funding Erickson and Keene's 2013 trip to Moscow. Responding to her proposal, Erickson ignored the fact that he was talking to someone with obvious ties to the Russian government and told Butina all she was missing was the money to make it work. He also provided a list of potential contacts.

"YOU HAVE ALREADY MET ALL OF THE AMERICANS necessary to introduce you to EVERYONE on that list. . . . All that is needed is for your friends to provide you with the financial resources to spend the time in America to TAKE ALL OF THESE MEETINGS," Erickson responded in late March 2015, in an email obtained by the Senate Finance Committee and the FBI. "Your potential sponsors either understand this or they don't."

Butina wasn't a secret agent in the traditional Hollywood sense. She didn't use clandestine methods of communications or engage in secret dead drops with embassy handlers. Instead, explained former FBI counterintelligence official Robert Anderson Jr. in a filing made in her case, she had two key objectives: first, to establish back-channel diplomacy that could be used to bypass more formal channels and undercut U.S. objectives; and second, to engage in a "spot and assess" operation that would identify sources Russian intelligence could potentially recruit in the future. Citing the reports Butina wrote to Torshin on American political figures over several years, Anderson said that "Butina provided the Russian Federation with information that skilled intelligence officers can exploit for years and that may cause significant damage to the United States."

In the service of her work, Butina would introduce herself differently to different people. She would varyingly announce her affiliation with the Russian Federation to some and claim to be just a humble student to others. She has introduced herself as a journalist, an interpreter, a gun rights advocate, and a staffer at the Russian central bank. Or perhaps she was simply a business owner and consultant, having started a mysterious company called Bridges LLC in South Dakota. "What makes her so dangerous is that the people who she's contacting don't know that she's there taking direction from the Russian government," said John Demers, the assistant attorney general for national security when Butina was later arrested.

But those who paid attention could recognize these cues immediately. Dimitri Simes is the CEO of the Center for the National Interest, a think tank founded by former president Richard Nixon. Simes became suspicious of Butina in part because her official role kept changing—she first appeared to him as a translator to Torshin, then later as someone professionally involved with Torshin and the Russian central bank.

"I cannot say with any degree of confidence that any of them, particularly Ms. Butina, were Russian intelligence agents," he later told investigators. "What I knew, [is] that she was not what she was trying to pretend to be, particularly because she clearly had multiple personalities in her discussions with Americans." Simes told his staff not to meet with her and barred her from entering their offices. Butina reported Simes's view back to Torshin in an online message: Simes "gave a direct order to his staff to not talk to me under the threat of being fired. He says I work for the SVR," she wrote; the SVR is a Russian intelligence agency.

Meanwhile, the National Rifle Association and its officials meandered past these suspicious clues. Erickson, whom Butina explicitly looped in on her plans and who was an outspoken advocate and facilitator on her behalf, overlooked it entirely. He also paid for her trips throughout the United States, some $8,000 to travel in the summer of 2015. After Butina moved to the United States under the pretense of being a graduate student, Erickson paid for part of her education and living expenses.

The NRA repeatedly opened doors for Butina and Torshin. By 2015 she had become so firmly ensconced in NRA circles that her itinerary for the NRA annual meeting was personally prepared by Nick Perrine, Keene's assistant. During the annual meeting, Torshin and Butina were heralded as international superstars:

Torshin gave remarks at an NRA dinner; they hobnobbed with an elite group of donors who had each given at least $1 million to the NRA, known as the Golden Ring of Freedom; and Keene hosted both of them for dinner.

Torshin and Butina were asked to observe the NRA board's international affairs subcommittee meeting, as well as its legislative policy committee meeting. For context, the public cannot even get a list of the NRA's committees and its members, let alone attend committee meetings where board members discuss strategy. Yet the two Russians just waltzed right on in. Thanks to Keene, Torshin and Butina received tickets to attend an ILA dinner and auction. Records show that Keene expensed these tickets—$1,000 for the pair—back to the NRA. Keene, who by this point had known Torshin for several years, gave the Russian government official a replica of a Civil War revolver, suggesting he use a diplomatic pouch to bring it back to Russia (Torshin declined to do so).

Before the 2015 conference, Butina asked for, and NRA staff provided, a list of American politicians who would be attending. Torshin and Butina were given access to the ILA Leadership Forum, where the 2016 Republican hopefuls were trying out for a spot on the presidential ticket.

The access provided by NRA insiders facilitated a meeting with Wisconsin governor Scott Walker at the venue. Butina would expand on that meeting, attending the Walker presidential campaign launch event in July 2015—she was tasked by Torshin to write a memo on this. She also sought to help the Russian ambassador at the time, Sergey Kislyak, identify a Walker adviser who apparently wanted to travel to Moscow.

Butina's effort was not the Russian government's only attempt to build ties with the National Rifle Association: there was a concurrent campaign by Ambassador Kislyak to develop ties with the gun group. Kislyak had been central to a number of storylines related to the Trump administration and Russia, because Trumpworld kept lying about their interactions with him.

Kislyak's conversations with former Trump national security adviser Michael Flynn led to criminal charges after Flynn lied about them to the FBI. And Kislyak's meetings with Jeff Sessions, who would later become Trump's attorney general, would spark one of the biggest storylines of the Trump era. Sessions had said during his confirmation hearings that he had not met with Russian officials during the campaign. When Sessions was found to have had two meetings with Kislyak, the attorney general recused himself from the Russia investigation, sparking special counsel Robert Mueller's probe.

Though Kislyak's story has been much less covered than those about Flynn and Sessions, this same Russian ambassador also took an active interest in the NRA, according to two Senate committee reports. Like Butina, he networked through Keene, who was at this time an NRA board member. Keene dined with Kislyak at the Russian embassy in June 2015, and then returned the favor by inviting the ambassador to visit NRA headquarters in Fairfax several months later. Keene and the NRA president at the time, Allan Cors, gave Kislyak a tour of the NRA museum and the rest of the building in a meeting that lasted for about three hours. They continued their engagements: the three of them had another lunch in April 2016 and were scheduled for lunch in June 2017. After Kislyak was recalled back to Russia, leaving the American capital under a cloud of suspicion about Russia's efforts to interfere with the presidential elections, Keene's wife, Donna, apparently attended his farewell party in D.C.

Butina was aware of the ongoing Kislyak-NRA outreach. Notes of a meeting she had with Kislyak, later obtained during a search by the FBI, showed that she had promised to share the name of a Walker adviser, and that Kislyak had explicitly told her that the NRA could become "one of the points of cooperation" between Russia and the United States. Prosecutors later said that Butina also previewed to Kislyak that she might take a trip to Moscow with an NRA delegation in December 2015—a trip that ultimately occurred. As the Russian government was attacking the U.S. political system, the NRA was cozying up to Russian government officials and furthering the networking of one of its unregistered agents.

While Russia's campaign to disrupt American politics did involve elements of in-person outreach, much of the influence campaign was carried out online through disinformation on social media networks during the 2016 election campaign. Central to this effort was the troll farm linked to the Russian government called the Internet Research Agency.

Twitter later identified a list of accounts it found to have been controlled by the Russian troll farm, allowing me to work with a data analysis firm to study its patterns. Based in St. Petersburg, the Internet Research Agency had a well-worn playbook: On every political issue, accounts controlled by the IRA aimed to create division. Using different usernames that purported to be genuine Americans expressing their opinions, the IRA would take extreme views on both sides of an issue to incite and amplify dissension within the American political conversation.

That is, on every issue except guns and the NRA. Internet Research Agency accounts overwhelmingly promoted pro-gun and pro-NRA messaging—an anomaly unlike anything else the Russian trolls usually did. It was as if someone decided to issue an edict: the National Rifle Association's messaging is so divisive that all they had to do is imitate them to achieve the goal of sowing massive discord and upheaval.

At times, the Russian social media agitators even plagiarized NRA language. The Internet Research Agency pushed some of its pro-gun content through an account on Instagram called "Defend.The.Second." The Internet Research Agency copied language used by the NRA's Institute for Legislative Action in one case; in another case, it copied the NRA's promotion of various firearms news stories. One of the Russian troll farm's posts celebrated Wayne LaPierre's visit to the White House in 2017. The National Rifle Association and the Russian trolls in St. Petersburg also did a lot of mirroring: the NRA on at least ninety occasions posted tweets similar to those of the Internet Research Agency—sometimes after the Russians had posted first.

The Russian troll accounts also had a suspiciously in-depth awareness of local American gun laws. They would write about state- or even city-level regulations, often writing in the aftermath of a violent crime that gun laws had not prevented a shooting. How Russians living in St. Petersburg would have the political knowledge to make critiques of local county gun regulations is still a mystery, as is the strange synchronicity that occurred between IRA and NRA social media accounts.

What's not a mystery is that Internet Research Agency accounts were publicly in contact with Torshin. They tweeted at him ten times from eight different accounts on Twitter, which was one of Torshin's and Butina's preferred mediums of communication. At one point, one of the IRA accounts sent him friendly well-wishes. In another, it quoted a line of Russian poetry: "A little oak leaf tore off from its branch / Was driven o'er the steppe by a cruel gale."

The report of the Senate Intelligence Committee's investigation into Butina has a final section that's completely redacted,
suggesting it includes classified information or could reveal sensitive intelligence sources and methods. But a footnote for that
section is only partially redacted and refers to the "IRA's influence operations during the 2016 U.S. election." Tantalizingly, it is
a public indication that somewhere in their investigation into
Butina, they found something related to the Russian troll farm in
St. Petersburg.

Butina had a habit of popping up all over America at various political events. Throughout 2015 she courted millionaire NRA donors and hobnobbed with NRA board members at one of their
meetings in Birmingham, Alabama. Being close with the NRA's
former president helped. In emails later obtained by investigators, Donna Keene, David Keene's wife, told Butina in April 2015
that the "NRA will pay your registration" for a conference organized by a conservative group called the Council for National
Policy. David Keene later expensed the NRA for $700 related to
registration costs for that meeting.

In the summer of 2015, more than a year before she would
begin graduate studies in Washington, D.C., Butina managed to
take the microphone at a Las Vegas libertarian conference called
FreedomFest and pose a question to then candidate Donald
Trump. It was the first question Trump had been asked about
Russia as a presidential candidate. It would not be his last.

"I am visiting from Russia. My question will be about foreign
politics," Butina said, glancing at prepared notes. "If you will be

elected as president, what will be your foreign politics especially in the relationships with my country? Do you want to continue the politics of sanctions that are damaging [to] both economies? Or [do] you have any other ideas?"

"I know Putin, and I'll tell you what, we'll get along with Putin," Trump said in his response to Butina. "I would get along very nicely with Putin. . . . I mean, where we have the strength. I don't think you'd need the sanctions. I think we would get along very, very well."

It had been a chance encounter, but Butina was very pleased with finally having interacted with Trump—she was so unable to restrain her excitement that she called Torshin from the restroom with her report on the exchange.

While at FreedomFest, Butina met Patrick Byrne, then the CEO of Overstock, an internet retail business he founded. She believed that as an adviser to Senator Rand Paul, who was also running for president that election cycle, Byrne could bring her deeper into Republican Party circles. Butina initially introduced herself as the head of a Russian gun rights group, and their first conversation involved flirtatious banter about Milton Friedman, Anton Chekhov, and John Locke. In their second encounter, the day after, Butina introduced herself as an aide to a senior official in the Russian central bank, Alexander Torshin—and Byrne agreed to lunch.

In an email to a friend, Erickson recalled how Byrne and Butina had met and alluded to how his romantic partner had used her looks to interest Byrne in a meeting. "When he met . . . Maria, his eyes lit up and his schedule cleared," Erickson wrote. "I think we now know how to capture his attention . . . and it ain't with women in burkas."

Byrne would later repeatedly pitch Maria Butina money for

sex, according to Erickson. In an email obtained by the Senate Intelligence Committee, Byrne "has found ever more creative ways to pitch a standing $1 million offer to her 'to have a baby with him,'" Erickson wrote to a friend. "He is utterly enamored of her imagined gene stock and believes that a baby would cement not only his familial line but also relations between our two nations." ("I had cancer when I was 22. I've been sterile since I was 22," Byrne said on a podcast, denying ever making such an offer, calling Erickson's suggestion a "delusion.")

Byrne's relationship with Butina would have long-term ramifications, and he would have something of a meltdown over it. In the three years after their meeting, the relationship between Byrne and Butina would turn romantic, off and on. After Butina was sent to jail, Byrne released an incoherent press release in his role as the executive of a publicly traded company, titled "Overstock.com CEO Comments on Deep State." His company's shares immediately plunged by more than 30 percent over two days. After divulging his affair with Butina, Byrne resigned.

Byrne later went on to allege that the FBI had directed him to pursue a relationship with Butina, something two former top FBI officials deny. He's spent the time since trying to get the Trump administration to pay attention to his allegations, to no avail, and, after Trump lost the 2020 election, was consumed by conspiracy theories about voter fraud. Add Byrne to the list of people who interacted with Butina whose lives were subsequently overturned. There would be more.

CHAPTER 13

Ackerman McQueen Power Grows

Wayne was always too socially awkward and afraid of confrontation to lead. He always needed a life raft. He needed someone to tell him how to deal with problems, someone to tell him how to talk, someone to tell him whom to hire and whom to fire. Wayne's character being what it was, he was always being manipulated by someone. It was mutually beneficial: Wayne needed reassurance from someone he felt was smart and he could rely on; while the other person could really stand to cash in on Wayne's malleability.

For this individual, there was a single prime directive: protect the golden goose. This one person's main goal would be to insulate Wayne from the problems he faced or else run the risk of a new, more resilient leader replacing him.

In the 1990s, during the earliest days of Wayne's tenure, the person who held this role was a man named Brad O'Leary, a heavyset Irishman who ran the firm PM Consulting, which primarily serviced Republicans. Before NRA insiders were complaining about Ack-Mac, they were complaining about O'Leary and PM Consulting. PM Consulting's playbook was similar to the one Ackerman McQueen would later adopt: charge exorbitant fees while riling up the NRA base through extreme rhetoric. Recall the incident in 1995 when George H. W. Bush publicly resigned from the NRA because the gun rights group had sent out a fundraising appeal calling federal agents "jack-booted government thugs." That was O'Leary's handiwork.

O'Leary was then making $50,000 a month—one profile in *Mother Jones* describes his compensation as including "a series of bonuses that would make a major league ballplayer blush." There was a familiar chorus: an NRA board investigation later found that PM Consulting was siphoning off nearly 20 percent of the NRA's budget.

But the person who was most influential, the longest, was Angus McQueen. In the 1990s, O'Leary and McQueen fought for Wayne's ear, and eventually Angus won out, a turn of fate that would alter the path of the NRA for decades. Angus McQueen, though not an NRA employee, was to spend much of the rest of his life as one of the true power centers of the National Rifle Association.

Small things could send Angus McQueen into fits of anger. An improperly closed door once sparked an outburst of rage, with Angus knocking items off shelves and screaming at staff for not shutting it properly. He had a tendency, in large groups, to pick the weakest, most vulnerable person in the room and humiliate them in front of the others. Whether in public or private, there were characteristic signs of an oncoming volcanic eruption: spit splashing from the corner of his mouth, furrowed brow, deafening voice. He was, a close friend noted, the male equivalent of Meryl Streep's character in *The Devil Wears Prada*.

Even his enemies would concede that he was a brilliant businessman and messaging strategist. "He was off the charts in strategic thinking and intellect," said a close friend. "He was [also] the meanest, ruthless motherfucking asshole. It would make you nauseated."

He was a fierce man with a strict father who had drilled into him the twin concepts of discipline and retribution. You could never hope to win an argument with a McQueen. The McQueen way was to fine-tune vengeance: if you strike out at me, I'm going to plot out my long, skillful, considered revenge—and when I strike back, it will not be to injure but to deal a fatal blow. He was proud of his Scottish ancestry—his family tartan was displayed prominently everywhere.

This simmering fury made Angus's personal mannerisms the subject of immense scrutiny. Those in his company paid close attention to cues that he might be set off at any moment. When annoyed, he would take his hands and brush off his pants, as if he were wiping off crumbs or whatever irritation was plaguing him. He might pick off nonexistent lint from his clothing, as if exorcising a troublesome issue from his life. While fidgeting, he had a tendency to shift his watch down on his left wrist. If he was pleased, he would lean back and take a pen or ruler and scratch his back with it. Unlike Wayne, who comforted himself by rocking back and forth while anxious, Angus was rarely frightened.

Angus was also masterful at his job, immensely skilled at selling to his clients and crafting the perfect pitch. While he never attended college, he honed his craft in his early career with the

Navy Office of Information during the Vietnam War. He later directed coverage of the Gemini and Apollo space missions for an NBC affiliate in Houston. In 1973 he joined Ackerman McQueen, cofounded by his father, Marvin, and was creative director when the firm first pitched the National Rifle Association with its services. "We're advertising people, we're optimists," he once said in a speech to accept an award. "Our work fills the spaces that distract the eye from tragedy."

During pitches, staff would often gather around television monitors to watch as Angus, from a nearby conference room, regaled clients with a near symphonic performance. Even those who hated him begrudgingly respected his oratory and salesmanship. "He was a brilliant speaker," recalled a former employee who otherwise had nothing positive to say about Angus. "He was really good at advertising."

Angus, who was CEO from 1987 to 2019, worked his employees down to the bone. "You gave your life to them," said one former Ackerman McQueen employee. "They pushed people as far as they possibly could." It was a sweatshop: sixty hours was a normal workweek, and it was not uncommon to work eighty hours a week. And even when you left the office, the expectation was you were on call. That expectation was driven from the top. Angus would say, "If you're not in your seat at eight-thirty A.M. on Saturdays, don't bother coming in on Monday." Staff would get burned out—and in extreme cases, have weeping, maniacal breakdowns at their desk under the stress and pressure. Much like at NRA HQ, an atmosphere of paranoia and fear prevailed—don't go outside the family.

The long hours made incestuous intra-office dating inevitable, and some employees even felt like they were encouraged to engage in this. "They liked it if you were dating within the agency," a former employee said. "They would try to set us up so we wouldn't create a separate family at home that distracted from work." Dozens of couples existed within the company, and anyone working there could tick off examples of marriages that resulted from dating within the office. Those who sought a life outside the office were not taken as seriously, some former employees said.

An unspoken sexist standard was the norm for staff at the ad agency, according to women who formerly worked there. Only thin and attractive women were welcome in the company's public-facing ranks, they said. Expensive brand-name dresses and skirts were the unspoken expectation: Prada, Louis Vuitton, Chanel, and Jimmy Choos were the standard, and those who didn't meet it did not last long. Good luck if you were a woman who tried wearing pants.

The staff servicing other clients, like Chickasaw Nation or Integris Health, for example, weren't expected to dress up in the same way. But the people on the NRA account were held to the same standard as advertising professionals on Madison Avenue in New York City. For Oklahoma City, this was a head-turning directive. Those working with the NRA might receive a nice bonus to help them along in the right direction. "We need our women to look hot for them," said one insider, summing up the attitude. Added another, "Women were paraded." There were a lot of women hired at the firm—but many felt that this belied the unspoken reality: looks were considered a key marketing tool. Bonus points if you were a woman who could shoot.

Ackerman McQueen responded to an inquiry about this section by saying that its employees worked hard, that they were ahead of the curve in hiring women for executive positions, that the team that worked on the NRA account was always a mixed team of men and women, and that the women executives on their team were always very capable.

⫙

Opposites attract. At heart, Wayne was a lobbyist; what he really wanted to do was count the votes. It was Angus who was the true believer in gun rights, the one who cared most about winning the strategic messaging war. "Fuck that shit," Angus would say when Wayne called with an update on the whip count for a piece of gun legislation.

Wayne lacked the confidence to do almost anything without consulting Angus, and would sometimes call him several times a day. During the time that Angus was a dominant partner, Wayne would not make a single major strategic decision without consulting him, as if the adman were his safety blanket. In Wayne, Angus had found a pliable partner who would pay his agency massive sums while helping him achieve his political goals.

Angus, like many others in the NRA orbit, realized that if he browbeat Wayne enough, he could get Wayne to do what he wanted. He would launch profanities at Wayne, as if Angus were the boss and Wayne were the client, rather than the other way around. And for years Wayne acceded to Angus's treatment, until the day he didn't. But that story comes later.

For decades, Angus ran the public messaging behind the NRA, and Wayne meekly conceded to all of it. Ackerman Mc-Queen built a cult around Wayne, writing his speeches, creating an image of a larger-than-life gun rights bulldog when he was anything but. The broader strategy was simple: clear, distinct positions, to draw a line in the sand and force the target audience to pick sides on gun rights. This often took the form of apocalyptic scaremongering: The United Nations was going to take away your gun rights. Congress was going to ban your guns. The Obama White House wants to seize your weapons.

The relationship between the two organizations was symbiotic, and for decades grew closer and closer each year. By 2016 there were around a hundred people working on the NRA account. The relationship was informal: Wayne, who didn't use email or texts anyway, would largely approve projects and bills verbally.

At the senior executive level, Ackerman McQueen and NRA employees were close to family: dining together, deeply enmeshed in one another's personal lives, and putting warm touches on the holidays by sending thoughtful, individualized gifts. At the middle or junior level, employees at the NRA would always wonder: *Why the heck are we required to use the expensive services of Ackerman McQueen for this or that? We've got better and more efficient staff in-house!*

"I witnessed a lot of selling just to sell. Let's sell our client this thing . . . and tell them they need it," said an internal witness to this Ackerman McQueen strategy. "It probably wasn't the best solution, but it allowed us to charge the most."

Wayne began the practice of routing NRA expenses through Ackerman McQueen, which would then bill it back to the NRA. Internally at Ack-Mac, it was referred to as the "Out of Pocket" project—where Wayne would direct shady bills, such as questionable payments for meals and cigars and hotels. Charges were often routed to the account through American Express cards, like the one Wayne used to pay for his travels in Europe.

Wayne would later claim to have no knowledge of this practice, but that was preposterous—he had daily conversations with Angus and other senior Ackerman McQueen staff, who ran approvals by him. Ackerman McQueen would send invoices to the NRA in a lump sum, without supporting receipts or documentation of the expenses, and request payment within thirty days.

The NRA's Out of Pocket project was treated differently from all the other business Ackerman McQueen had with the gun rights group. The separate bucket for Wayne's expenses existed since at least the 1990s, when he became the executive vice president of the NRA. There was an air of secrecy around it, as the ostensible reason for it was Wayne's confidentiality and personal security. Some Ack-Mac staff felt that they were trying to hide the documentation from the NRA's auditor.

Wayne used Ackerman McQueen to pay for all sorts of questionable costs. "LaPierre . . . used the pass-through arrangement to conceal private travel and trips that were largely personal in nature," the New York attorney general found. "LaPierre would also direct [Ackerman McQueen exec Tony Makris] to incur various charges—including hotel rooms, meals, cars, tips, and gifts for himself and VIP donors—and to submit those expenses to the NRA for reimbursement through the 'Out of Pocket' arrangement." Questioning in court proceedings indicated that these Out of Pocket expenses for travel and entertainment exceeded $560,000 in 2016, and were billed back to the NRA.

In January 2018, Wayne, notoriously paranoid about health concerns, asked Makris, the president of the Akerman McQueen subsidiary Mercury Group, to travel with him to visit with doctors at the Mayo Clinic. Makris had been in Las Vegas for a gun show, and Wayne called him in a panic. "He called me, distraught, and he said that his local doctor in Washington had given him a very severe diagnosis," Makris later recalled. Wayne asked for him to accompany him to the clinic in Scottsdale, Arizona, and said he would redirect the private jet to Las Vegas to pick him up. Wayne booked a stay at the Four Seasons during this health scare, and the lodging ran $9,550, dutifully charged to Ackerman McQueen and passed on to the NRA. The private jet cost was directly paid for by the gun group. (They ultimately went twice to the Mayo Clinic, and the health scare turned out to be a false alarm.)

"One of the reasons Wayne ran so much of his financial stuff through Ackerman was because we didn't trust his own accountants," wrote his former chief of staff after he left the NRA. "Classic NRA protocol: rather than fix the problem, Wayne came up with a somewhat paranoid and backasswards work-around."

When Wayne traveled, he wasn't accompanied by an NRA "body man," the term used for a personal assistant that travels with powerful political figures like the president. Instead, he required Makris to travel with him along with copious amounts of cash. At one point, Makris spent $7,500 in gratuities over just three months of traveling with Wayne. Wayne was "worried about security and worried about confidentiality," Makris later said, explaining that especially in L.A. and Las Vegas Wayne wanted to maintain a good relationship with doormen and staff so that no one would tip off the press as to where he was.

·ᛁᛁᚹ·

Perhaps the most notorious Ackerman McQueen product that Wayne LaPierre bought into was NRATV. The advertising agency pitched its clients on the concept of branded news: bypassing the mainstream press by launching a news outlet catering directly to its target audience.

The NRA branched out into the news business after the 2002 passage of a campaign finance law called McCain-Feingold. The law put limitations on how groups could campaign, and the NRA wanted to bypass the rules by creating its own news organization. It was originally called NRA News when it launched in 2004. (Wayne was considering all sorts of wild ideas at this time, including a pirate radio station in international waters that could be broadcast onto American soil.)

Ackerman McQueen upsold Wayne in later years, promising that an online media arm called NRATV would help create a more diverse NRA, draw in younger members, and eventually pay for itself with sponsorships from companies that wanted to reach this audience. Wayne approved the idea, and the NRATV project formally launched in 2016. But Angus's promises were never realized, and the NRA found that not only were very few people watching it, but of those people who did watch it, very few were contributing money to the NRA through the project.

NRATV marked the latest turn after Sandy Hook: away from a strict focus on gun rights and toward a broader conservative culture war. Ackerman McQueen hired a number of people who knew little about national politics or firearms to lead the project, including Tammy Payne, a news director who also happened to be Angus's girlfriend.

Payne was obsessed with what Fox was talking about on any given day, rather than what the gun issues of the day might be. NRATV content did center on firearms but also came to be known for extreme rants on race wars, sharia law, immigration, and the media. NRATV sold an official T-shirt with the slogan "Socialist Tears"—the marketing asked: "Want to make a socialist cry?" It became totally unhinged—Newsmax without the viewers.

Dana Loesch, hired to be one of the faces of NRATV, embarrassed herself on a number of occasions, most infamously when she mocked Thomas the Tank Engine for promoting racial diversity. "This is horrible," she ranted while broadcasting an image of train engines with Ku Klux Klan hoods. After Trump's election, she called journalists "rat bastards of the earth" and said that she was "happy, frankly, to see them curb-stomped." These rants obviously had nothing to do with guns or the NRA's core mission.

The non-gun content irritated longtime NRA members who wanted the group to stay laser-focused on firearms. "They have been narrowing and narrowing the demographic that they are appealing to among gun owners. Targeting social conservative Christians only, to the exclusion of everyone else, is a great way to get the best return on your investment in terms of fundraising, but it's a horrible way to lobby for gun rights, because you alienate others," said Rob Pincus, an NRA member who is a critic of Wayne's tenure.

Even legendary NRA board member and Wayne ally Marion Hammer spoke out against NRATV, releasing a rare public statement denouncing the project after Loesch's KKK incident. "Since the founding of NRATV, some, including myself and other board members, have questioned the value of it," Hammer said. "Wayne has told me and others that NRATV is being constantly evaluated—to make sure it works in the best interest of the organization and provides an appropriate return on investment."

Wayne was apparently furious about the incident, but he did not speak out publicly about it or take any action to discipline anyone for it.

It ultimately became more trouble than it was worth. Costs skyrocketed over the years as the concept developed, rising to $25 million a year by 2018. Only forty-nine thousand unique visitors viewed NRATV in January 2019. Rather than use an existing platform like YouTube, Ackerman McQueen developed an NRATV website from scratch—a time-consuming and expensive project. Conversely, NRATV received little promotion or advertising, so not many people knew about it.

When Josh Powell, Wayne's chief of staff, asked Ackerman McQueen how many viewers NRATV brought in, the firm said it could not provide internal metrics. Powell and Wayne once went to talk to Angus about the costs of the TV channel. Angus went ballistic, according to Powell.

"Angus just blew up at Wayne and me, screaming profanities and claiming we didn't know what we were talking about," Powell wrote. He claims Angus said, "Wayne, I will cut your fucking tongue out if you do anything to NRATV!"

Buoyed by the millions of dollars his company was receiving from the NRA, one of his most lucrative clients, Angus lived a lavish lifestyle. With cash flowing in the door, problems were often solved by throwing money at them. Stressed-out staff? Money. Problem with equipment? Money. Tight schedule? Money. Go fix it.

While what Ackerman McQueen was doing might have been unethical at times, it wasn't illegal. The firm never hid the fact that it was trying to make money. It was, after all, a for-profit business. It was Wayne who could always be counted on to approve their bills without much oversight. The NRA board, a rubber-stamp panel, wouldn't care to look deeply, and if there were problems, they could always retroactively approve it. And so it went for years.

CHAPTER 14

Moscow Bound

Moscow in the second week of December 2015 was *the* place for scheming. At the Metropol Hotel, future Trump national security adviser Michael Flynn had dinner with Russian president Vladimir Putin. On December 8, a delegation of NRA officials and bigwigs arrived in the Russian capital. They were greeted by a striking redhead, and an equally striking sign that read WEL-COME TO RUSSIA COMRADES, featuring the side-by-side logos of the National Rifle Association and its Russian equivalent, the Right to Bear Arms.

Most of the delegation had just finished an NRA-sponsored trip to Israel. After landing at Sheremetyevo airport, the arriving Americans were ushered to the same hotel that Flynn and Putin would later dine at. Their agenda, painstakingly prepared by their Russian hosts, read "THE PROGRAM of the visit of the delegation from The National Rifle Association of America (The NRA) to Moscow."

The December 2015 trip had been organized by Butina in consultation with David and Donna Keene. David, the former NRA president, was now a board member. Donna, like Susan LaPierre, considered herself just another NRA volunteer. The NRA helped pay for some of the delegation's expenses—an inconvenient truth that would undercut its efforts to distance the organization from the trip later. NRA staff had also been instrumental in putting the trip together by preparing itineraries and briefings and helping arrange tourist visas. The delegation took advantage of the NRA's travel agents for logistics, and the NRA provided the trip's members with NRA-related gifts to present to Russians they would meet along the way, a Senate Finance Committee report concluded.

"We will be escorted and spoiled," Donna told the participants before they arrived, listing an NRA staffer as their contact for any issues they might have with the trip. But why did the Russians want to spoil them? It was not a puzzle: members of the NRA delegation were directly briefed that Torshin needed them to illustrate to the Kremlin how influential he was in American politics. A U.S. intelligence report later concluded that the Russian government had approved Butina's infiltration of the NRA and that Kremlin officials had internally discussed the NRA trip to Moscow.

"Russia believes that high level contacts with the NRA might be the BEST means of neutral introduction to either the next American President OR to a meaningful re-set in relations with the Congress under a (God forbid) President Clinton," Erickson told incoming NRA president Pete Brownell before the trip, about why the trip was being organized. (Brownell did not respond to a list of questions regarding this book.)

In organizing the delegation, Butina had been obsessed, as usual, with how politically influential the attendees were. She was less interested in their professional experiences and more interested in assessing how they might be useful to her and her cause in the future. "I strongly need the information about how are people below important POLITICALLY," she wrote in a planning email. "I do not need bio. I need how influential they are in the USA politics."

Joining the Keenes and Brownell in Moscow were a number of NRA heavies: top-dollar donors Dr. Arnold Goldschlager and his daughter Hilary Goldschlager; Jim Liberatore, the then CEO of the Outdoor Channel; David Clarke, the former Milwaukee sheriff and Fox News fixture, and his spouse; and Joseph Gregory, who chairs the Golden Ring of Freedom recognizing those who have given more than $1 million to the NRA.

The NRA president at the time, Allan Cors, was originally scheduled to attend but had to pull out, citing health reasons "after a month-long argument with my doctors." In a note on NRA letterhead, he explicitly designated Keene and Gregory to "represent the NRA. . . . I am sorry I won't be with the delegation and appreciate the arrangements you made on behalf of the NRA and of me." Incoming NRA president Brownell, who was set to replace Cors, had already been in Russia for several days when the delegation arrived.

The unseasonably warm Muscovite air was thick with plots. Yes, the NRA delegation took in the sights of the Red Square and caught a ballet performance at the Bolshoi Theatre. But most delegates had other schemes they hoped to tack onto the trip— schemes that, despite their representation as an NRA delegation, had nothing to do with the National Rifle Association or promoting their nonprofit organization's mission.

Brownell, the owner of a massive gun distributorship called Brownells, had been in discussions with Butina about business opportunities in Russia all year. Butina had been in touch with Brownells staff about finding Russian-made ammo and also about expanding their operations in Russia surreptitiously without risking the broader Brownells brand. This "would DEFINITELY be profitable," Butina told Brownell as she tried to convince him to go.

Brownells had a business partner in Russia that was distributing its products, though not under its name, and staff were very worried about the damage that could occur to the brand's reputation if they were seen to be expanding their business in Russia, given their lucrative government contracts and America's adversarial relationship with Russia. So Brownell was eager to keep the trip a secret and conferred with Wayne's close aide Millie about how to tell Butina that he would not be doing media interviews while he was in Russia.

The risk of discovery was outweighed by the potential of future sales. Brownell went to Russia days prior to the remainder of the delegation's arrival to explore personal commercial opportunities and "to introduce our company to the governing individuals throughout Russia," he explained to his staff. He was accompanied by Butina, who had promised that Russian gun companies were ready to talk "export and import deals."

Brownell was told directly about Butina's contacts with the Russian intelligence service the FSB. In fact, it was alluded to in the planning for his trip. Butina had "moved heaven & earth and manipulated the Russian FSB (the current incarnation of the old KGB) and gotten you cleared for a tour of one (1) Russian arms factory . . . probably because most of the FSB agents 'assigned' to her want to marry her," Erickson told Brownell in an email obtained by the Senate Finance Committee.

Liberatore, the CEO of the Outdoor Channel, which has business relationships with the NRA, had other commercial opportunities in mind. He wanted to develop a show called "Unknown Russia" for his channel, and later paid Butina thousands of dollars in vain to help get Putin to appear on it. Butina had bragged about having close contacts with Putin's office, and she was ultimately paid $20,000 to help make the connection, the Senate Intelligence Committee found. Torshin told Butina that he had reached out to Putin's deputy chief of staff to facilitate this and had spoken to another party who was interested in helping. Butina's contract with the Outdoor Channel was ultimately canceled after she made no progress in securing Putin's cooperation after four months.

Keene had his own ask. He had joined the conservative *Washington Times* as the opinion editor after leaving his post as NRA president. Keene sought an interview with Vladimir Putin for the paper and worked through Butina and Torshin to get one. Torshin tried to get it done, but later noted in a message that he was blocked by "a tradition that [Putin] gives an interview to a particular foreign media outlet only on the eve of his visit to that media outlet's home country."

Gregory, who chaired the group of NRA million-dollar-plus donors, was there for a joyride. Through his lawyer, he told the Senate Finance Committee that the NRA had often reimbursed him for trips to Israel, and that historically the NRA paid for his expenses on international trips like this. There is no obvious reason related to the NRA's stated nonprofit mission that the NRA should have paid for Gregory's trips to Israel. Instead, there was an expectation among NRA bigwigs that the NRA would foot the bill for their international jaunts.

Butina used Putin as a lure, not only suggesting to Keene that she could make an interview happen and to Liberatore that she could get him for his television channel, but also tempting Brownell by indicating he could meet the Russian president during the trip. Brownell seemed particularly intrigued by the idea, writing in an email it would "be a very interesting meeting." They never did meet Putin, although the day after Butina suggested it was a possibility, Brownell agreed to join the delegation to Moscow.

They did, however, meet with Putin's inner circle. The itinerary that week in December 2015 was packed with a parade of Russian diplomats, government officials, and wealthy businessmen. The NRA delegation had meetings with Russian foreign minister Sergei Lavrov; Igor Pisarsky, introduced as the man who runs Putin's presidential campaigns; and Konstantin Nikolaev, the oligarch who had funded Butina's gun rights group in Russia.

They also met with Putin's deputy prime minister, Dmitry Rogozin; and Igor Shchyogolev, a special assistant to Putin—both of whom had been economically sanctioned by the United States because of the Russian invasion of Ukraine in 2014. For all the organization's public messaging associating gun rights with patriotism, the NRA delegation had no problem privately meeting with America's designated adversaries, only eighteen months after the sanctions were imposed.

Rogozin undercut his NRA guests by subsequently posting a photo with Brownell and Gregory on Twitter, surprising Torshin and Butina, who had wanted to keep the meeting secret. There was a consciousness of guilt here: in private messages Torshin and Butina said at the time they were worried that the tweet could "create problems" for the delegation.

It did. After I began asking questions about the 2015 Moscow trip years later, Keene claimed that the meeting with Rogozin was purely nonpolitical and that Rogozin was merely the chairman of the Russian Shooting Federation. Butina would later testify that they talked about gun rights. Brownell's lawyer would try to argue that the meeting was a chance encounter. But contemporaneous documents show that the handout NRA members received on arrival included a biography of Rogozin, who was described as "Deputy Prime Minister, in charge of [the] defense and space industry." They knew who he was, they knew or should have known he was sanctioned, and it was no surprise to meet him.

The group received gifts from a Russian sniper rifle company, with photos dutifully posted on social media by former sheriff David Clarke. And, as Donna had promised, they were spoiled. "They were killing us with vodka and the best Russian food," Arnold Goldschlager recalled later. Butina knew that the NRA delegation owed her and Torshin for the successful trip. "We should let them express their gratitude now, we will put pressure on them quietly later," she wrote to Torshin after the delegation had left Moscow.

In another image of the trip, the NRA delegation members are all smiles as they take in a lavish meal at a Moscow hunting club called the Trophy House. They wouldn't be smiling about this trip forever. Years later, Butina would be charged with—and plead guilty to—being a secret Russian agent. Brownell would depart his post as NRA president early, an unprecedented occurrence. Keene's work with Butina would be exposed. Liberatore would spend thousands of dollars and ultimately abandon his plans in Russia. Many of the delegation's members would be subject to investigations by Congress, the FBI, and the press—and play a game of hot potato, blaming other NRA officials for organizing the trip.

The bottom line is that the National Rifle Association, for all its culture-war noise and reliance on patriotism as a selling point, was more than willing to meet with America's designated adversaries for personal gain. And in doing so, it served as a conduit for a Russian government agent who was secretly trying to build back channels between Russian and U.S. officials in order to undercut American interests.

Following the trip, there was the issue of money: Butina likely spent tens of thousands of dollars on the trip, but came up a few thousand dollars short because of the late addition of Jim Liberatore and his wife. Butina shelled out $6,000 from her own bank account and asked the NRA for reimbursement. To hide the transaction, Butina created what a Senate Finance Committee report would call a "U.S. domestic shell company"—South Dakota's Bridges LLC.

Butina testified later that she didn't want the money directed to her Russian gun rights groups because it "would be seen very badly." But it wasn't a PR problem she was worried about. At the time she specifically wrote to Donna Keene suggesting they wire money to her U.S. account to "avoid international economic sanction problems."

The money problem would make its way to the NRA. Brownell emailed Millie asking for Butina to be reimbursed, and Millie responded that the NRA could cover the costs via the NRA president's office budget. Ultimately, a series of transactions occurred in which Brownell paid about $21,000, and the NRA paid Brownell back a similar amount. Millie submitted an invoice with two line items: "NRA special project. [$]15,535,10" and "NRA special project, $6,000."

"The NRA appears to have simply moved those expenses, which it originally paid when the trip was organized, from a travel account to the president's office account," a Senate Finance Committee investigation eventually concluded.

More than two years after the Moscow trip, after I wrote about the NRA delegation to Russia, congressional investigators began their own investigation. Once Senator Ron Wyden, the top Democrat on the Senate Finance Committee, reached out to the NRA with questions, the gun rights group asked Brownell to pay back $17,000—so as to, as Brownell's lawyer put it, get "the trip off the NRA's books."

Millie didn't get thrown under the bus: she gently placed herself underneath it as it ran her over. She was ready to protect Wayne. In sworn testimony, she said that Wayne didn't want the NRA to pay for the Russia trip but confirmed that she had written an email stating, "Wayne approved these special projects involving outreach that Brownell has done." She also added, "I do not remember specifically whether I talked to him about [the Russia] invoice." Millie was not subsequently punished in any way.

Contemporaneous documents, messages, and actions undercut explanations crafted later, after investigations into the behavior started. The NRA had full visibility into who its officials, board members, and donors would meet on this trip, in part because its staff helped organize it and its delegates were members on the trip. The NRA's argument after it came under scrutiny was that Wayne opposed the trip. If that's the case, why didn't he, as the executive vice president of the NRA, stop it? And further, why were funds from the NRA approved by his closest personal aide? The NRA was unable to provide any actual evidence that Wayne had objected to the trip, other than its say-so.

Another argument the NRA used was that its delegates were there in their personal capacities. The argument would have worked better if NRA staff had not helped to arrange visas, organize itineraries, and work with travel agents to schedule flights. It would have worked better if an NRA aide wasn't designated as the delegation's contact for follow-up issues, and if the NRA president hadn't written a letter on the NRA's letterhead designating Keene and Gregory as leaders of the NRA delegation. And it would have worked better if the NRA had not paid for more than $20,000 in expenses until investigators began asking questions.

The connections Butina made during the December 2015 Moscow trip became the foundation for everything that would follow. She spent much of the next twelve months, a presidential election year, branching out from the contacts she made in Russia.

After the NRA Moscow trip, participant Joe Gregory became another sponsor of Butina's, hosting her for several days in Nashville in early 2016, before flying her on his private jet from Bristol, Tennessee, to Washington, D.C., to meet with Torshin. The three of them then flew to Las Vegas for the annual Safari Club International convention, with Gregory picking up the tab for their lodging. Gregory didn't pay for everything though: the National Rifle Association also chipped in for Butina's and Torshin's

expenses. Using Woody Phillips's credit card, the NRA paid
for Torshin and Butina to become members of Safari Club International, and for their convention registration costs, for a total
of $520.

Gregory also played the important role of introducing Butina
to the organizers of the National Prayer Breakfast. The breakfast,
attended annually by some of the nation's most prominent political and religious luminaries, was where Butina would seek to expand her influence next. Torshin and Butina were stars at the
2016 breakfast—and Torshin at one point used the ol' Butina
trick: puffing up his importance by suggesting to an organizer
that he might be able to bring Putin to next year's breakfast.

That year at the breakfast she met a member of the Rockefeller
family, George O'Neill, who, like so many other men in her orbit,
became absolutely enthralled by her and her mission. Erickson
joined in on the sweet talk with O'Neill, encouraging him to join
in Butina's goal of improving U.S.-Russia ties. In one email, Erickson tells him that Torshin and Maria are "very serious about
improving relations between [America] and Russia" and brags
that "they have the desire and authority to listen." O'Neill, like
Erickson, begins to fund her graduate studies at American University, which she would start in the fall of 2016.

In a memo, Butina dutifully reports to Torshin about the
meeting with the Rockefeller heir and begins to craft another series of proposals, which she passes on to the Russian government.
In a February 2016 memo titled "Note on Organizing a Channel
of Informal Communication between Russia and the USA," she
wrote that her goal was to "generate the necessary background
for promoting pro-Russian sentiment in the USA."

To do this, Butina, backed by O'Neill, set up a series of

"friendship dinners" in New York City and Washington, D.C., to promote the topic. But she needed permission first. In an email to O'Neill, she wrote that her Russian government contact Torshin had "confirmed his desire in our Russian-American project . . . he talked to some people in Presidential Administration—they also gave a <<green light>> as Russians say for building this communication channel." Butina added in the email, "All that we needed is <<yes>> from Putin's side. The rest is easier."

Torshin and Butina had a specific prediction for how 2016 would play out, Erickson explained in one email outlining their strategy, and it was a triple bet: "that [Republicans] are a better match for diplomatic relations with Russia, that a [Republican] will win the 2016 presidential contest and that the [National Rifle Association] is the best back-channel into any [Republican] administration." As it turns out, they were right on all three counts.

CHAPTER 15

Butina's Back Channel

By the time the 2016 National Rifle Association annual meeting came around, it was Maria Butina's third convention, and she had carte blanche access to whatever it was that she wanted. In an email to Pete Brownell, long known to be the next president of the NRA, she wrote as if Brownell were some sort of subordinate. She sent a list of Russians she wanted the NRA to issue official invitations to and twenty-two events that "we usually were invited to," including a private breakfast with Wayne LaPierre. She also asked Brownell about a "possible meeting with Trump's sons," which appears to be one of her priorities. NRA staff dutifully complied with her requests, issuing invites to the Russian nationals and creating a personalized itinerary for Butina and Torshin.

Torshin needed to seek approval from his "boss" to go to the United States for the NRA convention and asked Butina to write him a memo that would justify the international travel. It was never specified who this "boss" was.

Butina complied. In her memo she suggested that it could be

an opportunity for the Russian central banker to meet Donald Trump and influence the Trump campaign's view on Russia. She stressed that the "influence of the NRA on election results is critically important for the Republican Party," and she emphasized the VIP treatment Torshin would get because of the already deep relationships the two had developed with NRA leadership. She also hinted that there would be possible networking opportunities at the conference with Trump "and his entourage that will help form Trump's correct view of Russian-American relations." Torshin's "boss" subsequently approved the trip.

Torshin was more concerned about the NRA than Trump personally, writing in a message to Butina that it might be less useful to interact with Trump during the campaign, while deeper ties with the NRA would "certainly prove useful."

Throughout the 2016 campaign, Butina wrote reports about Republican presidential candidates for Torshin, which were then shared throughout the Russian government. As Trump inched closer to securing his spot as the Republican presidential nominee, they narrowed their approach to focus on influencing his campaign's position on Russia.

There were multiple, overlapping efforts by various conservatives to arrange a meeting between Donald Trump and Butina. Erickson wrote to Rick Dearborn, a Trump campaign aide, with one such ask. Using the subject line "Kremlin Connection," and when the world was not yet concerned about Russian interference in elections, Erickson explicitly laid out his position, according to an email obtained later by the Senate Intelligence Committee:

Happenstance and the (sometimes) international reach of the NRA placed me in position a couple of years ago to slowly begin cultivating a back-channel to President Putin's Kremlin. Russia is quietly but actively seeking a dialogue with the U.S. that isn't forthcoming under the current administration. And for reasons that we can discuss in person or on the phone, the Kremlin believes that the only possibility of a true re-set in this relationship would be with a new Republican White House.

Referring to Torshin, Erickson said that "Putin's emissary" was planning on attending the NRA annual meeting in Louisville, Kentucky, and that Torshin wanted to make "first contact" there. Erickson added, "Putin is deadly serious about building a good relationship with Mr. Trump. He wants to extend an invitation to Mr. Trump to visit him in the Kremlin before the election."

Erickson's effort did not succeed. But it was clear that Butina was trying to set up the meeting through multiple channels. Conservative Rick Clay also reached out to Dearborn, writing that Butina and Torshin had been designated by Putin to ask for a meeting, and pitched Dearborn on a proposal whereby Trump would come to Russia during the campaign so that Putin and Trump could send a message about the persecution of Christians in the world. Clay had two asks: for a senior Trump campaign aide to meet with Torshin and for Trump to do a short meet-and-greet with Butina and Torshin. The Trump campaign ultimately rejected this effort.

Butina also targeted Trump's son, as hinted in her request to Brownell. During the conference itself, Butina met a friend of Donald Trump Jr., Bobby Hart, who relayed to Trump Jr. Butina's desire to meet up. Although this, too, was not to succeed, Torshin and Butina did happen to meet Trump Jr. by chance. The two of them joined Donna and David Keene for dinner and ran into Brownell, who was arriving with Trump Jr. and others. Brownell, long a fan of Butina, promptly introduced him to the duo, and they took photos.

The Senate Intelligence Committee did not explain how exactly, but wrote in the dry language of its investigation, "The Committee assess[es that] the Russian government did have insight into this meeting."

To those not utterly enamored by Butina, it was obvious that there was something fishy about the woman with the ever-morphing title and Russian accent. Somehow word of the meeting between Trump Jr. and Butina had gotten back to Chris Cox.

"I understand that someone introduced a Russian gal to you this week. I'll fill you in this week but I would steer clear if she tries to reach out to you," Cox wrote to Trump Jr. "OK cool just let me know," came the reply.

Cox later lamented in an email to NRA colleagues that his friend Trump Jr. had run into Russians on the single night during that conference that they hadn't been together. (He jokingly added in another email that Millie should be designated by the NRA to testify to Congress on the subject—to which Millie responded, "Niet! Dude.")

The chief NRA lobbyist didn't have any concrete reason to mistrust Butina, but his gut instinct said there was something wrong about the whole picture. "I had concerns about her well before the 2016 annual meeting. On its face, quasi-attractive, twenty-something-year-old Russian women don't hang around older American guys for no reason," Cox explained later. "I had steered clear of her and was annoyed that someone put Don in a situation where she was given the chance to be introduced. While

I understood the interaction was a brief 'hello,' I wanted to let him know—as a friend—that I didn't trust her."

Susan LaPierre also had the foresight to avoid Maria Butina, who had made herself at home among the women of the NRA. Maybe Susan didn't like Butina's looks, or her charm, or where she came from. But from the start, Susan indicated she didn't want to be anywhere near her. Wayne's former chief of staff Josh Powell also stayed clear. "Hey, do you think that woman is a Russian agent?" Susan once asked Powell. "One hundred percent," Powell responded. "She's probably with the FSB."

⫼

By the fall of 2016, as Election Day neared, Butina had begun her graduate studies at American University. Butina had, through her networking and "friendship dinners," positioned herself nicely should Trump pull off an unlikely upset against Hillary Clinton. "I talk to all of Trump's Russia advisors . . . I have a couple of people on his staff," she once wrote Torshin.

But news that Russia had hacked and dumped the Democratic National Committee's emails—an unprecedented foreign intervention in America's elections—was seen as incredibly disruptive to Butina's operation in D.C. Erickson and Butina's communications at the time reflect the panic they underwent as the political universe sought to understand this latest development.

Erickson worried that the news "complicates the hell out of nearly a year of quiet back-channel diplomacy in establishing links between reformers inside the Kremlin and a putative [Republican] administration." Meanwhile, Butina told Torshin that her work might have to be put on hold. "I'm sitting here very quietly . . . my all too blunt attempts to befriend politicians right now will probably be misinterpreted, as you yourself can understand," she said, according to a later government filing. Torshin tried to reassure her by saying that she was "doing the right thing."

But none of that could dull their joy regarding the election outcome. Against all odds, Trump won the presidential election on November 8, 2016. The National Rifle Association and Butina had both bet on the right horse. As the nation digested this unlikely news about the next occupant of the White House, Butina stayed up late into the night to gather information and report it back to Torshin. It was a moment of absolute ecstasy: they were, in their view, about to become very, very influential.

"I'm going to sleep. It's 3 am here," Butina wrote to Torshin. "I am ready for further orders."

CHAPTER 16

The NRA and the 2016 Campaign

By the time of the 2016 presidential election, the NRA had completed its metamorphosis from a gun organization into a conservative culture-war organization. The campaign wasn't merely about gun rights, declared top NRA lobbyist Chris Cox at that year's annual meeting, but a "do or die fight for the soul of our country."

The National Rifle Association has a *Field & Stream* membership with a *Fox & Friends* leadership. For example, the silent majority of its membership supports universal background checks, the defining component of Manchin-Toomey. But the organization is largely controlled by the diehards who show up. And those diehards are generally politically active campaign junkies with a dedication to the Republican Party.

The 2016 NRA convention was a critical moment for the gun rights organization, due to the perceived risks of a Hillary Clinton presidency. But Cox opened his speech not with a conversation about firearms, but with a screed against the media and the culture. "The media tells [our kids] that Bruce Jenner is a national hero for transforming his body, while our wounded warriors, whose bodies were transformed by IEDs and rocket-propelled grenades, can't even get basic health care from the VA," Cox began. After eight years of the Obama administration, he said, "the America we know is becoming unrecognizable."

Cox's speech was part of a broader strategic messaging push within the NRA. They weren't there merely to stand up against their opponents on gun rights, but to push back against all that was changing in America, to fight for all that conservatives felt was slipping away from them. "In times like these, Americans turn to places they trust the most," Cox said. "For moral guidance, they turn to their churches. For mutual support, they turn to their families. And for a champion who will bring the fight to those who want to destroy our country, they turn to the National Rifle Association of America."

It was good for business: by 2016 membership had risen to more than 5 million members, according to the group—up from 4.5 million in 2013. Revenues had climbed to $412 million in 2016, giving the NRA a swelling war chest to use during that year's campaigns. Cox told the assembled crowd that year that the election of Hillary Clinton would be the end of individual freedom in America—Antonin Scalia's seat on the Supreme Court was vacant, and his replacement could determine the future of gun rights in the country. They turned to Clinton's opponent for help: the Republican Party's standard-bearer.

The National Rifle Association's relationship with Trump started in 2015, when few took him seriously as a presidential contender.

Before he launched his campaign with a famous escalator ride in June 2015, he did a test run with the members of the NRA at the 2015 annual meeting the previous month.

Donald Trump had a concealed carry license from New York City and at one point had owned at least two handguns. But the key relationship was between his son Donald Trump Jr. and Chris Cox. Donald Trump Jr. was a lifetime NRA member as well as a devoted hunter and fisherman. (Later, near the end of the Trump presidency, Trump Jr. was rumored to be considering a campaign to replace Wayne as head of the organization. However, Trump Jr. himself has a troubled background with nonprofits. He was an officer of the Trump Foundation, which was disbanded by the New York State attorney general after a misuse of funds. Trump Jr. had to reimburse some money and undergo mandatory training on nonprofit law.)

Trump Jr. and Cox had been friends for years, having bonded over their mutual love of hunting, and they spent more and more time together as the elder Trump ramped up a campaign for the presidency. Trump campaign aide Corey Lewandowski convinced Cox to give Jr.'s father a speaking slot at the NRA-ILA leadership forum—a cattle call for prospective 2016 GOP White House hopefuls.

"While I had closed off the invitations due to the fact that we had a long list of contenders, I made the decision to invite Donald Trump as I thought the members would enjoy hearing from him," Cox explained. "The fact that he wasn't a current or former elected official made for nice change in the lineup. At the time, I wasn't convinced that he was serious about running for president . . . but that changed quickly."

NRA-ILA was one of the few organizations to take the businessman seriously enough to provide him a platform—and so he spoke that day in April 2015 alongside Republican Party contenders like Jeb Bush, Marco Rubio, Ted Cruz, Scott Walker, Rick Perry, and Bobby Jindal. "I love the NRA. I love the Second Amendment, so you have to know that," the future president said.

Eight months later, the stakes of the election shifted drastically for Chris Cox. With the death of Justice Scalia, the cause for which Cox had worked his entire adult life was now at risk. If Hillary Clinton won the presidency and appointed a left-leaning justice to replace Scalia, the Supreme Court decisions in *Heller* and *McDonald*, which held that the Second Amendment included an individual right to keep and bear arms, could be overturned. Trump wasn't whom Cox had pegged as his first choice to be president of the United States, but Cox did like the man's disruptive nature, and he could see the writing on the wall: the NRA's most politically motivated members were wild about Donald Trump. In spring 2016, Cox visited with the members of the NRA's board and pitched going all-in for the Trump campaign, asking for an additional $15 million to support Trump.

The NRA had endorsed presidential candidates only four times in its history. In fact, it had spent the first 109 years of its existence not endorsing presidential candidates at all. Chris had to convince Wayne to go along with endorsing Trump. The real estate mogul was a loyalty-conscious man, Cox reasoned, and he would remember who endorsed him early. The assessment was right: throughout his presidency, Trump's main point of contact on gun issues was Chris Cox, rather than Cox's theoretical boss Wayne.

Usually the NRA's main strategic question when it came to backing a Republican presidential candidate had been how to make its members comfortable with the nominee. Such had been the case for Mitt Romney, the former Massachusetts politician who had supported a ban on assault weapons in the 1990s ("that's not going to make me the hero of the NRA," he said at the time) and later as governor signed into law a permanent ban on that category of firearms. John McCain, the GOP nominee in 2008, had said of the NRA some years earlier, "I don't think they help the Republican Party at all." The NRA had responded that McCain was "one of the premier flag carriers for the enemies of the Second Amendment." McCain had also infuriated the NRA with his creation of the McCain-Feingold campaign-finance reform package, which sought to limit the power of advocacy groups like the NRA. He had also expressed his support for eliminating the gun show loophole. "Over the years, I haven't agreed with the NRA on every issue," McCain acknowledged to NRA members during the campaign. Both McCain and Romney would eventually receive the National Rifle Association endorsement, but it was half-hearted, more a reflection of the Republican Party coalition and the necessary trade-offs that come in a two-party system than a glowing seal of approval. The NRA's endorsements of McCain and Romney were made late in the presidential campaign, in October of their respective election years. There was no other choice: the NRA wasn't going to endorse Barack Obama instead.

Trump was a different animal entirely. The NRA's politically minded members were absolutely head over heels for his candidacy. While the NRA had traditionally focused on how to make sure its millions-strong membership voted for the GOP candidate, with Trump it could focus its resources more broadly, assured that its base was already on board.

On May 20, 2016, with Trump slated to speak before the NRA

annual meeting, Cox took the step of endorsing Trump. It was the earliest in an election cycle that the NRA had ever endorsed a presidential candidate, and at a time when the Republican Party primary was still being contested. The GOP had not united around Trump, and there was even talk that party leaders would buck the nominee at the Republican convention. The endorsement was an early sign of support that the Trump campaign desperately needed.

"Now is the time to unite," Cox told the crowd, making the announcement moments later, right before Trump was to appear onstage. "If your preferred candidate dropped out of the race, it's time to get over it."

Told just minutes before that the endorsement was coming, the NRA's staff was caught off guard. Usually there would be strategic discussions about how to maximize the impact of the announcement. In this case, it was all done over a two-day period with many people left out of the loop.

With their view of the stakes, Cox and the NRA had no other choice but to go all in on Trump and his party. And so they did: the NRA dedicated more than $50 million to candidates in the 2016 elections, 99 percent of that on Republicans. It was by far the most the NRA had ever spent in any election cycle. And most of the focus was on the presidential race. The NRA spent more on boosting Trump's presidential campaign in 2016 than it did in boosting the GOP's presidential campaigns in 2008 and 2012 combined. In fact, the NRA spent $30.3 million on the Trump election effort, more even than the leading Trump super PAC, which spent a paltry $20.3 million. By comparison, the NRA spent $7.4 million on the McCain campaign and $12.3 million on the Romney campaign.

Over the course of the campaign, the National Rifle Association morphed from a Second Amendment organization into a Trump organization. Because it didn't need to motivate its base, the NRA focused its election polling and in-depth focus groups not on gun owners but on understanding voters who were negative about both Trump and Clinton and using that knowledge for Trump's strategic advantage.

NRA-ILA zoomed in on Democrats and disillusioned Republicans, particularly women. In one advertising spot, a woman awakes to a figure lurking outside her window. "She keeps a firearm in her safe for protection, but Hillary Clinton could take away her right to self-defense. And with Supreme Court justices, Hillary can. Don't let Hillary leave you protected with nothing but a phone," the narrator said darkly, noting that the average 911 response time was eleven minutes. An NRA spokesperson said that the ad was "designed to run up the score with . . . Trump voters."

A critical moment in the campaign was the release of the *Access Hollywood* tapes in October 2016, in which *The Washington Post* published Trump saying that "when you're a star, they let you do it . . . grab 'em by the pussy." Close allies and supporters of Trump's campaign withdrew their endorsements and denounced his comments. Republican Party leaders had secret discussions about how to dump Trump off the presidential ticket. The NRA, on the other hand, actually increased its advertising buy after *Access Hollywood*, according to two sources with knowledge.

Not only that, but the NRA's advertising was extremely effective in countering the fallout from that scandal. After the release of the *Access Hollywood* tapes, the Trump campaign needed to shore up support among women horrified by his conduct. An ad the NRA ran in October, around the time the tapes were published, centered on a lawyer named Kristi McMains. She had used a gun to fend off an attacker in a parking garage in Louisville, Kentucky. "A man attacked me . . . tried to stab me with an eight-inch knife. But I carry a pistol. I fight back. That's why I am still here," McMains said in the ad. "Every woman has a right to defend herself with a gun if she chooses. Hillary Clinton disagrees with that. . . . Donald Trump supports my right to own a gun. Defend your rights. Vote Donald Trump for president." The NRA spent $6.5 million on that ad, its largest advertising buy of the cycle. The ad ran in the battleground states of Virginia, North Carolina, Ohio, Pennsylvania, and Nevada, as well as on national cable. Republican pollster OnMessage surveyed eight presidential swing states following the election and found that gun rights were a central reason why female voters who weren't conservative Trump voters ended up choosing him over Clinton.

"There are many claimants to the honor of having nudged Donald Trump over the top in the presidential election," wrote Fred Barnes, formerly an editor at the now-defunct conservative magazine *The Weekly Standard*. "But the folks with the best case are the National Rifle Association and the consultants who made their TV ads."

Despite most predictions to the contrary, Donald Trump narrowly won the election in November 2016. In the early hours of November 9, as it was becoming clear he would pull it off, NBC anchor Chuck Todd stressed the NRA's role: "Trump did not get a lot of help from a lot of Republican institutions, but he did from the NRA, and they came through big, and this is a big night for the NRA, and they just bought a Supreme Court seat." Cox was more than happy to gloat: he was one of the few who had genuinely believed that Trump could actually become president.

But the irony is that by endorsing Trump and ensuring his victory, the NRA sowed the seeds of its own destruction. Everyone who follows the NRA knows that the association does better under Democratic presidents. With Trump so wildly popular among its most engaged members, the NRA had set itself up for failure: it had no fear left to monger.

And what's more, the organization had done next to no strategic planning for how to weather the financial hit a Trump victory would yield. It was such an obvious question, but no one at the senior levels of the group had tried to find an answer.

The NRA's financial situation was already dire by the time Donald Trump entered the White House, and its execs knew it. Alarm bells were ringing for anyone reviewing balance sheets at NRA HQ. But the budgets simply did not reflect the coming reality: belt-tightening was necessary, but no one wanted to make any cuts.

Revenue dropped almost immediately: the NRA brought in $330 million in 2017, compared with $412 million the year before. Membership dues collapsed by about $36 million in that same time frame. This happened even as spending ballooned on projects like NRATV. The NRA faced a nearly $18 million deficit in 2017, adding to the $46 million deficit that the group had racked up in 2016. Wayne would later call that period of catastrophe a "Trump slump."

"Whenever there's a pro–Second Amendment presidency," Wayne told *The New York Times* years later, "it's more difficult to raise money. Because so much of it is the air, the energy, the atmosphere and the threat to people's rights."

Wayne was cognizant of the need to incite in order to stay in power. "Frequently, in the middle of a political fight, he would say—[for] speeches and [for] direct mail [fundraising letters]—'I need gasoline. I need gasoline,'" former Wayne confidant Tony Makris later testified, explaining that this was Wayne's way of asking for "words that would stimulate the NRA membership to join the fight."

The NRA had accumulated millions of dollars in corrupt spending over the Obama years, and now it was about to run full speed into a brick wall: the reality of fundraising during the Trump era. The shift, and the incoming investigations, would yield disaster.

CHAPTER 17

Butina's Downfall

The decor at Cafe Deluxe, a restaurant near American University in Washington, D.C., didn't usually look like this on Saturday nights. It was several days after Donald Trump's shocking election in 2016, and the mood in the air was celebratory. An ice sculpture sat in the middle of the table, imprinted with the Soviet hammer and sickle.

These were heady days for Maria Butina, and she was celebrating her birthday. The event was thrown with a "Stars and Tsars" theme, and she had dressed up as the Russian empress Alexandra, while her boyfriend Paul Erickson had shown up as Rasputin. Erickson and Butina loved dressing up—they had a romantic relationship that some might view as a little *too* saccharine. On one occasion, they wore costumes to visit F. Scott Fitzgerald's grave. Butina showed up with a flapper's silver headband and a pearl necklace, while Erickson appeared with a bottle of rum in one hand and *The Great Gatsby* the other.

Butina must have been overjoyed. In a matter of a few short years, she had managed to alter the trajectory of her life, forging a path from Siberia to Moscow to Washington, D.C. Her ambition and hard work looked to be finally paying off. Her networking had led her deep within conservative circles, thanks to the NRA, and the Trump administration looked like it could be responsive to her entreaties.

In the days around her birthday party, she had written new memos for Torshin and the diplomats at Russia's Ministry of Foreign Affairs. She excitedly tapped out a new paper outlining her contacts within the Trump orbit and proposed to "use the existing personal groundwork" she had established through the NRA to create "informal relationships in U.S. political circles . . . for the purposes of assessing, monitoring, forecasting, and developing the politics of the [Russian Federation] vis-a-vis the United States."

In another memo she proposed organizing a conference to shape Russian-American relations under the incoming Trump administration, arguing that it should be a "private initiative" as opposed to a "government undertaking" so that they could influence relations without official government involvement.

But all her success had worn away at prudence and caution. Drunk off the intoxicating news of Trump's win—and maybe a little vodka—she began to brag. She told friends at her birthday party that she was a link between the Russian government and the Trump campaign. She may have spoken a little too loudly: American political circles were still reeling from the news that Russia had systematically attempted to interfere with the elections, and in subsequent months, news story after news story would drop about Russian malign activities. And she was about to be at the center of one of them.

I started looking into Butina's online footprint: she had been an active blogger and had given a number of interviews. Her classmates at American University and one of her professors told me that she had claimed to be linked to the Russian government. Some in her orbit had seen her at public events with Paul Erickson, himself prone to bragging loudly about his importance and political network. I found that Butina had registered a mysterious LLC in South Dakota. I found Torshin's tweets about Butina and a video of David Keene giving a speech in Moscow in 2013.

I reached out to Torshin for comment, and he in turn asked Butina how she thought he should handle it. "Under no circumstances should you contact him. You didn't even see the letter at all," she told him at the time.

I put all that I knew in a February 2017 story about Butina for *The Daily Beast* titled "The Kremlin and GOP Have a New Friend—and Boy, Does She Love Guns." Two weeks later, I broke another story, about the 2015 NRA delegation to Moscow, noting that the group had met with a sanctioned Putin deputy.

The publication of the stories sent Butina, Keene, Torshin, and Erickson into a meltdown. Donna Keene made calls trying to find out who my sources were. David Keene would scrub his website of references of Torshin. Butina realized that I had spoken to people who were in her inner circle. "Somebody really threw the three of us under the bus. Furthermore, this someone is well-informed," Butina wrote to Torshin at the time. In another email, she realized that her operation had been compromised. "It's better to keep a low profile now. For some time," she told Torshin.

The FBI, which, unbeknownst to me, was already investigating Butina, wasn't happy either—and tried to figure out who was going to the press. The FBI had begun looking into her after receiving what appeared to be a routine tip that Butina's activities in Washington, D.C., appeared to be outside the scope of her student visa. It turned out to be a much more complicated case. The FBI began interviewing Butina's friends and classmates, and eventually placed her under physical surveillance, which at one point captured her speaking to a Russian intelligence officer.

Things did not improve for Maria as time went on. Russia was a dominant political topic throughout 2017 and 2018, and she got pulled into the maelstrom. Numerous lawmakers demanded documents and answers from Butina and the National Rifle Association, most prominently Senator Ron Wyden, the top Democrat on the Senate Finance Committee. When Democrats took control of the House after the 2018 midterms, lawmakers in the House, too, turned their attention to this topic as an investigative priority.

November 22, 2017, was a dreadful day for Butina—the day she got her first letter from a congressional panel demanding that she answer questions about the NRA's 2015 trip. It would not be her last. In early 2018, Wyden formally started an investigation into the NRA and its Russian ties. By that spring, she had submitted eight thousand pages of documents to the Senate Intelligence Committee, which had launched a much broader, years-long investigation into Russian efforts to interfere in the 2016 election.

Shortly after, the Senate Intelligence Committee pressed Butina to come to Capitol Hill to provide testimony. She gave testimony under oath for eight hours, providing information that the committee later found to be "frequently incomplete and misleading."

The National Rifle Association was also being unhelpful. Wayne had designated Bill Brewer, a Dallas-based lawyer with little to no experience on Capitol Hill, as the lead lawyer to deal with this investigation. Chris Cox was livid and nearly quit over this incursion into what was clearly his jurisdiction. "Mr. Brewer . . . doesn't know his butt from his elbow about the Congress of the United States," NRA board member Oliver North said.

The NRA's strategy was to stall: it would ignore questions it found objectionable, and it never produced to the Senate Finance Committee all the documents it possessed. The Senate Intelligence Committee later rebuked the National Rifle Association for only providing requested documents "sporadically"—and then some of them much too late to be of use to the probe. "It is not clear to the Committee why the NRA's production was delayed so significantly," the Senate Intelligence Committee's ultimate report noted.

Not everyone felt that way. Within the NRA, the finger-pointing had begun. Brownell, by this time president of the NRA, had been keenly aware of the risk a trip to Russia would be to his business, and he was fed up. He felt that if he didn't cooperate with the congressional investigations—and get ahead of the press with his side of the story—he could ultimately be involuntarily hauled before a congressional committee by subpoena. So he handed over stacks of communications and itineraries related to the 2015 Moscow trip. (The emails he turned over revealed just what a brownnoser Erickson was, sucking up to Brownell by calling him "International Man of Mystery" in one email and "Weapons King" in another.)

The FBI closed in on Butina, interviewing more associates, then raiding her home. Just over a week after her testimony to the Senate Intelligence Committee, more than a dozen FBI agents wearing tactical gear showed up with guns drawn at her front door. They were there to search her house and electronics for evidence of criminal activity.

During the raid, they found tens of thousands of photos, seized more than a dozen boxes of documents, and collected terabytes of data. In one of their searches, the FBI had found a note titled "Maria's 'Russian Patriots in Waiting' Organization." The handwritten note included questions like "process for green card/work visa?"; "how many Russian ex-pats in US?"; and "how to respond to FSB offer of employment?" They also found contact information for employees of the FSB on her contact list.

The net continued to slowly close in on Butina as she finished her graduate studies at American University. She was arrested as she was packing up her Washington, D.C., home, ostensibly to move to South Dakota. She would later say that she thought when the FBI came a second time, it would be to apologize. That was very much not the case—it was to put her in handcuffs. She had the Wimbledon men's final on television with Erickson when agents pounded on the door of apartment 208. Three FBI agents pulled her into the narrow hallway and placed her under arrest.

She was charged with acting as an unregistered agent of a foreign government, and also charged for engaging in a conspiracy to violate that law, known as 18 U.S.C. § 951. That law requires that those who are working under the control of foreign governments register with the attorney general before operating in the United States. The National Security Division of the Justice Department described Section 951 violations as "espionage lite," usually resulting from "espionage-like or clandestine behavior or an otherwise provable connection to an intelligence service, or information gathering or procurement-type activity on behalf of a foreign government."

It's a law that is used by the Justice Department—helmed at the time by Trump administration appointees—to charge conduct that is similar to espionage, while avoiding the requirement that national security information be involved.

Wearing a green jumpsuit in a federal courthouse in D.C. in September 2018, Butina stared ahead as a federal judge denied her release pending trial, citing the risk of the Russian government spiriting her off to the Russian embassy before she could properly face charges.

Her attorney, Robert Driscoll, had mustered a comically bad defense. The morning of that hearing, he had angered the judge by trying to submit a last-minute piece of video evidence. It was a professionally made video of Butina and Erickson singing "Beauty and the Beast" at a recording studio while looking deeply into each other's eyes—something Driscoll claimed was evidence that their love was genuine. "I'm not sure what on earth the relevance is," the judge said. "The Court does not find those videos to be at all relevant on the issue of Ms. Butina's risk of flight."

Driscoll's other claim was that if Butina had truly been a covert Russian agent, why hadn't she fled when I wrote in 2017 that she had ties with Torshin, the NRA, and the Russian government? One doesn't need to be an attorney to see the weakness of this argument: it was if he were saying, "Your Honor, if my client were a criminal, why wasn't she a *better* criminal?" Butina said nothing. But the former Siberian furniture store worker must have been thinking: *What the hell have I gotten myself into?*

Her thirtieth birthday was marked alone, in solitary confinement, in cell 2FO2 in the Alexandria Detention Center, not far from the Ackerman McQueen offices in Old Town. She eventually pleaded guilty to one count of conspiring to act as an unregistered foreign agent of Russia, though she has always denied being a spy in the strictest sense. In April 2019, the Russian agent was sentenced to eighteen months, including time served. In the wake of her arrest, the FBI would see to it that at least sixteen foreign nationals in the United States had their visas revoked because of the Butina scandal, a source briefed on the matter said.

In April 2018 the Treasury Department included Torshin on a list of Russians who were to be sanctioned for that country's "malign activities." Through the Freedom of Information Act, I later obtained the Treasury Department internal evidentiary package, which justified the sanctions designation. It details Torshin's and Butina's meetings with government officials and makes reference to Torshin's alleged links with Russian organized crime, particularly the Taganskaya organized crime group. The sanctions would mark the end of his travels to the United States. Any assets he might have had on American soil would have been seized, and he would be considered persona non grata to global financial institutions.

Erickson was not prosecuted for anything related to Russia, even though he had a major role as one of Butina's primary American boosters. But federal investigators who were monitoring Butina started scrutinizing his businesses. It turns out that while helping Butina infiltrate the NRA, he was also defrauding investors through business scams for more than a decade. He pled guilty to a charge of money laundering and a separate charge of wire fraud. He was sentenced to seven years in federal prison—far in excess of what Butina eventually served. President Trump, as he was leaving office in 2021, pardoned Erickson—meaning Erickson was off the hook for nearly $3 million in restitution to his victims. Trump called Erickson's crimes "minor."

Throughout her years in the United States, Butina was aware her memos were being circulated throughout the Russian government, which would use the information she gathered for strategic advantage. And the NRA colluded with her, financed her activities, and helped her expand her networks the entire time. It did not pay off for the NRA.

As of April 2019, the NRA had spent more than $5 million to investigate the fallout from the Russia trip and its own ties to Butina, its former president Oliver North wrote in a memo. This is likely an underestimate. To conduct an internal review, the NRA hired Elaine Lammert, who heads George Washington University's homeland security master's degree program and was previously the principal deputy general counsel at the FBI.

The scandal also exposed ongoing, years-long tension between staff who worked at the NRA and those who worked at NRA-ILA. ILA staff were left bewildered at how their non-lobbyist counterparts could have messed up this situation this badly, and expressed frustration that they had to deal with the fallout of a controversy they weren't responsible for. Responding to a news story about former NRA president David Keene's attempted business dealings with Butina, NRA-ILA official Scott Christman wrote in an email, "We should be kicking him to the curb for getting us in this mess. We did nothing."

An NRA spokesperson similarly showed disdain for his NRA-ILA counterpart. As the Butina controversy was unfolding, NRA-ILA spokesperson Jennifer Baker forwarded a reporter's inquiries to NRA spokesperson Andrew Arulanandam. Arulanandam shared the reporter's questions with other colleagues, noting that he wouldn't be responding to the inquiry. "Fuck him and our team player Jen Baker," Arulanandam wrote acidly in an email.

Ultimately, no substantial amounts of money flowed from

Russia to the NRA—which had been a topic of investigation on Capitol Hill and, reportedly, by the FBI. The NRA acknowledged in 2018 that it had accepted contributions from twenty-five Russians and that the total sum contributed was just over $2,500, a drop in the bucket. The NRA told the Federal Election Commission that it accepted only one donation from Butina: $520 for a silver necklace and earrings set she purchased at an NRA fundraising auction. And it claimed to have collected just $1,000 from Torshin when he paid NRA membership dues in 2012.

But money did flow from the other way: from the NRA to the Russian agent. The NRA formed the foundation for almost every significant interaction Butina had in the United States. It was critical to her effort to establish an unofficial back channel with U.S. political actors. Without the NRA, she would have had no foothold. In its willingness to be used as a piggy bank for its senior officials, the NRA had directly facilitated the work of a Russian seeking to advantage her country over the United States.

As Erickson plotted with Butina and Keene, he seemed to reckon with how surreal their undertakings were. "It might be a novel someday," Erickson wrote once in a moment of self-reflection. In the end, Paul, it will at least be a book.

CHAPTER 18

The Start of the End

The shootings at Marjory Stoneman Douglas High School in Parkland, Florida, would irrevocably change the gun control landscape by mobilizing America's students. Between the massacre at Sandy Hook in 2012 and February 14, 2018, there had been 332 incidents of gunfire on school grounds. On that Valentine's Day in 2018, a gunman walked into the school and killed seventeen people with an AR-15 semiautomatic rifle. Young adults were spurred to action by the deadliest high school shooting in U.S. history, culminating in the March for Our Lives, when hundreds of thousands of protesters demonstrated in Washington, D.C., for changes in gun laws.

Just as the National Rifle Association had failed to come up with a strategy to counter Everytown for Gun Safety, again it seemingly had no plan to answer March for Our Lives. While the NRA said it had between five and six million members, it acted sluggishly to defend its turf—half because of the inertia that comes with being so historically dominant, and half because it was so distracted by the chaos occurring internally.

Part of the NRA's slipping bipartisan support was due to the political polarization that was happening in America, regardless of the NRA. But the part the NRA could control—coalition building and outreach—its leaders did not engage in effectively.

This arrogance has cost them. Since Sandy Hook the NRA had not been reaching out to moderate Democrats who could be a firewall against more gun control. And rather than speak to the millions of Americans who aren't members but could be persuaded of its view, the NRA had spent the years since embroiled in the culture war. In the wake of the shootings in Parkland, more than a dozen states with Republican governors passed some form of gun control legislation—including in Florida, where Governor Rick Scott, who had an A rating from the NRA, signed a bill. Corporate partners of the NRA began to abandon the organization, refusing to do business with it. A series of cyberattacks were levied against the NRA's servers.

Wayne responded to Parkland the way that he always did after a mass shooting. While others in the NRA were consumed by research into the facts—what kind of firearm was used, what messaging to put out into the public—he was consumed by self-pity, those around him observed. After a mass shooting, the security detail at his home was typically increased from one full-time security guard to two.

In public, he often disguised himself in a ball cap, jeans, and sunglasses—he believed that the more beat-up the clothing, the less chance he'd be recognized. He also sometimes wore a bulletproof vest beneath it all. Ironically, this meant he rarely wore suits—Zegna or otherwise—when he was in public. "I don't really put on a suit except when I have to for NRA work. I get so harassed. The minute I put on a suit, I get ID'ed and somebody starts yelling at me," Wayne once said.

"Wayne's safety became an all-consuming issue for him," his former chief of staff Josh Powell would later write. "I wouldn't be surprised if he suffered from PTSD. . . . He would often disappear, to God knows where, for a few days, or a week or two at a time, checking in but not divulging where he was. There was never a week that went by when Wayne didn't talk about leaving or quitting."

The heightened security risk was the excuse for what was nearly another big Wayne payday. Months after the Parkland shootings, Wayne and Susan huddled with Ackerman McQueen executives in the firm's Dallas office. Ackerman McQueen CFO Bill Winkler almost didn't recognize Wayne, who had shown up to the meeting in a disguise. "He was saying he couldn't go to his house, he didn't know where he was going to be safe," Winkler recalled. "He was extremely scared."

In April 2018, as the Officers Compensation Committee (OCC) approved a new compensation package for him in the millions of dollars without broader NRA board approval, Wayne and Susan toured guarded, gated homes in the Dallas region alongside a realtor. They eventually settled on a ten-thousand-square-foot mansion in an exclusive golf community located in Westlake, Texas, that was worth about $6.5 million. The NRA's Woody Phillips, negotiating with Ackerman McQueen, agreed to invest $6.5 million for a 99 percent stake in an LLC set up to purchase the home called "WBB Investments," according to the NY AG.

Susan was intimately involved in the process, taking the lead on various elements of the French-style country estate. "My wife was at her wits' end," Wayne later explained, stressing the security threats they faced after Parkland. In a May 21, 2018, call, according to notes taken at the time, Susan complained about the amount of closet space and the home's cabinetry. They planned on a July closing and an August move-in, as well as the purchase of two vehicles and social membership to a nearby golf club.

A shady LLC sent the NRA a bill for $70,000 under the description, "Investment in Security Assets." NRA staff then cut a check for that amount, which was deposited by the LLC. Later, the arrangement was canceled and the money was returned.

Ackerman McQueen later claimed that Wayne had asked it to do the mechanical activity of setting up the LLC so that it would not be in Wayne's name for security reasons. Angus aborted the deal after learning about how Wayne wanted membership at the exclusive Vaquero golf club next door to the mansion, according to this version of the story. It just didn't add up. "The confidentiality, the security . . . it just wasn't correct," Winkler later stated. "You couldn't have a membership in a golf club and [have] people [not] know where you live."

Wayne's story is that he was hoodwinked. He told lawyers later during a deposition that Angus had suggested that Ackerman McQueen buy the home as an investment for the advertising firm, and that Wayne could live there for safety purposes, only to later ask the NRA to foot the bill. Wayne claims to be the hero of the story. "I killed it. No one else did. . . . I said, 'We can't use NRA members' money to do that.'"

Left unexplained is what incentive Ackerman McQueen would have to buy a property and let Wayne live in it without charge, or why the NRA cut a check to WBB Investments if Wayne had not wanted it so, or how Wayne and Susan had been so clueless about a transaction they had been so personally involved in, down to the closet space.

⊶||⊷

As the Parkland shootings reverberated across America's political landscape, further eroding the NRA's power and exacerbating Wayne's anxieties, the most urgent issue for the group was money. The foreseeable decrease in revenue during the Trump era had not been addressed, and every department within the organization resisted the cuts that Wayne sent Josh Powell to make. Meanwhile, the cost of NRATV continued to rise. The problem got so bad that by the end of 2018, the NRA struggled to pay staff salaries.

The NRA begged vendors for more time to pay bills, and for those they had loans from to give them more time to pay debts. Within the organization, a lawyer named Bill Brewer was beginning to have an outsize role on the costs of the National Rifle Association. Brewer had been brought on to handle New York State's inquiries into an insurance program that the NRA was running, and his bills were beginning to mount as his clout with Wayne increased.

The cash-strapped NRA had a flow in which it paid bills: pay Brewer, then payroll, and then vendors and lenders. Brewer had directly intervened to make sure his legal bills were prioritized over those of others, according to NRA whistleblowers and other inside sources, which caused a cascading cash crunch that jeopardized the NRA's ability to pay its own staff. It was only due to a fortunately timed legal settlement in the millions that the National Rifle Association was able to make payroll.

Cuts came that year, squeezing the NRATV project and causing a series of layoffs at the struggling network. Cameron Gray, a producer and sometimes guest host, was fired just short of his ten-year anniversary. Dan Bongino, a conservative firebrand whose reputation and fan base had skyrocketed because of the channel, left NRATV in December 2018 after hosting a show for less than a year.

Employees at NRA HQ began to see their salaries cut. Travel considered as "non-mission-critical" was prohibited in order to bring down expenses. The situation was so strained that the NRA even temporarily stopped offering coffee to its employees, a flashing alarm bell of financial distress if there ever was one. The blow to morale within any organization would be enormous, but at the NRA it was an early hint of how bad things would become. The rank-and-file employees, always subjected to a different set of rules than the execs, were being made to pay for the sins of their leaders.

Support for the NRA's core missions also fell: a 22 percent cut to the education and training programs; a 61 percent decline for hunter services; and a 51 percent drop in spending on field services, which includes organizing volunteers. The cuts were not enough to put the NRA in the black, however—despite revenues of $352.6 million, the NRA posted a $2.7 million deficit.

It seemed like everything was getting cut—everything but Wayne's salary. The Officers Compensation Committee, a panel made up of the NRA's most senior board members, generally makes a recommendation to the wider NRA board as to what executives should make. In August 2017, the OCC paid a consultant to assess how senior NRA executives should be paid, based on, for example, the salaries of comparable execs at comparable organizations. But it was just for show: the OCC made a recommendation for Wayne's salary without waiting for the consultant to write the report, according to the NY AG probe.

Asked about it in 2019, Wayne could not name his own salary. "I think it was one six—one five—one six, seven, somewhere in that range," Wayne told lawyers in a deposition. In fact, even as his organization made deep cuts, Wayne was paid $2.15 million in 2018, a 57 percent pay raise. His base salary was $1.3 million, with bonuses and other reportable compensation making up the difference. When the OCC suggested Wayne's $455,000 bonus, it did not list any benchmarks or achievements he had reached in order to justify the extra money.

That's not all. As he was overseeing deep cuts in the organization, he was also laying the groundwork for a decade-long income stream. For years he had talked about leaving the NRA: now he was putting in place a plan that would let him make just as much money as ever, without having to do much work at all.

In April 2018, NRA president Pete Brownell authorized a "post-employment contract" that paid Wayne $1.3 million in 2019 and $1.5 million annually over the following six years, regardless of whether Wayne actually stayed on as executive vice president. The reason for this contract was, among other reasons, the "security concerns" Wayne faced.

From 2026 to 2030, Wayne would be employed as a "consultant," and the NRA could use his name and likeness (an earlier chapter has discussed how much work "consultants" are typically expected to do). During this time he would be paid $1.5 million for three years, then $1.3 million for the final two years. Wayne had managed to put together a compensation package that would pay him $17.4 million before bonuses over twelve years.

Wayne had various iterations of this "post-employment con-tract" in place for years, should he not be reelected as executive vice president or otherwise leave the organization. He later claimed that he did not approve of the generous terms in his contract, which was signed by him and other NRA officials. "I noticed that and kind of shook my head at it when I saw it," Wayne testified later. "I didn't ask for this contract. It's what was presented to me and I signed it and it never went into effect because I stayed on as EVP."

Wayne had created a path where he could leave and be paid about the same as he had been as CEO and EVP, but not have any of the responsibilities. He imagined it might involve some fund-raising but little authority or responsibility. But the trajectory he was already on, the corruption he had already engaged in, had put him in so much legal peril that he would later not be able to leave without a fight.

That same year, Letitia James, the New York City public advocate and an outspoken gun rights critic, became a candidate for at-torney general of New York. She had made no secret of how much she despised the National Rifle Association: on her campaign website she said that the "NRA [was] waging a full-throated pro-paganda campaign to thwart any common sense gun laws," and promised as the first plank in her gun violence prevention plan to "investigate the legitimacy of the NRA as a charitable institu-tion." She went even further in an interview with *Ebony* maga-zine: "The NRA holds [itself] out as a charitable organization, but in fact, [it] really [is] a terrorist organization," James said.

It was an existential threat: the possibility of a serious investigation from an incoming attorney general from the state where the NRA was incorporated as a nonprofit. The prospect of James winning the election sent NRA officials scrambling throughout the year to see what they could do to come into compliance with the law. With all the corruption swirling around internally, a reckoning was about to come due.

The senior levels of the organization were not in compliance with the law in a number of ways. The Ackerman McQueen pass-through arrangement, if discovered, would create a public relations and legal fiasco. Other vendor agreements could be publicized. The ability for the NRA to keep its tax-exempt status could be threatened. In the madness that followed, the NRA would turn to Bill Brewer to try to bring the organization into legal compliance.

In November 2018, James won the election, but the next New York attorney general's forthcoming probe wasn't the only investigation that the NRA was worried about. A number of Senate committees had launched investigations that touched on the NRA, and after the midterm elections, a new Democratic-controlled House would launch even more. The National Rifle Association continued to produce documents in connection with these investigations but begrudgingly—and not in full. Those investigations alone ran the NRA into the millions of dollars.

Chris Cox was pissed off, and he had had enough. The NRA's top lobbyist had kept a steady hand at the tiller of the NRA's lobbying shop, but NRA HQ was falling apart, and there was little he could do about it. He thought, then and now, that Ackerman McQueen was consuming far too much of the NRA's budget, and took steps to insulate his fiefdom from the advertising firm's influence.

The constant tension between ILA and Ackerman was an irritant, but it became more so following Parkland. One month after the shooting, students participated in the National School Walkout to protest gun violence. The NRA's lobbyists were concerned about possible gun legislation. So in a video the same week as the walkout, Cox announced an NRA-ILA openness to gun control legislation known as "red flag laws," allowing a judge to order a temporary seizure of an individual's guns if it is determined that they are a danger to themselves or others. Ackerman McQueen and NRA HQ, concerned primarily about amping up their base, decided to antagonize the protesters, posting a photo of an AR-15 on the day of the walkout with the caption "I'll control my own guns, thank you." The rifle was the same style of firearm used in the Parkland shootings.

Cox was the natural successor to Wayne. In fact, Cox said, Wayne had said for years that he wanted Cox to take over for him eventually. This was a nightmare among gun control advocates, who saw Cox as charismatic, professional, and competent—someone who, unlike Wayne, could go on television and forcefully defend the NRA's position.

"I certainly believed that I could not only do that job but do it very, very well—partly due to the fact that I would have immediately made changes that I believed were desperately needed," Cox said, reflecting back on Wayne's promise.

But it was clear that this was not going to happen anytime soon. Cox was hearing murmurings within the organization about emergency meetings, whistleblower reports, and a cash crunch. His house had been defaced by protesters, who had poured fake blood on the exterior twice; his wife's interior design business had also been the site of a demonstration.

He was also furious about Bill Brewer's ascendance within the organization. As congressional investigations began into the NRA, Cox was muscled aside by Brewer's team, who had no experience in probes led by Capitol Hill committees. Despite Cox's objections, Brewer was given the portfolio, leading Cox to threaten to quit.

Just a month after a series of NRA whistleblowers began raising their concerns internally, Cox began planning an exit. His contingency plan was to use the relationships he'd developed on Capitol Hill to start a lobbying organization that could do PR, government affairs, and consulting. The website for his firm, Capitol 6, was created in August 2018, as was the LLC he registered in Delaware to start the business.

On October 24, 2018, a number of the NRA's most senior leaders gathered at NRA president Oliver North's offices near Dulles Airport in Virginia. On the agenda, the topic was marked as "succession issues": what to do about Chris Cox's pending departure. North had also been hearing from people that there weren't clear rules about how Wayne could be replaced and was concerned about putting in place a plan to replace Wayne if he were to leave.

"There's friction here," North told Wayne and Chris. "What do you want?" North, like many others in the NRA, preferred that Cox stay, because they needed someone who could feasibly replace Wayne at some point down the line. North also felt that Wayne needed assistance. The financial situation was abysmal, and the 2018 midterms were coming up. For the first time in modern history, gun control groups would outspend the NRA. "I don't need any help," Wayne insisted.

Cox could have walked away then. In 2018 he had received a

17 percent increase in his pay, with his compensation rising to nearly $1.4 million. He had a generous retirement package, and he could have spared himself the drama that followed.

Wayne, North, and a top NRA lawyer lobbied Cox hard not to leave. "Chris was the natural heir apparent," North explained. "You know, if a doggone freight train ran over Wayne LaPierre, Chris Cox was the guy everybody wanted." Cox allowed himself to be talked into staying on the condition that his staying meant that he was going to be Wayne's successor. It was a decision Cox would regret.

CHAPTER 19

Whistleblowers and an Angry Mother

A pissed-off mother set off the immediate chain of events that would culminate in the National Rifle Association's dirty laundry being aired to the public. NRA president Pete Brownell's wife, Helen Redmond, had been simmering for years. A teacher and president of the local school board, Redmond is a progressive who supported Hillary Clinton in 2016—a vibrant contrast to her husband.

The two are avid philanthropists to a number of local causes near their home near Grinnell, Iowa—population of around nine thousand, some fifty miles east of Des Moines. Using their wealth, much of it derived from Brownell's success in selling firearms, ammunition, and accessories, they backed a robotics team at the high school, an arts program, a community garden and skate park, and a program at Grinnell College to bring local students to the school.

Brownell's ascension to president of the NRA caused new problems for both of them. Brownell was a simple, soft-spoken, deferential, "Iowa nice" kind of guy who had expanded his father's business into a gun-industry behemoth. Like his father before him, he had been active with the NRA—Brownell had donated more than $1 million to the group, earning him a spot in the Golden Ring of Freedom. He had seen the presidency of the NRA as a prestigious post within the firearms community, something that might be useful to help him further expand his business.

But following the trip to Moscow in 2015, Brownell had faced congressional and media inquiries into his role. As the Senate Intelligence Committee and Senate Finance Committee investigated the National Rifle Association's relationship with Butina, he decided he would not be scapegoated. He cooperated with the congressional investigations, handing over schedules, emails, and other notes from his trip. He wanted to shape the narrative early.

As the gun debate heated up, more and more neighbors in the Brownells' small town began to take note of who was behind the money sustaining their community. Concerned residents began to raise questions about whether the family's funds should be accepted by local organizations, such as Grinnell College. Locals organized an event titled "26 Days of Action Against Gun Violence"—one day for each victim killed at Sandy Hook Elementary School.

Pete Brownell's work with the National Rifle Association was making it uncomfortable for them to live in their own community. After Parkland, stickers emblazoned with the Brownells store logo were posted throughout downtown Grinnell with the caption "Brownells, where school shootings are good for business."

Redmond eventually put her foot down. She was on the other side of the gun debate entirely and had silently seethed with disdain for the NRA. Redmond made clear to others that her husband's views were his own, but it had become far too much trouble. She told him that she would divorce him if he took a second one-year term, as was customary for NRA presidents.

Brownell chose his family. He was already expressing quiet concerns about the direction of the organization under Wayne. This is not to say he was some sort of profile in courage: the month before he left as president, Brownell signed off on the compensation package that pays Wayne millions of dollars until 2030. And despite stepping down as president, he remained on the NRA board. But his conscience was beginning to speak to him. "I drank the Wayne Kool-Aid," he confided to a friend. It was not until later that he started seeing the patterns of financial misconduct inside the organization.

Brownell served one year as president, from May 2017 to May 2018. As he stepped down, Brownell told Wayne that the consequences of his role were too much for his family to bear. "He was undergoing constant harassment at home, constant harassment with his family's involvement with a college out . . . in Iowa," Wayne later recalled in a deposition. "The harassment was never ending for the family. . . . Pete's decision was totally based . . . [on] family reasons." Oliver North, the person who would replace him as NRA president, said that the Russia probes "created a conflict" for Brownell that contributed to his leaving. "His business was being severely damaged by this," North recalled.

Pete Brownell's unexpected departure as president wouldn't have, in and of itself, been a problem for the NRA. Presidents were typically figureheads and fundraisers who didn't stir the pot. But when choosing Brownell's successor, Wayne made a critical mistake—he chose a leader who demanded details, who inserted himself into problems so as to solve them, and who was willing to cause massive amounts of trouble to accomplish both.

·⼁|⼁·

The National Rifle Association suffered from extremely lax financial oversight, led by individuals uninterested in or unqualified for the task. The person primarily in charge of ensuring that the nonprofit organization was following the law was general counsel John Frazer. He was an NRA lifer. He had received his undergraduate degree at Bowdoin College and then a master's degree in government and foreign affairs from the University of Virginia. He spent some time working with remodeling firms in northern Virginia, then joined the NRA's research division in 1993 after answering an ad in *The Washington Post*. His first job was fielding phone calls and responding to mail from NRA members about firearms-related issues. He would spend nearly the next thirty years working at the gun rights group.

Frazer attended George Mason University's law school at night while working at the NRA and rose until he was the director of ILA's research and information division. He left for a sixteen-month period between 2013 and 2015 to practice law independently but returned in 2015 as general counsel of the NRA.

He was described by those who know him as cerebral, thoughtful, and intelligent. Frazer is self-assured, the kind of person who doesn't need to speak up in a group just to prove he's smarter than the others. Some described him as quiet—but that may just be in comparison with the kind of people who surrounded him in the workplace. Unlike most of the men who work at the NRA, he is not boisterous or loud or garish. He's not flashy, and he's not

particularly interested in the high life. When the New York attorney general later named him in the NRA complaint, he was
not accused of personal corruption—he was accused of noncom-
pliance with nonprofit law.

And this was his big problem: Wayne and others in the NRA
had installed as their general counsel someone wholly unqualified to lead regulatory and legal compliance for an organization
that brought in $400 million in annual revenue. Prior to leading
a team of lawyers for this task—as of 2020, he led a team of five—
Frazer had never done any work of this sort.

The New York attorney general's investigation later concluded
Frazer was not familiar with the New York laws relating to not-
for-profit corporations and had failed to maintain a framework
to comply with them. This was a feature, not a bug, that investigation found: LaPierre hired Frazer and others "despite their lack
of skills or experience" in order to "facilitate his misuse of charitable assets."

Wayne had brought on Frazer as the organization's top lawyer
without reviewing the candidate's familiarity with nonprofit law,
without reviewing his previous legal experience, without reviewing his prior legal writings, and without ensuring a comprehensive check of his background was conducted. LaPierre told the
NY AG's office that he "assumed" Frazer understood nonprofit
law and that the HR department had done a review of Frazer's
history and background.

Similarly, the NRA's audit committee, the panel of NRA board
members charged with overseeing financial controls within the
organization, was outrageously incompetent. Those who chaired
the committee didn't understand the law, didn't understand their
role, and took no steps to address this.

The chair of the audit committee, Charles Cotton, told the attorney general under questioning that he had *zero* understanding of New York law relating to conflicts of interest, audit committees, or whistleblowers. He also testified that he could not remember when he last reviewed the NRA charter, which lays out the audit committee's role. He believed that his role was merely to act as a liaison with the NRA's external auditors and testified that in his nineteen years on the NRA board, there had never been internal auditing at the NRA.

Under the law and NRA policy, the audit committee has the job of reviewing whistleblower complaints. So when there was a major legal and financial problem—as there was when a series of NRA staffers became whistleblowers in 2018—there were no adults in the room.

The group of whistleblowers was led by a woman named Emily Cummins, a true believer in gun rights who had become the director of tax and risk management at the organization. She is a hunter and competitive shooter who collects AK-47s—so not the kind to blow the whistle for ideological reasons.

She joined the NRA in 2006 as its first staffer employed as a risk manager. "When our organization's leadership is doing what's right for the mission to protect law-abiding gun owners and looking at the big picture, [the organization] will succeed in the long term," she said in an interview with *CFO* magazine in 2016.

In late 2017, Cummins and other members of the NRA Treasurer's Office—Woody's team—began putting together a list of legally and ethically dubious financial transactions that had occurred within the NRA. "We were asked as an accounting department to do some things . . . that we were not comfortable with at all," one whistleblower later said. "We kind of started talking to each other about compliance issues."

By this time, the organization was already feeling the cash crunch that would be the dominant internal problem throughout the course of this year. At least five staffers at the NRA would ultimately blow the whistle.

Their end product was a one-and-a-half-page document with the heading "List of Top Concerns for the Audit Committee," which they presented to the panel on July 30, 2018. The chair of the audit committee, who was aware they were going to be presenting allegations of misconduct, left the room before the presentation began. ("I had to leave to catch a flight," he claimed later.)

Cummins briefed the audit committee on their memo, which laid out the NRA's practice of paying out "overbilled, deceptive, vague invoices" to its contractors and alleged that the NRA often acted in the best interests of its vendors, in particular Ackerman McQueen. She presented allegations on the myriad conflicts of interest within the organization as well as the outrageous contracts to former NRA employees. And, she said, the NRA board had been kept in the dark about all these arrangements. Her memo included an exhortation to the NRA board, that it should "step up + fulfill its duties!"

Rather than directly investigate and address these concerns, the New York attorney general found, the NRA took "affirmative steps" to cover up this audit committee meeting, including omitting any mention of the whistleblowers from the official report outlining the meeting that day. The notes also say that the NRA's external auditors were present at the meeting, when in fact they were not. Later, when the audit committee interacted with the external auditors, they never disclosed the whistleblowers' complaints.

Meanwhile, the rotten smell of some of these arrangements began slowly bubbling up to the surface. Rumors began circulating in the NRA orbit about whistleblowers and financial misconduct. *The Wall Street Journal* had one of the first stories on the topic, outlining conflicts of interest between NRA senior officials and some of its vendors: "NRA Awarded Contracts to Firms with Ties to Top Officials" read the title of that story, in November 2018. Other reporters also began sniffing around.

In the face of the allegations outlined to the audit committee, some abandoned ship. Cummins resigned in November 2018, changed her phone number, and moved to an entirely different part of the country.

Cummins's boss, Woody Phillips, had left two months prior, in September 2018, with a golden parachute. Woody was a key figure in the Ackerman McQueen–NRA relationship, and his departure would leave Ack-Mac shorthanded in the internal power struggle that was coming. When Angus heard about Woody's planned departure, he called him up to beg him to stay: "You can't do that. You're not leaving!" Angus said. Woody could not be swayed—he left with a five-year, $1.8 million "consulting" package.

As for the substance of the whistleblowers' allegations, the audit committee turned exclusively to Bill Brewer's law firm to investigate the complaints. By this point, Brewer's influence on Wayne and the National Rifle Association was growing stronger by the minute.

CHAPTER 20

Brewer Replaces Ackerman McQueen

It got to be almost a joke. What's Wayne going to do? If he doesn't know yet, [it is because] Bill hasn't told him.
—LIEUTENANT COLONEL OLIVER L. NORTH (RET.)

A few years before the events of these chapters, the left-leaning attorney Bill Brewer convinced himself that he needed to obtain a firearm for his own personal safety. The lawyer got ahold of a handgun and brought it home. He recalled to associates that while fiddling with it he accidentally set it off with a loud bang. Alarmed, he placed it away in a little fingerprint-reader safe that he kept near his bedside and tried to forget the whole messy episode.

Brewer is a flashy man, fond of pristine menswear: he ordered well-fitting, tailored suits; chose flamboyant ties; and had a habit of never wearing socks. In the time that followed the incident, he noticed that he had a hole near the lapel of a custom-made suit, which he purchased at thousands of dollars apiece. Suspicious of moths, he cast the garment aside and chose another. It was then that he realized what had happened: he had discharged a bullet right through his closet, destroying a small fortune in expensive suits that were all lined up in a row.

This is the man whom the National Rifle Association would

choose to represent them, and who would ultimately suck tens of millions of dollars out of the organization into his law firm's coffers.

·|||·

It is not an exaggeration to say that vultures are often spotted literally circling the building where Brewer keeps his office, on the fifty-ninth floor of the Comerica Bank Tower in Dallas. He is a paranoid, neurotic, incessant lawyer whose "Rambo tactics" over his career have led observers to say that he bills his own clients to death. The vultures simply add to the ambience.

Bill Brewer founded his firm—Brewer, Attorneys & Counselors—in 1984, originally under the name Bickel & Brewer, with partner John Bickel. "Both of them were considered fairly obnoxious people, and apparently someone at a social event said, 'You know, you two need to meet each other,'" recalls a former close friend. Their aggressive tactics and take-no-prisoners style earned them the title of "the bad boys of the Dallas Bar."

His personal style reflected money and the finer things, yes, but more importantly, he was thrilled by the chase of the biggest prey: the Big Case, the litigation that was On the Map. This approach to lawyering never garnered much respect in the genteel Dallas legal community. The Long Island–born attorney found a way to alienate most everyone in that group. In 1998 the *Dallas Observer* described him as "a not-so-great Gatsby who craves status and wealth and importance and then provokes the very people who can give it to him."

While not an especially large law firm, Brewer's organization punched above its weight, drawing in high-caliber—and expensive—clients. The result was an extreme work environment: new associates could expect to be thrown into trial almost immediately upon hiring. However, they were paid handsomely, and the image-conscious Brewer provided perks: the firm once had access to a Gulfstream business jet and had available to it an apartment near their New York offices off Park Avenue. Brewer also leased a house in East Hampton during summer months, where favored employees could be invited.

By establishing a high-tempo, high-stakes work culture—and justifying it with high wages and bonuses—Brewer could shade his expectations and corporate toxic expectations with masculine bravado. "Joe Blow is a pussy, he couldn't handle it; he ain't a man, that's why he left," paraphrased a former employee on Brewer's response every time an attorney moved on. "We are in stratospheric levels of practicing law, we breathe pure oxygen, and some people aren't cut out—that's why he left."

The reputation of Brewer, a New York lawyer in a southern state, grew more and more infamous by the case. He was accused by more established firms of outrageous efforts to delay cases by being overly pedantic or by producing excessive paperwork, or just of being a jerk to other lawyers. In chasing the Big Case, Brewer would put six lawyers on a case where one might do.

His clients would be prepped to make the litigation process as painful and laborious as possible, slowing depositions down by claiming ignorance of words like "where" and "when." They would be taught to admit to nothing; to never back down; to concede no singular point where the opponent—the *enemy*—could gain an advantage. "In practice, we wound up with a lot of witnesses who just wouldn't say anything," said a former Brewer employee. And Brewer never shied away from any of this. He savored his reputation as edgy, confrontational, militant even. He fancied himself the Rambo type—without the guns or actual violence.

Brewer is charismatic—of that there is no doubt. But he is not particularly disciplined. He once entered a jury box and flirted with a female juror, resulting in a mistrial. Brewer also flirted with ethical lines. In 2016 a Texas judge sanctioned him for actions that might have tainted a jury pool (it was later overturned in 2020).

Longtime NRA attorney Steve Hart was the first to reach out to Brewer to ask if he'd be interested in working with the NRA. Hart had worked with him in the past and Hart's daughter had previously been an intern at Brewer's firm. Brewer was not an obvious choice for the NRA. After all, Brewer was not supportive of the Second Amendment and had never before worked a Second Amendment case. He had also been a longtime supporter of Democrats like Hillary Clinton and Beto O'Rourke.

But the New York–born lawyer's Democratic leanings actually made sense from the perspective that New York State's government was controlled by members of that party, and Brewer sold his political connections as filling a niche the NRA lacked. He'd do it, but at a rate of $1,400 an hour, of course.

"Bill's representation of the NRA is a classic example of 'servicing the client to death,'" former Brewer law partner Hal Marshall told ProPublica. "We tried to leave no stone unturned in our cases, and it often yielded great results. On the other hand the bills were hefty."

From the start, Brewer's work with the NRA was arranged improperly: the NRA has a number of internal rules requiring that contracts above $100,000 be signed off by the president and a vice president. Brewer's no-bid contract was approved by Wayne and others at NRA HQ on March 7, 2018, without signatures from the president and a vice president, effectively hiding the deal from the NRA's board of directors. "It was an error on my part," NRA general counsel John Frazer said later.

Brewer had been brought on specifically to represent the National Rifle Association in early 2018 to address the litigation over Carry Guard, an insurance that the NRA used to offer.

But he had eyes on expanding the scope of his work for the NRA from the beginning. As he took the job, he told Wayne's chief of staff Josh Powell that he would do this, but only if Wayne let him "get into all the issues at the NRA." Powell and Brewer became extremely close, coordinating daily on legal compliance issues and their internal investigations—working into the night and early morning so often that Wayne nicknamed them the "Vampires."

Here's a twist: Bill Brewer was also Angus McQueen's son-in-law. There was tremendous bad blood between the two of them, a rivalry that had existed for decades. In private conversations, Angus told close friends that he was especially displeased about Brewer's marriage to his daughter Skye. Angus was uncomfortable that his daughter was marrying a man with three children and twenty years her senior. Angus paid the bills for their New York wedding—Brewer's fourth marriage—as a sort of fuck-you. Everything was a competition between them about money and power, and payment for the wedding was as much a slap in the face to his son-in-law as it was a gift of generosity and affection to his daughter.

Bill Brewer and Angus McQueen butted heads because they were so similar. Both of them engender love and hatred—from the same people, at the same time. Both of them were so monumentally arrogant, so egotistical, so narcissistic—they couldn't stand the other. Angus was the patriarch of the McQueen family, and Brewer couldn't stand being in a room without being the most powerful one present. There could be only one alpha in the McQueen clan, there could be only one power center within the McQueen clan, and there could be only one richest man in the McQueen clan.

"I have personal knowledge that Brewer's relationship with Angus was strained at times and have personally witnessed numerous instances of disrespectful conduct from Brewer toward Angus," wrote Angus's son, Revan, in a later declaration filed in court.

Before he was hired by the NRA, Brewer was critical of Ackerman McQueen for its relationship with the NRA. Brewer, after all, was an opponent of the way the NRA views gun rights. But that was before money was involved. In 2018 and 2019 Brewer's firm sought to replace Ackerman McQueen as the NRA's most trusted vendor, and Bill Brewer sought to supplant Angus as Wayne's closest adviser and confidant. Brewer had for years heard about the Ackerman McQueen–NRA relationship, given his closeness with members of the McQueen clan. He now used that knowledge to overthrow Angus.

It began with small things that Ackerman McQueen had historically done for the NRA. Brewer's office began drafting press releases, writing speeches, and providing public relations advice.

By preying on Wayne's fear of jail time and other legal exposure, Brewer's strategy worked. In just two years, the NRA racked up $54 million in legal bills with Brewer's firm.

With Brewer getting more and more entrenched as the number one Wayne confidant, he began directly intervening in the

NRA's finances. After she had departed the National Rifle Association, whistleblower Emily Cummins wrote a memo about what she saw at the organization. She claimed that Brewer had provided "unrealistic and duplicative billing" that drove up expenses. In 2018, as the NRA faced an unprecedented financial crisis, Brewer demanded to be paid first—intervening with the NRA's accounts payable department to make sure that his bills were paid immediately, before the overdue bills of other vendors and even the NRA's own staff, she wrote in her memo.

Brewer solidified his position inside the gun rights organization by compiling research files on key NRA personnel. They became known as "burn books": white binders that contained embarrassing or damaging information about these individuals. On its website, Brewer's firm brags about having an in-house "Investigative Group" with backgrounds in journalism and government, which would have been useful for this purpose.

"I witnessed Bill Brewer compile what became known as burn books to accumulate enough knowledge of each individual's pressure points in order to keep them acquiescent," Cummins claimed in her memo.

These burn books were compiled on board members, senior NRA staff, and Susan LaPierre, and included information about their backgrounds, possible criminal histories, and other sensitive matters. Wayne learned definitively about Millie's criminal history only after Brewer told him, for example. Brewer's supporters argue that they were not "burn books" at all, but necessary research placed in binders done to prepare the organization for coming litigation and legal problems. Wayne, later questioned about them, said that he had never heard of these burn books. Neither Brewer nor a spokesperson for his firm responded to a list of questions about him, his firm, nor this book's general contentions about either.

⊹∥⊹

As Bill Brewer's power grew, fate struck. Angus McQueen was dying. He had been diagnosed with lung cancer on June 1, 2018. Brewer was ruthless. He took each parcel of Angus's declining health as a sign of weakness and an opportunity to expand his power more deeply, Angus's son alleged. In its first year representing the NRA, Brewer's firm charged the group some $19 million in legal fees. Brewer's scope grew to include close to twelve different legal matters, set out in a complex series of engagement letters that outline his work with the NRA. While these contracts outline the firm's legal work, Brewer also began to do public relations work, which he mixed in with his legal invoices, NRA lawyer John Frazer later testified.

This may be a familiar refrain by this point, but Wayne said that he had been unaware of the full scope of Brewer's bills for millions of dollars. He had never sought to know what the law firm was charging the NRA as it sucked millions of dollars out of coffers largely filled by middle-class American gun owners. Asked whether he had seen the bills, Wayne said, "I did not . . . that's not my job."

As Angus grew more ill, Ackerman McQueen began pushing back on certain NRA requests. The deal surrounding the $6.5 million mansion for Wayne and Susan fell apart. The NRA had approached Ack-Mac to do PR on the Russia and Butina issue, but it had declined. And Ackerman McQueen began to resist paying thousands of dollars for the travel agency that booked

Wayne's private jets and other travel arrangements. The reluctance to do these jobs came at a time when Brewer's firm seemed willing to do anything and everything—and Brewer's personal stock with Wayne kept surging.

Brewer took Angus's illness as an opportunity to begin criticizing Ackerman McQueen's speechwriting services, including the speech that Ackerman McQueen had written for Wayne for the annual Conservative Political Action Conference in 2018. Those at Ackerman McQueen observed that Brewer's hostility increased as Angus became sicker.

Ultimately, as Brewer's scope expanded, the charismatic lawyer slowly convinced Wayne that only he could keep Wayne out of jail, those around him observed. By the summer of 2018, Wayne had become convinced this was the case. Driven as always by fear, Wayne gave Brewer the keys to the operation, providing permission to investigate all the NRA's relationships with its vendors so that they could be in compliance with the law. It was the chance Brewer needed to eliminate Ackerman McQueen.

In August 2018, the National Rifle Association sent out hundreds of letters to its vendors. In an effort to come into compliance with the law, it set out guidance on the details that would be required for invoices and new expense-reimbursement procedures. Ackerman McQueen also received a curious letter from Woody Phillips, demanding that the NRA be able to look at all Ackerman McQueen's financial records. Woody later said that Brewer had written this letter on his behalf.

Brewer's hostility toward Ack-Mac continued to escalate. "His letters and communications to AMc's attorneys became increasingly inaccurate, adversarial and incorrectly claimed that AMc was actively breaching its obligations," Revan McQueen later wrote in a sworn court filing. The tension was quite alarming to Ackerman McQueen: in 2018 the National Rifle Association made up 41 percent of its gross revenue.

Executives at Ackerman McQueen began to feel as if they were under siege from their most important client, with an inquisition led by their own CEO's son-in-law. Brewer demanded and received an on-site review of Ackerman McQueen's financial records in September 2018—but his staff were unwilling to say what their objective was. Over two days, Brewer accountants reviewed financial documents related to the Out of Pocket project—Wayne's method for routing his expenses through Ackerman McQueen. Those at the ad agency thought Brewer was on a witch hunt to find anything wrong in the financial records that could help him end the NRA-Ackerman relationship.

Trapped between his own potential legal jeopardy and an expensive, demanding lawyer, Wayne began to complain to confidants that he felt like he was "just a pawn on Brewer's chess board." But Wayne was the chief executive officer and the executive vice president of the NRA. He never sought to act like an executive, like a leader, like someone who might be responsible for running an organization that brought in up to $400 million a year in revenue. He never sought to question or review Brewer's bills, which would rise to around $100,000 a day. He never acted like someone interested in finding the answers to elementary financial questions within his own organization. But you know what they say: nature abhors a vacuum.

CHAPTER 21

The Colonel

*It's almost like a volcano, you know, you feel a little bit of
rumbling and all of a sudden it blows up.*
—LIEUTENANT COLONEL OLIVER L. NORTH (RET.)

Wayne had approached Oliver North in the spring of 2018 with a problem: the National Rifle Association's president, Pete Brownell, was bowing out early and they needed someone to replace him. Wayne had assigned Millie Hallow to make the original suggestion, then followed up with the personal ask himself.

The pair met on April 22, 2018, at North's offices near Dulles Airport, in a building that once featured a manufacturing plant that produced body armor. NRA board counsel Steve Hart, Millie, Wayne, and North were present, while Susan LaPierre retired to a nearby office and didn't take part in the meeting.

"I need you, the NRA needs, you, the country needs you," Wayne told North. "You need to be the new Charlton Heston." The NRA's cash crunch was getting severe, and he desperately needed a popular president who could fundraise and build the NRA membership. Wayne's strategy was to distract from the story of Brownell's departure by presenting a shiny new object to the press: that of a famous new NRA leader taking the reins.

Wayne appealed to North's patriotism and laid on the flattery.

North was enormously popular in the Second Amendment community, Wayne said, and consistently received the most votes among NRA members to be on the organization's board. Wayne also appealed to their personal friendship. Wayne and North had been friends for at least a quarter century—the NRA and North's foundation Freedom Alliance had coordinated on fundraisers. North had been elected to the NRA board in 1998, recruited in part by Wayne. And of course, North had been at Wayne's wedding.

North had a number of reasons to hesitate about the offer. He had heard rumblings about trouble in the organization, issues that would be difficult challenges to confront. "I had already heard things about the Russia trip, you know, in the newspaper, I'm getting anxiety from inside the NRA," he recalled.

He had also been with Fox News for nearly twenty years by then, and would have to give up a lucrative contract he had just extended for two years. Meanwhile, his wife, Betsy, was seriously ill, and he could not take on a job that did not have top-tier health insurance.

To add to the problem, the role of NRA president was typically not paid, which was a huge roadblock with North, who made about a quarter million dollars in salary at his gig at Fox News, and a fortune more giving speeches and writing books. "[The NRA presidency] is a non-compensated position and I knew it," North said.

The solution was to find some way that allowed North to make an income while taking on the technically unpaid NRA presidency role. Enter Ackerman McQueen. Ack-Mac had done some work with North through NRATV and had twice previously made him job offers. North had turned both offers down in favor of Fox News, which he viewed as a stable place paying him a stable income.

In the meeting with North, Wayne presented his plan: North would become the uncompensated president of the NRA and would also receive a job with Ackerman McQueen that would address all his monetary concerns. "We'll iron all of this out," Wayne promised, making both pitches at once. Left unsaid between them was that Ackerman McQueen would funnel all the bills for North's salary back to the NRA.

"Look it, Wayne LaPierre suggested as the means of making me the president of the NRA that I take the job with Ackerman McQueen," North later said at a sworn deposition. "I didn't make that suggestion. He did."

North summarized the conversation in a fax to Millie, in a memo dated April 23, 2018, titled "Deal Points." It laid out their arrangement, including that North would have a "key role in formulating strategic direction of NRA." Having heard gossip about the troubles bubbling up in the organization, North didn't want to be a mere fundraiser—he sought to be a part of solving problems as they arose.

"I wanted to make it very clear that when I'm president of the NRA . . . I'm going to have a key role in making those decisions. I'm not a bump on a log. I'm not just out there as a figurehead. I'm not just a guy who signs letters and they use my name to raise money," North said. "I'll do all that, but I want at least a voice at the table as the president of the NRA."

North brought the attitude of a commanding officer. He also wanted to be able to freely approach NRA staff as needed and take their temperature on ongoing projects, just like a Marine Corps lieutenant colonel might. "I wanted to be able to just walk in the door and introduce myself as the new president of the NRA and say do you like your job, what are you doing, how are you doing," North recalled. "My success as a United States Marine was not to be a wilted flower and a dry face."

According to North's sworn testimony, Wayne agreed to all these conditions. Wayne had hoped that North would follow the model of previous NRA presidents. But instead he brought on board a Marine who was going to be nosy, persistent, and hands-on.

The agreement was all hashed out in a discussion in Dallas in 2018 during the NRA annual meeting. Senior NRA officials and Ackerman McQueen executives met and agreed on North's salary, benefits, and conditions. North would host a show for NRATV called *American Heroes* and take on the presidency of the NRA. No one appeared to have any issues with it or expressed confusion about the arrangement.

North's compensation would be $2.1 million in year one, $2.3 million in year two, and $2.5 million—ten times what he made at Fox—by year three. All these reflected the "Deal Points" memo that he had sent to Millie. Ackerman would pay North for the show, but the NRA would be billed.

North would immediately go to work for Ackerman McQueen, then formally assume the NRA presidency in September. Through their machinations, Wayne and North created a secret deal hidden from the public so that the grassroots-driven organization empowered by its members would have no choice, no input, and no knowledge.

᛫ǁ᛫

Oliver Laurence North is a graduate of the U.S. Naval Academy, class of 1968. Called Ollie by close friends, and Colonel by those who know him only professionally, he is an exacting and disciplined man. His father was a Penn Wharton School graduate who fought in Patton's Third Army during the Second World War and ultimately left the service as a lieutenant colonel, the same rank the younger North would eventually obtain.

All Ollie North had ever wanted to do was lead men into combat as a U.S. Marine Corps infantry officer. It had been his life's highest ambition to be a Marine. Returning from combat in 1969, however, he was scarred by the traumatic memories that he brought home. He received an award during his tour for more than seventy-six successful ambushes on enemy troops. Like so many young Americans, he was enthralled by the thought of war, but the reality of it haunted him. "When I came back from the war I basically stopped hunting and the kinds of things that I enjoyed as a youth in large part because I killed a lot of people," he recalled later. "I just got—I just stopped killing things." It was Marine Corps officer and NRA president Joe Foss who got him interested in guns and hunting again. In 1993 North became a life member and contributor to the National Rifle Association.

No stranger to controversy, North was a central figure in the Iran-Contra Affair. In 1981, he was posted to the National Security Council. In this role he took part in a scheme in which weapons were sold to Iran, and part of the proceeds were secretly funneled to the Contra rebels in Nicaragua, in apparent violation of congressional laws passed to limit just this kind of financial backing. As part of the resulting fallout, North was fired from the NSC, but stayed in the Marine Corps until he was indicted in 1988. He was charged with, among other things, obstruction of Congress and for making false statements to Capitol Hill; with illegally accepting funds to pay for home security; and with improperly using a tax-exempt organization to raise funds for arms.

While he was convicted on a number of counts, these convictions were later vacated on appeal.

North likes to write in ALL CAPS when he drafts memos and other documents. He likes to say "look it" to get your attention. He's the sort of person to write his zeros as 0s with slashes through them so you won't confuse them for the letter *O*—a discipline that is the polar opposite of Wayne's head-in-the-clouds demeanor.

Oliver North had never wanted to be a television personality. He had never wanted to be famous. He had only ever wanted to be a colonel in the Marine Corps, and he had been forced out as a lieutenant colonel. It was permanently embedded in his psyche: when he negotiated contracts with television and radio, he always made outrageous requests for compensation—it was never what he wanted to be doing with his life in the first place. He wanted to be leading Marines in combat.

North would sign some of his formal letters with the following: "'SEMPER FIDELIS' IS MORE THAN A SLOGAN FOR U.S. MARINES. 'ALWAYS FAITHFUL' IS A WAY OF LIFE." You don't bring in a Marine Corps officer to be a mere figurehead. A more astute manager than Wayne would have known that.

As North started his work at the NRA, the audit committee gathered and approved his arrangement with Ackerman McQueen, concluding that it is "fair, reasonable and in the best interest of the NRA" to green-light the contract he had with the ad agency while serving as NRA president. This will be important later on when Wayne claims there was a coup and the NRA claims to be absolutely shocked that North had a deal with Ack-Mac.

North had lofty goals: to raise the membership of the gun rights group from between five and six million to fourteen million. But that was before he looked under the hood. Almost as soon as he started in his new role, he immediately realized that he had entered an organization in crisis. The NRA was just months away from a crisis in which its payroll was nearly not paid out; expenses were rising, especially legal costs; and the numbers of donors and contributions were down.

"People would come up to me and they would say things like, 'what the hell's going on, you guys are sending out letters about you're running out of money,'" North said later. "Within the time frame . . . we're turning off the . . . free coffee, and water coolers . . . and it was a constant refrain about the problems that NRA was confronting, of which I knew nothing before I took over as president."

One of the things he did after realizing the urgency of the situation was to take a pay cut, dropping his salary from $2.1 million to $1.75 million for all three years of his contract—still a hefty income, but one that would allow him to look others in the eye while he asked them to make cuts too. "I want to be—you know, a good leader can never ask a subordinate to do something that they themselves will not do or cannot do," North said in his deposition. "That's why I'm still alive today. My Marines kept me alive."

Wayne went ballistic when North proposed cutting his salary, admonishing him while scribbling all over his signature yellow pads. "You can't tell me not to cut my own pay," North shot back.

North also gathered a group of advisers that he called his "kitchen cabinet." As someone who had spent decades working on his own foundation, Freedom Alliance, he was familiar with nonprofit law and his responsibilities as president of the board.

And he had been immediately alarmed by what he saw happening inside the NRA.

North's interest in investigating the root causes of the crisis met with immediate pushback. Wayne had expected North to bail him out of the crisis by crisscrossing the country and fundraising, not to get all nosy about why the crisis itself was happening. It was a cycle that would occur for months: North inquiring about financial issues and expressing concern about legal jeopardy, and Wayne telling him to butt out, that he didn't need any help.

What shocked Wayne most was having a president who actually wanted to put in work. "I learned later on that I spent more time in the president's office at the NRA than any of my predecessors in a thousand years," North said. Sensing a lack of leadership, he began to fill the vacuum by taking charge.

Even though he was essentially the chairman of the board, North began to operate as if he were an executive. He began calling staff meetings, to the chagrin of the actual executives inside the building. He'd enter NRA HQ and be welcomed by a chorus of "Good morning, Colonel!" as if staff were Marines giving him the greeting of the day. He operated as if he were in charge, so in the absence of better instructions, people began acting as if he were.

While he no doubt would have been a better, more organized manager than the rest of the executives in place, this attitude led to pandemonium. An *Animal House* atmosphere reigned because no one knew who the boss was, no one knew what the chain of command was. The confusion emboldened members of the seventy-six-member NRA politburo—aka the board—who began haranguing staff members, demanding answers on their pet projects. It became utterly dysfunctional.

Wayne was incensed that North was getting involved with the management of the organization, even though North had explicitly made his interest in the strategic direction of the organization clear. The way Wayne saw it, North was interfering with his work, whatever the hell it was Wayne was doing in the first place. Wayne didn't like it, but he perpetuated the problem by not issuing clear guidelines or taking charge.

Wayne was allergic to accountability and responsibility—but North's command presence was making him look bad. So Wayne couldn't have that either.

The real breaking point was when North began asking about Brewer. The lawyer had been hired to work on a single NRA case, but his portfolio was quickly expanding to encompass a litany of legal issues—and a whole host of other projects beyond just legal representation.

North began digging deeper: Why was Brewer handling that congressional Russia probe, despite having no experience with Russia? How did he become an attorney for the NRA? Did he ever disclose his antagonistic relationship with Angus McQueen before he was hired? Had he properly disclosed to the NRA his sanction—then not yet overturned—in Texas? None of the answers was forthcoming, creating escalating tension among senior NRA officials.

North demanded the legal agreements that had been drafted in order to hire Brewer. He asked for documents showing how Brewer's responsibilities had expanded. "Look it, I had questions about his integrity, his greed, his ability to do the job, and the fact that the outcomes were rarely what we expected," North later testified.

The colonel discovered a whole host of issues. "I asked for the paperwork on the initial engagement letter, and it turns out that, holy mackerel, none of this stuff was done properly," North recalled. NRA policy had not been followed, rules about contracts over $100,000 had not been adhered to—the whole thing was a mess.

Wayne at first said that North could examine the books and see what Brewer was costing the NRA, but sent NRA general counsel John Frazer to do the unenviable deed of telling North that Wayne had changed his mind. Wayne was always willing to be in the room for the generous yes, and always looking for a way to avoid being in the room when the unhappy decision of *no* was being presented.

"I can protect you, Wayne, I can protect us as an institution, and it's going to be good for us to self-correct before we end up with these investigations," North pleaded. Wayne and Brewer ultimately put up a fierce fight, at various points even refusing to tell North what Brewer's overall compensation was.

North had been asked to fundraise and save the NRA at a critical moment for the organization. And when he traveled the country, he was getting constant questions about why the NRA was in a financial bind to begin with. Why should wealthy donors put money in an organization that is bleeding money, they would ask. "I'm getting challenged by various people as I go around, 'Well, whiskey tango foxtrot, why is this costing so much?'" recalled North, using the NATO phonetic alphabet to express the abbreviation "WTF?"

North, who is apparently more familiar with nonprofit law than quite a number of people in this story, realized that the NRA could save itself significant heartburn down the line by self-correcting before government regulators found problems. North suggested an independent audit to look at the NRA's finances, including the Brewer invoices.

What followed for the NRA's higher-ups became known internally as the Letter Period. The back-and-forth between ad hoc factions consumed the attention of all the senior staff at NRA HQ. North would write letters to Wayne, demanding transparency on the Brewer bills. "This is a fiscal emergency," North wrote in one such letter. The Brewer law firm at this point was drawing NRA coffers at an incredible rate: $97,000 per day around early 2019. In the first quarter of 2019, the NRA paid the Brewer firm more than $2.9 million per month. In the first twelve months Brewer was retained by the NRA, the gun rights group paid it $19.2 million.

Between February and April 2019, North wrote at least six letters to senior NRA officials making the case that he and the board should be given access to the Brewer firm's invoices.

"It was not designed to go out and get Wayne LaPierre. It was designed to help Wayne LaPierre, who reminded us all frequently 'I'm in charge of the NRA.' He said it all the time to me and to others. Well, you need help," North claimed later.

John Frazer, who had worked at the NRA for the vast majority of his career, was caught in the middle. He confessed to his wife that he was in constant fear of crossing one side or the other and losing his job. "I was in an extremely difficult position," he said. "I had my CEO strongly at odds with my board chairman." He decided to adopt Wayne's strategy of the turtle pose: retreating out of the situation as much as possible and trying to avoid involvement. Frazer later testified that during this period he did not seek to investigate Wayne's expenses or review the travel billings from Gayle Stanford, Wayne's travel agent—basic tasks that a responsible general counsel might be expected to do in the face of serious allegations of misconduct.

Because North was an employee of Ackerman McQueen, Brewer and Wayne began arguing that North could not inquire about Brewer's legal activities, because Brewer was, among other things, looking at Ackerman McQueen's billing, and thus North had a conflict of interest. Confused yet?

As North began digging into Brewer's billing, Brewer responded with petty lawfare—suggesting that North was conflicted, and also that the NRA had been shocked to discover that North was an employee of Ackerman McQueen. "Brewer manufactured and concocted conflicts at every turn," North later fumed.

Brewer would draft letters on Wayne's behalf, pushing back and telling North to "cease and desist," that North was exceeding his mandate, that it was inappropriate for him to inquire. "As a highly compensated full-time employee of Ackerman McQueen, Colonel North must desist immediately from efforts to burden or obstruct NRA's engagement of outside counsel on matters pertaining to Ackerman," read one such letter.

North was not looking after Ackerman's interests, the colonel would respond, but instead was interested in the monstrous legal bills. "I regarded the payments to the Brewer firm to be excessive on the face and urged to avoid criticism and to avoid the inevitable exposure of all of this that we conduct an outside independent audit," North later said.

Brewer and Wayne became fixated on North's contract, demanding that he show them the contract that Wayne had been an active part in negotiating. "Colonel, I'm just trying to protect you," Wayne would say. When shown the contract, the goal posts would move: Oh, we need to see it again. Oh, actually now we need a hard copy of the contract.

This bureaucratic hairsplitting went on and on for months and months. North, a steel-willed Marine, was doing everything he could to turn up the temperature on Wayne. *This is Wayne LaPierre we're talking about,* everyone who knew Wayne thought. *If we push him to his limits, he'll yield.* North made demands, verbally and in writing. He yelled. He began having letters hand-delivered to Wayne at odd hours of the night to amp up the pressure, to make Wayne feel vulnerable and unsafe at all times. Wayne felt it: in a later interview the self-pitying CEO compared it to torture: "It was literally, weekly, weekly, weekly, like this waterboarding of me."

North even tried appealing to him personally. "Wayne, there's nobody who cares more about you than we do except maybe your wife, Susan," he once said. None of it worked. Wayne was totally under Brewer's spell. "Wayne totally rejected any idea that Brewer could not walk on water," North later recounted. Backed by Brewer, Wayne stood his ground. It was a Wayne LaPierre unfamiliar to those who knew him best, one who would turn his back on all the people who had made him so powerful to begin with.

In a sworn deposition, North repeatedly claims never to have talked to anyone at Ackerman McQueen about Brewer's invoices or work for the NRA, and was never told by anyone at Ack-Mac to look into this matter. "Never once did I ever discuss any of that with anyone from Ackerman McQueen or Mercury Group," he said, adding that he never raised any objections about Brewer looking into Ack-Mac.

Wayne and Brewer continued to claim not to know that North was an Ackerman McQueen employee, even though Wayne himself had suggested the arrangement and was well aware that North needed to be an employee of Ackerman McQueen in order to get sufficient health care for his wife. There was a personal outrageousness to the lie: Wayne had met with North's wife on a number of occasions and surely knew that her illness—which was obvious—necessitated North to seek formal employment to secure health insurance. "He knew exactly why I needed that benefit," North later said. Here's how Wayne answers questions about this later, at a deposition:

Wayne: "It was never my idea for him to become an employee of Ackerman McQueen. . . . I actually did not learn that he was an employee of Ackerman McQueen until way, way, way later on."

Lawyer: "But you knew he was going to be paid by Ackerman McQueen."

Wayne: "I did."

Lawyer: "And that the NRA would pay Ackerman McQueen for whatever . . . it was paying Oliver North."

Wayne: "I did."

Lawyer: "Okay."

Despite the distractions and counter-allegations, North was not dissuaded. Around the one-year mark of Brewer's engagement by the NRA, North authored yet another letter in which he outlined his criticism of Brewer's multimillion-dollar bills and demanded an outside, independent audit of Brewer's work.

"They fought it hammer and tong to keep that independent outside review of the finances from ever being explored," North said. He kept warning Wayne, "You're swimming in a pool of sharks." But Wayne wouldn't listen to him.

The battle lines were drawn: North, his friend and fellow NRA board member Richard Childress, and NRA board lawyer Steve Hart on one side, and Brewer and Wayne on the other. "There was a coordinated effort to try to deal with Bill Brewer, this has been reconstructed as a conspiracy against Wayne," Hart later testified. Hart, as you might recall, was actually the lawyer who had recommended the NRA hire Brewer in the first place. He obviously came to regret that decision.

North's life became a walking nightmare. The Marine would spend a grueling schedule on the road, delivering speeches, four or five at a time some days. The work didn't bother him so much as what he was working for. As he prepared for bed, he would look at himself in the mirror and realize what all that effort was subsidizing. "I didn't raise enough money today," he would tell himself. "I've got to try harder tomorrow because I didn't cover Mr. Brewer's bill for [the] day."

To this day, North has never gotten his hands on Brewer's invoices. Wayne, the CEO, claimed never to have examined them either.

Brewer was fighting a two-front war. As he battled the NRA officials seeking to get into his bills, he was also set on destroying Ackerman McQueen's relationship with the gun group by digging deep into the ad agency's bills. He was demanding a careful dissection of Ack-Mac, including multiple audits, while refusing any examination of his own practices.

Angus McQueen was livid. He was a man unaccustomed to being powerless, especially when it came to Wayne LaPierre. He erupted in conversations with Wayne, cursing at him. "No one is going to look at our records," he told Wayne. There were a ton of vendors who had been pissed off with Wayne since the fall of 2018, when the NRA began putting new standards in place for its contracts and reimbursement policies. "It was just me getting yelled at," he said. Officials at David McKenzie's company called him up to curse him out too. But "the worst . . . was Angus," Wayne recalled. "You know, a million cuss words."

By this time Brewer was fully in charge of the organization's legal strategy—Wayne was vaguely aware that the NRA was conducting audits of Ackerman McQueen but not at all familiar with what was being directed in his name, and his organization's name. "It got to the point where it was all in the lawyers' hands, and I just kind of stepped out of it, to tell you the truth," Wayne recalled.

Wayne had signed off on a broad effort for Brewer to inspect the financial records of the NRA's vendors to preempt what the group's leaders expected would be a vigorous investigation by the New York attorney general. Brewer took the latitude and ran with it. In September 2018 the Brewer firm directed a multiday audit reviewing Ackerman McQueen's financial documents. Wayne later said in a sworn deposition that he had not specifically authorized it.

Lawyer: "Who requested the September 2018 examination? . . ."
Wayne: "I don't know."
Lawyer: "It wasn't you?"
Wayne: "No."

Ackerman McQueen thought of these as assault audits— lawyers examining their financial documents for any hint of a problem so that it could be brought up in possible future litigation.

These sorts of adversarial visits had not been common in the decades-long NRA–Ackerman McQueen relationship.

Angus tried to convince Wayne to sideline Brewer, and for a time it appeared that this might happen. Board members led by North were pushing for Brewer to go—or at least be more transparent about his fees. Wayne agreed: "We've got to get rid of Bill," he told his chief of staff. "I'm getting too much pressure from the board."

The NRA brought in a different law firm, Cooper & Kirk, to review Ackerman McQueen's financial records. But in another round of silliness, Cooper & Kirk didn't have the expertise to do forensic audits—so it hired Brewer's team to assist in the effort, but this was aborted after Ackerman discovered the bait-and-switch. "And around we went," observed Powell.

In October 2018 the tension came to a head at a meeting in Dallas. "It was an emotional meeting," Ackerman McQueen CFO Bill Winkler recalled. "There were some real problems going on." Execs at Ackerman McQueen felt that they had been constantly threatened and harassed by the Brewer firm. And Angus was especially affronted because this had to do with problems involving his biggest client and his son-in-law: "You're dead to me. Don't you understand it? You're dead to me," Wayne remembers Angus telling him.

Despite the decades-long relationship between the two groups, Ackerman McQueen was ready to resign the NRA's business. "He begged us not to resign the account," Makris later testified. "He said, 'please don't leave me, please stay with me . . . I need you, please stay with me.'" Wayne promised that Brewer would soon be gone.

But Brewer had his hooks in Wayne and returned to the fold

in December. Four days before Christmas, Brewer's law firm demanded new information from Ackerman McQueen, including about its other clients. It was an intrusive demand at absolutely the worst possible time for the company. By this point Angus was going through a painful process of radiation and chemotherapy. Wayne was no longer phoning his former Ack-Mac allies for advice. "It's measurable, when you've known somebody for almost 40 years, and you know how often they called you . . . and how often they sought advice. When it all of a sudden stops, it's palpable," Makris observed later.

By January 2019, Brewer's firm was helping with writing Wayne's Conservative Political Action Conference speech—a task that traditionally had been conducted by Ackerman McQueen. Brewer had laid the groundwork by pointedly criticizing the speech Ack-Mac had written for Wayne the previous year. Now Brewer would be running the show.

Ackerman McQueen executives seethed with betrayal and confronted Wayne in person. Makris had catered to Wayne's personal and professional needs for years: shuttled him to medical appointments, played amateur therapist to his anxieties, and even once went to San Antonio to help Wayne's nephew pick out an apartment.

"We had been close friends, and I had done a lot of, let's say, service, both personal and professional, for him," Makris recalled. "I said, I don't understand, what has you so scared that you're going to forsake everybody that has helped you for thirty-eight years? Turn your back on us all and turn your entire life in this organization over to a guy you barely know, who is a professed Democrat . . . who doesn't even like the Second Amendment. What has you so scared?"

In a room full of people, Wayne responded by admitting his great fear. "Bill Brewer's the only one who can keep me out of jail," Wayne said, according to Makris's sworn testimony. "He's the only one between me [and] the guys with the handcuffs, [between] me and an orange jumpsuit." (Wayne has denied saying this.)

In 2019 the NRA demanded yet another audit of Ackerman McQueen's financial records, announcing that it had hired a Dallas company called Forensic Risk Alliance. FRA examined records relating to Wayne's Out of Pocket expenses, the names of Ack-Mac staff whose work was billed to the NRA, and Ack-Mac's media buys on behalf of the gun group. Left unsaid was that Susan Dillon, a member of Brewer's team, had surreptitiously moved to FRA in order to be part of the team examining the documents.

Internally, the FRA called its project the North Project and gave it the code O-N, suggesting that the Brewer-directed auditors were hunting for irregularities or problems with North's arrangement with Ackerman McQueen. The auditors ultimately stayed for days longer than they had originally planned.

Asked about it later, Wayne said he didn't know the details about this audit either—neither what the auditors were doing nor whether they were allowed to see the records. He didn't authorize the audit. He didn't know whether the audit led to a report of conclusions. And, he said in a later deposition, it was "probably" the Brewer law firm who gave it the green light.

⊲‖⊳

In early April 2019, Angus told his family that his medical condition was improving. Meanwhile, North was told that he had been reelected by NRA members to another term on the board, from

2019 to 2022, winning more votes from the membership than any other candidate up for election that year.

On April 11, North sent the audit committee a copy of his contract with Ackerman McQueen, asking them to again review it, as well as the amendment in which he takes a pay cut. "I don't anticipate any problem," came the reply from audit committee chairman Charles Cotton.

But the next day, as Angus lay recovering, the NRA did what for years would have been unthinkable. Brewer and Wayne filed a lawsuit against Ackerman McQueen, sending a decades-long working relationship to a screeching halt. It includes a claim that the NRA had not seen the North contract, a copy of which had been provided to Frazer the day before. In its first complaint, the NRA claims Ack-Mac had violated the terms of their contract, and demanded business records relating to Oliver North. Things would escalate from there, with subsequent claims and counterclaims being filed that demanded tens of millions of dollars in damages.

"Let loose the dogs of war," NRA lawyer Steve Hart wrote in an email, reacting to the news of the first lawsuit in mid-April 2019. "Brewer just picked a fight with the folks with all the dirt on expenses for the last 30 years."

Asked about this lawsuit later, Wayne expressed his most common sentiment: he didn't know, and it wasn't his job to get involved in this critical NRA matter. "It's not my role to be in the middle of it. . . . All I know is the whole thing was an ungodly mess at that point, and people were all over the board on everything," he said at a deposition. He first acknowledged that he "signed off on it," then later substituted that explanation for this phrase: "I knew they were doing it."

The NRA filed the lawsuit without informing its own general counsel, John Frazer; its president, Oliver North; or its board of directors. The board never got a chance to vote on it.

It was a sign of how deep Brewer's influence over Wayne had become: a seismic event in the history of the NRA, and none of the senior officials who should have had input or knowledge of this was looped in. The NRA's president learned about the move from public news reports. "I've got nothing. I have no guidance. I have no information," North said about this time. The NRA's actions sent the gun group into a downward spiral. It was about to get a lot worse: the organization's annual meeting was in two weeks.

CHAPTER 22

Wednesday, April 24, 2019

The NRA was in deep distress. It was two days before the annual meetings, held this year in Indianapolis, and everyone could sense that upheaval was coming. Typically this was a joyful time on the NRA calendar, an occasion for glad-handing donors, grassroots organizing, fundraising, and hobnobbing with the thousands upon thousands of dues-paying NRA members who turned out for the show. This year President Trump and Vice President Mike Pence were booked to address the crowd, and staffers and board members were frantically trying to tie down last-minute arrangements. But everyone knew that a public reckoning was already taking shape.

Just a few days prior, *The New Yorker* had published a piece that blew the lid off the corruption inside the gun organization, revealing for the first time to those outside that things were dangerously amiss. The story touched on the NRA's shady ties with Ackerman McQueen, inappropriate contracts, the failings of NRATV, the whistleblower reports, and the organization's catastrophic financial situation. It was explosive.

In the lead-up to this day, North had not backed down after Brewer and the NRA filed the lawsuit against Ackerman Mc-Queen. In his mind, that had nothing to do with him—he was interested in the separate matter of legal bills, the only topic of corruption he was aware of at the moment. In yet another letter leading up to the convention, he doubled down on his demands regarding the Brewer bills, calling the amounts invoiced excessive, the secrecy around them "alarming," and the arrangement with the NRA "inconsistent with industry standards." The board of directors had a "fiduciary duty to oversee massive expenditures of NRA funds," North said.

Separately, Ackerman McQueen was putting the squeeze on Wayne. It had ratcheted up the pressure on the NRA's executive vice president, but unlike every other time in the past, he now refused to give in. Josh Powell and Brewer were the main reasons for this, they realized, and resolved to turn the pressure up even higher.

On April 22, 2019, coincidentally the one-year anniversary of when Wayne and North hashed out details about the presidency of the NRA, Ackerman McQueen showed their hand. In a series of private letters to NRA officials, including Wayne LaPierre and Steve Hart, Ackerman outlined in not-so-subtle terms that they had ammo on the organization's CEO. They said they needed to talk to Wayne and the NRA about these odd travel costs, these dining expenses in Europe, the $274,695.03 he spent on suits—and, oh, by the way, what is the deal with this apartment you arranged for an intern? (These letters would later leak to *The Wall Street Journal*.)

Later that evening, at 6:07 P.M., NRA board attorney Steve Hart sent an email to NRA execs and board members about the information he received related to the previously unknown travel reimbursements routed through Gayle Stanford and her travel company. The way he wrote the email, Hart clearly expected he would be punished for disclosing the information. "As I write this email I am still counsel to the board. As such, I cannot sit on this information. Knowledge brings responsibility," Hart wrote. He left it unsigned.

Within hours, Hart was fired, after working with the NRA for more than a decade. John Frazer sent an email at 10:21 P.M. with the subject line "Message from Wayne LaPierre regarding NRA board counsel, confidential and privileged." The message read, in part, "Effective immediately, Steve is no longer counsel to the NRA."

Wayne was just making the rules up as he went. "What authority did you have to terminate the general counsel for the Board if that general counsel served the Board?" he was later asked in a deposition. "Yeah, I know, it's kind of crazy," Wayne responded. The NRA later argued, through Frazer, that Hart was hired to advise the NRA on board matters, not to specifically represent the board, and that Wayne could hire and fire Hart as he pleased.

It was the latest Brewer-Wayne power move. They were slowly stripping away North's ability to act, as Hart had been a key adviser. It also sent a message: "The purveyor of bad news to the management of the NRA was something that you would get fired for," North recounted later. He was not consulted before Wayne fired the board's lawyer. North, of course, was the president, the theoretical chairman of the board, but was not kept in the loop about this decision.

The move also sent another message, this one perhaps less

intentional: that Wayne was totally in step with—if not outright controlled by—Brewer at this time. Wayne LaPierre never writes emails. He certainly doesn't write sentences like "Effective immediately, Steve is no longer counsel to the NRA." North later testified that he believed that Brewer had written the statement and put it in front of Wayne to sign.

As Wednesday, April 24, 2019, arrived, Wayne was under enormous strain: Board members were demanding to talk to him. Firings, public airings of controversy, an ongoing deficit—all were bouncing around Wayne's head in the run-up to the annual meetings. And that was before the actual yelling started. Wayne was due for a meeting with NRA senior officials held in North's suite at the JW Marriott. He had spent the morning strategizing with allies in his own suite, and now was arriving late.

Entering North's suite, Wayne ran into Richard Childress, a NASCAR driver turned businessman who at the time was a senior member of the NRA board. Childress had allied himself with North as a figure on the NRA board demanding answers about the Brewer bills. His relationship with North had been noticed. Wayne had been working overtime behind the scenes to marginalize the two of them, contacting key members of the board in an effort to prevent them from being reelected to senior NRA positions at that convention. Childress didn't mince words, pointing a finger directly at Wayne after he had entered the room: "You've told every member of the nominating committee not to renominate the colonel and me!"

Wayne, with his aversion to confrontation, claimed not to

know anything. Wayne said he didn't know what the nominating committee would be doing. In reality, Wayne knew two things: First, if North stayed on as president, North could reshuffle the audit committee and push forward with an audit of the Brewer bills. Charles Cotton, the chairman of the audit committee, had come to Wayne urging him to marginalize North. "If Ollie gets reelected, I'm a dead man," Cotton told Wayne. And second, Wayne knew that the board wouldn't act in a way other than how he wanted them to act—he had stacked it with members loyal to him.

Wayne had long made up his mind. Ollie North had to go.

"What's the nominating committee going to do?" North asked Wayne.

"Colonel, I really don't know what they're going to do. I'm not the nominating committee. They can do whatever they want to do," Wayne responded.

"Yeah, but if you support me I get reelected," North said. "Are you going to support me?"

Wayne stared at North, whom he had known for some thirty years. Everyone thought that surely Wayne would yield under pressure, as he had yielded so many times before.

"No, I'm not," Wayne said, looking directly into North's eyes.

As one former close friend of Wayne put it, hyenas normally scavenge, but they can be ferocious if they have to be. Wayne was a wounded animal, backed into a corner. He finally stood firm.

Millie's phone rang. She stepped out to take it.

On the line was an NRA board member named Dan Boren, a former Democratic congressman. Boren had been calling Millie all morning, but not recognizing the number, she hadn't picked up. Finally, Boren had texted her, identifying himself as a board member who needed to talk to her. Now, in the wake of Wayne's confrontation with North, Boren laid out what he knew: embarrassing info about Wayne LaPierre was threatening to spill out, just days before Trump would arrive to address NRA members at the convention.

Millie felt like she had been punched in the stomach. According to Millie, Boren said that serious allegations of misconduct would be publicized unless Wayne resigned. "I have intel that in the next two or three hours Ackerman McQueen will file a lawsuit that will have negative implications and impact for Wayne," Boren said. Millie promised to get the information to Wayne immediately. "I will see if I can buy a couple hours," Boren said.

Ackerman McQueen had been Wayne's brain for decades, and now it was on its way out. The marketing firm was not going to take it lying down—not from that weak-willed, backstabbing traitor Wayne. Not while Angus McQueen was still alive.

Millie walked back into North's suite. She had been separated from them by a sliding wall. A group of the NRA's most powerful officials were huddled together, including North and Wayne. She briefed them on the call she had just had with Boren, and Wayne absolutely erupted. He is almost universally a mild-mannered man—not easily angered, and not prone to swearing.

"That son of a bitch Angus McQueen!" Wayne shouted, before storming out of the room.

Millie began to cry. "This is not right," she said.

The other officials were left sitting there, stunned. Millie began to poll the room, asking Childress if he wanted Wayne to step down. "Every man has his prime, and every man has his time," came the folksy answer from Childress. Millie was stunned—

until this moment she had not known how deep the opposition to her boss had been among the NRA board.

She turned to her friend Oliver North.

"Do you want Wayne to resign?" she asked.

"Not today," North responded.

◦║║◦

North and Boren connected by phone later that day. North's first instinct was to try to mediate. He volunteered to get on a plane to talk to Angus, to bring the temperature down a little between the two parties. North, reflecting on it later, said he wanted to "ameliorate the hostility." North didn't think Wayne would resign abruptly, because leaving the NRA could put him in even more jeopardy—isolated, without the protection of the gun rights group or its shrinking but still vast resources. But he did think Wayne could be coaxed out with a generous succession plan in place.

"Wayne LaPierre is not going to quit just because somebody's threatening to say bad things about him," North recalled later. "This is a gun fight going on . . . friendly fire, shooting at each other."

North received a readout from Boren as to the nature of the allegations against Wayne. The laundry list of misdeeds—travel expenses, lavish meals, suits, and on and on—came as a shock. "I had no idea about the things that Wayne LaPierre was being accused [of]. We'd never gotten that far in any of the investigations. I was stunned and, quite frankly, it's the first sense that I had that Wayne LaPierre might actually be corrupt," North recalled.

North thought he could address the crisis by moderating a

conversation between the two sides. "That was, you know, obviously blissfully naive on my part," he later said. Instead he would be sucked into a conspiracy theory crafted by Brewer and his allies to save Wayne's job: that of a coup against Wayne.

⊰⊱

That afternoon Wayne's suite was a hive of activity, the room abuzz with the chatter of lobbying: temperature-taking, strong-arming, cajoling, whipping. Over the course of the day, dozens of NRA board members and Wayne himself were on the phone, calling other board members to see if Wayne had the support to stay on.

At around 4 P.M., Chris Cox had asked Wayne to come to his suite. Cox had also spoken with Boren, who had called him with details of what Ackerman McQueen had on Wayne. Cox was a longtime antagonist to Ackerman McQueen, but he was adamant that the madness had to stop. Over a thirty-minute conversation, Cox asked Wayne to back down from his confrontation with Ack-Mac.

"Man, Wayne, you need to withdraw that lawsuit against Ackerman McQueen. . . . You need to go along with these guys. You need to alleviate the pressure," Cox said. "If you don't . . . they are going to smear you to a point where you will not be able to walk down the street."

For years, these executives with the NRA and Ackerman McQueen had reveled in their shared camaraderie, this fellowship they supposedly had with one another. That was in good times, when the money flowed freely. Now it was difficult to see how any of them genuinely liked each other to begin with.

"I'm telling you as a friend," Cox said. "That's what they're go-ing to do."

⼷

Wanting to convey what he had learned from Boren, North tried frantically to get in touch with Wayne, but couldn't reach him. He next tried Millie, but couldn't get through—Millie had lent Wayne her phone so he could lobby anxious board members. Millie called back using a borrowed phone.

Millie was an emotional mess, having been crying at several points during the day. But she gathered herself enough to grab a notepad and sit on a chaise longue in the suite. She wrote down what North was saying: Ackerman McQueen had evidence of fi-nancial mismanagement, sexual harassment allegations against Wayne's aide Josh Powell (which he has denied), clothing expen-ditures by Wayne, and an apartment that had been inappropri-ately rented for someone close to Wayne and Susan. But all this could go away if Wayne agreed to an eventual departure, North said, and the window was short.

North was trying to convey what Boren had told him, and Millie sensed no hostility from the colonel, whom she had never heard say a single negative word about her boss. North said he wanted to help Wayne by giving him an exit plan followed by a comfortable retirement.

Millie and North were close. Both had experienced the impact of cancer and had bonded over it, and Millie had on occasion signed emails to him, "Love, Millie." North had noticed that Mil-lie was always kind to Betsy, his wife, and had found Millie to be warm and straightforward. "Millie's the kind of person I can pick up the phone and say whiskey tango foxtrot is happening," North would later say. But now Millie was torn between her friend and her boss. When North had started talking about a retirement package, she realized that North was no longer supportive of Wayne staying on at the NRA.

Millie stumbled back into the room where Wayne was and read aloud from her notes. NRA board members allied with Wayne immediately seized on the information to cast North as the villain. "This is extortion," they said. Millie got on the phone to Wayne's chief of staff. "Get your ass up here," the normally mild-mannered woman told Josh Powell.

Here's the story that Wayne, Brewer, and their staff came up with: North, whose contract Wayne had helped arrange, had secretly and unbeknownst to Wayne been an Ackerman McQueen employee. North was conspiring with Ack-Mac and other senior NRA officials to oust Wayne in order to prevent Brewer from examining Ack-Mac's NRA financial files, which in reality had by this point already been audited multiple times.

"I think others have intentionally mislabeled that as a threat or as—what did they call it, a coup. It's anything but. I was trying to save—still trying to save Wayne LaPierre but deeply concerned that what was being said was corruption," North later said in a deposition. In a nod to his national security background, he added teasingly, "A coup is something run against a head of state. I mean, I know. I ran a few, right."

If there is solid, clear evidence of a conspiracy to oust Wayne, it hasn't been provided to the public. Not in the press, not in the numerous lawsuits that followed, and not to me. There are some vague and circumstantial messages that suggest NRA officials were discussing the crisis as it happened, but nothing definitive. In the New York attorney general's investigation, North is portrayed as an NRA official determined to carry out his fiduciary responsibilities, and stymied by Wayne, Brewer, and their allies.

Months later, surrounded by lawyers, Oliver North gave his sworn testimony.

"So were you engaged in any kind of arrangement or agreement with Ackerman McQueen to try and force Mr. LaPierre to resign as the executive vice president of the NRA?" a lawyer asked.

"No," the former Marine Corps officer responded.

CHAPTER 23

The Weekend from Hell

This is so far beyond reality, John Grisham would have a hard time laying it out in a novel and yet it happened.
—LIEUTENANT COLONEL OLIVER L. NORTH (RET.)

It was like a montage of slow-motion assassinations from a Mafia movie. Wayne, with Brewer firmly at the helm, was methodically moving through the senior ranks of the NRA to eliminate opposition. Steve Hart had been the first to go. Chuck Cooper, who had been providing legal services to the NRA for some thirty years, would be fired in the wake of this weekend in Indianapolis. So would Michael Volkov, a lawyer hired to advise the NRA on congressional investigations, who would leave the organization the same day as Cooper. Soon, Chris Cox would also be pushed out. But first for Wayne and his cohorts was the matter of Oliver North.

Unfazed by the events of April 24, North made his move the next day. The NRA president has the authority to appoint special committees. North tried the only maneuver he could: using this power to form a special panel of NRA directors to investigate the organization's financial troubles. On Thursday, April 25, 2019, just before 8 A.M. on the day the NRA's annual meeting was to kick off, he sent a confidential memo to the NRA's executive committee. "I HAVE FORMED A SPECIAL COMMITTEE ON CRISIS MANAGEMENT AND AM IN THE PROCESS OF ASSIGNING MEMBERS," North wrote in his signature style. "DO NOT HESITATE TO CALL WITH ANY QUESTIONS."

This was a real problem for Wayne and Brewer. By filling a special committee with board members interested in an audit, North might just pull it off. And North, as president, also had the ability to replace the existing members of the audit committee. For Wayne, there was no other choice: North had to be ousted, and the committee shut down.

North was fired through an email, sent formally by Millie but blessed by Wayne. "This note confirms that [Wayne] will not endorse you for another term as N.R.A. president," the email read. Millie was asked to hand-deliver the message to North, but she refused. She had been through the ordeal of being asked to sign the notice, which she did reluctantly. But she couldn't look North in the eye while handing him a pink slip.

She loved her friend Oliver North, but she liked the idea of keeping her job more. It was also a signal of Wayne's personal cowardice—he allowed the effort to fire North to grow around him, and even condoned it, but he refused to pull the trigger on his friend in person.

North decided he would leave the annual conference. "Why are you doing this?" Richard Childress asked. "I'm going home. Humility is a virtue. Being humiliated is a sin," North replied. "I'm not going to stay for this."

As he reflected on this moment, North thought of a Bible verse, Psalm 26, which reads in part: "I do not sit with the deceitful, nor do I associate with hypocrites / I abhor the assembly of evildoers, and refuse to sit with the wicked."

North bought a one-way ticket out of Indianapolis and left the annual meeting quietly. His special committee was ultimately disbanded before any investigation could be started. North never saw or spoke to Wayne again.

·|||·

With North gone, Wayne and his advisers began the process of painting Wayne as the victim. He had run a similar play when he was threatened in the 1990s, falsely accusing Neal Knox's camp of a fake conspiracy to oust him. Now he sent a letter to the NRA board with the tone of a valiant, stoic hero: "Leaders in every walk of life must often choose: between what is true, and what is polite; between what is convenient, and what is right." He said that he had been extorted by the NRA's president, Oliver North. Wayne said North had threatened him on behalf of Ackerman McQueen, and dropped what was to the public a bombshell: North had been making money from Ackerman McQueen.

"It is regrettable that threats now emanate from our fiduciaries and friends. But so long as I have your confidence—an honor that humbles me, daily—I will not back down," Wayne wrote. "Serving this Association has been the greatest honor of my life, and not one I'm willing to forfeit in exchange for a backroom retirement deal."

Reading it now, the letter doesn't hold up. Wayne acted surprised about North's employment at Ackerman McQueen, as if it were a secret organized behind his back, as opposed to an idea he came up with and pitched to North. Wayne claims that North threatened him, when in fact North was offering him a way out of the situation. Wayne said that he wouldn't take a "backroom re-tirement deal," when he knew he already had a very generous multimillion-dollar retirement package waiting for him, negoti-ated in secret. It was a loud, clumsy attempt to create a conspiracy where none existed, and push a narrative whereby Wayne was the courageous victim rather than the progenitor of this entire rot-ting mess.

But this spin on the news got out quickly: the letter to the board was soon leaked to reporters in Indianapolis, hungry for news about the NRA's inner turmoil. With no counter-narrative and no evidence to the contrary, Wayne's claims were quickly broadcast to the public.

The crisis within the NRA soon drowned out what was origi-nally set to be the big news of the weekend: President Trump's speech at the conference on Friday. He would be the first sitting president to address the NRA's annual conference since Ronald Reagan. The assembled thousands were the base of his base. "Chris Cox, Wayne LaPierre, Oliver North—I've been following Oliver for a long time. Great guy," Trump would say during his speech. "Three extraordinary champions for the Second Amendment."

But behind the scenes, Trump was anything but oblivious to the turmoil at the NRA. He knew how critical its tens of millions of dollars had been in securing his victory in 2016 and was count-ing on them showing up again in 2020. He closely followed the internal struggles at the gun rights group and was concerned the NRA might not be able to support him as it did in 2016.

Backstage before his speech, Trump told Chris Cox and Wayne that the NRA's legal team was "lousy." On Twitter, then Trump's favorite medium, he acknowledged that the NRA was facing troubles, urging it to "get its act together quickly, stop the internal fighting, & get back to GREATNESS—FAST!"

·||·

Though some gossip made its way through the membership in the alcohol-soaked events around the Indiana Convention Center Friday night, most of the NRA's members had no clue Oliver North had quietly left town. On Saturday morning, the annual members' meeting was set to occur. It was a throwback to when the grassroots had a firmer grasp on the comings and goings of the gun organization, an occasion when dedicated members of the NRA could put forward resolutions and question its leadership.

The meeting started with a shocking announcement. On the stage, a place set out for Oliver North was empty, with no one sitting behind the name placard. His friend Richard Childress was left to break the news. "I just found out last night at seven o'clock that I'd be standing here, standing in for the president," Childress told the crowd.

Childress then delivered a message written by Oliver North. "Please know, I hoped to be with you today as NRA president, endorsed for re-election," the note began. "I'm now informed that will not happen." He explained how he had agreed to come on at the NRA along with a salaried role with Ackerman McQueen, that he had urged for an independent audit of the Brewer firm's invoices, and that he was deeply concerned over press reports about the NRA's alleged financial misconduct.

But it was clear from the letter that North, while he was to remain on the board, would not be staying on as president of the

NRA. "Should you ever need me in the future, just call," the letter ended. "I will come." The crowd sat in stunned silence.

North was not the only NRA member deeply concerned about corruption and Wayne's role in it. A substantial portion of the grassroots in the audience was interested in accountability, in passing resolutions demanding a change in senior leadership, and in the NRA's financial practices. Usually Ackerman Mc-Queen would have been tasked with running Wayne's "ground game," his strategy for handling the floor—but Wayne had jettisoned the firm.

Wayne's allies tried to adjourn the meeting immediately after pro forma statements made by senior NRA leaders, but the hundreds of people in the audience were not having it. The reformists in the crowd voted that suggestion down immediately.

"I demand the right to be heard!" shouted one reformist, citing NRA bylaws. The rebels submitted a motion to oust Wayne LaPierre as CEO of the National Rifle Association, forcing John Frazer to read their resolution in front of a grim-faced Chris Cox and Wayne, who sat silently onstage.

"The ultimate responsibility for the situation for the last 20 years rests with the executive vice president of the association Wayne LaPierre. . . . Therefore be it resolved . . . [that NRA members] do hereby express our disappointment and frustration and lack of confidence in Wayne LaPierre's ability to guide the association out of the dangerous mess he has created and call for his immediate resignation," stated the resolution, authored by NRA member Frank Tait of Pennsylvania. It went on to state that the members had no confidence in the board members on the audit, finance, and executive committees.

The rebels in the audience took to microphones in support of their case, demanding evidence be presented regarding alleged financial misconduct. "Just tell us what the allegations are!" one NRA member shouted, stamping his cane on the ground. Wayne's allies also took to the mics, arguing that this was not a fight that should be publicly discussed and that ongoing litigation prevented many of the details from being revealed.

Marion Hammer, the staunch Wayne ally on the NRA board, took to the microphone to urge unity. "The lifeblood of this organization is on the line," Hammer said. "We are under attack from without. We do not need to be under attack from within."

It was high drama, and revealed to the public for the first time the extent to which the National Rifle Association was in absolute disarray. Reporters, including myself, were frantically trying to live-tweet the event while taking notes and preparing to file reports. After a lot of shouting and contentiousness, the resolution to oust LaPierre was eventually defeated and referred to the broader board for further consideration, where it would languish.

The weekend from hell could get worse, and it swiftly did. That evening, as members of the NRA were still reeling from the news that its president had stepped down and that its CEO/EVP was the subject of numerous allegations of financial misconduct, the New York Attorney General's Office made an announcement.

A spokesperson for Letitia James told me and other reporters that their office had begun an investigation into the NRA, including the issuance of subpoenas and document preservation requests. This would be added to the pile of congressional investigations already under way, as well as the litigation that the NRA was already engaged in.

"The NRA will fully cooperate with any inquiry into its

finances," Bill Brewer said in response to the news, speaking on behalf of the NRA. "The NRA is prepared for this, and has full confidence in its accounting practices and commitment to good governance."

The NRA had a contentious nine-and-a-half-hour board meeting the Monday after the weekend from hell. It was held mostly behind closed doors and in "executive session," meaning that the board members were prevented from disclosing details of the meeting to the public.

It had been arguably the worst week in the history of the National Rifle Association. Reformers on the board who sought change and accountability were stymied—North and his allies were out or on the way out, and the board began to close ranks around Wayne. Any opposition to Brewer, or any support of transparency, was seen as de facto evidence of support for the so-called coup against Wayne.

During the board meeting, Chris Cox rose to support Oliver North and praise his character, all the while declining to make eye contact with Wayne. Cox had been reappointed as the NRA's top lobbyist that weekend, but he would soon be under suspicion, and later, on his way out. Wayne viewed his friendly comments about North as a statement of great betrayal.

Former congressman Allen West was a board member who had been vocal about the need to investigate allegations of Wayne's financial improprieties. "I think it's very important that we put in the right type of organizational reforms that are necessary if we do find that there has been financial malfeasance—and then we've got to report it back to the members," he told reporters that weekend. There was a rumor that West would challenge Wayne for the job, but that never materialized. No one put their name forward to challenge Wayne, so he was reelected by acclamation during the private, closed-door session.

"United we stand," Wayne said in a statement after his reelection. "The NRA Board of Directors, our leadership team, and our more than 5 million members will come together as never before in support of our country's constitutional freedoms. . . . I am humbled by the Board's vote of confidence and its support of my vision for the future."

Wayne's opponents had calculated that he would fold if enough pressure was applied in the right places and at the right time. Instead, Wayne held on. He would at least nominally lead the NRA for years to come as it confronted a series of threats to its very existence.

CHAPTER 24

Rebellion

It's the most painful period of my life.
—WAYNE LAPIERRE, TO *THE NEW YORK TIMES*

In the 1960s, during the height of the Cold War, when paranoia ran high throughout the nation, the National Rifle Association administered a loyalty test to potential members: to join the association, they had to pledge that they were not, in fact, interested in the overthrow of the government "by force and violence."

More than half a century later, Susan LaPierre was in a similar state of mind. She had seen what had happened to her husband in Indianapolis, and with the Women's Leadership Forum's own annual meeting approaching in September 2019, she was looking to stamp out any hint of insurrection within her corner of the NRA.

The LaPierres, especially Susan, were in a paranoid and vindictive mood. If there were any of those anti-Wayne subversives in her crowd, she wanted them found and tossed, according to those who were later told about the event. At the Women's Leadership Forum meeting, she gathered her elite donors together and, along with her cochair, demanded that they pledge their loyalty to the current regime.

The members of the Women's Leadership Forum executive

committee, as they were known, were given an ultimatum. If those gathered were not willing to pledge their loyalty, she wanted their resignation. You're either for us or against us, Susan conveyed, before breaking down in tears. She added dramatically: And there are some people against us in this very room!

Some donors, who had given sizable fortunes to the NRA, did not appreciate being talked to that way. But most fell in line. The National Rifle Association, their membership in the WLF—that was part of their personal identity, who they were as human beings. And they didn't want to lose that part of their lives.

The WLF executive committee had gathered at La Cantera Resort in Texas. Along with speeches from the Republican politicians Governor Kristi Noem and Representative Debbie Lesko, they were treated to a speech from Susan about how she and Wayne were the *real* victims in this whole saga.

Susan's rant followed a long, drawn-out exodus from the NRA. Board members who sought answers were generally ignored. Singer-songwriter Ted Nugent, one of the NRA's most popular board members, asked repeatedly to speak to Wayne about the allegations of financial misconduct. But he received no response.

Those who pressed harder were dealt with more harshly. Board members and officials who objected to the LaPierres' leadership were accused of being part of pro-coup, anti-LaPierre forces.

Three board members—Sean Maloney, Esther Schneider, and Timothy Knight—stepped down in August 2019 after demanding oversight of the NRA's finances. They had asked for an independent investigation and information about money paid to board members, salaries for NRA execs, and the Brewer law firm's legal representation of the NRA.

These requests were ignored, and those who spoke out were retaliated against. "We have been stonewalled, accused of disloyalty, stripped of committee assignments and denied effective counsel necessary to properly discharge our responsibilities as Board members," they wrote. "We are left with no other choice but to resign as members of the Board of Directors."

Pete Brownell, the former NRA president, separately decided that he had experienced enough and resigned from the board that same month, claiming that his business needed his full attention. Privately, he confessed to a friend that the ongoing probes into the NRA could be just what the association needed and that he hoped Wayne and a large portion of the board would be replaced. "I'm a religious person," Brownell confided to the friend. "[New York Attorney General] Tish James' investigation could be what they need, the archangel burning everything down completely. The NRA could survive, but it's going to take everything being burnt down."

Dan Boren resigned in November. Ultimately twelve board members either chose to resign or were prevented from being renominated to the panel following North's 2019 departure from the presidency.

Reflecting on it now, some once connected to the NRA lament their affiliation. "You are only as good as the dollar you gave today," Schneider said. Schneider had given generously to the NRA and had been friends with Susan, but she was tossed from the in-crowd as soon as she spoke in favor of an independent financial investigation into the group. During the speeches at La Cantera Resort, Schneider was specifically cited as an example of disloyalty. Schneider points to one nasty Facebook post by Janet Nice, Susan's co-chair on the WLF. The post falsely accused

Schneider of saying mean things about Susan. "That is absolutely fabrication," Schneider said, "and it pitted a lot of people against me, that I was out to get the NRA, which couldn't have been further from the truth."

Schneider had been personally recruited to the board by Susan and joined the NRA's board of directors in 2016. Having served on the boards of more than a dozen nonprofits before, she was shocked by the fact that the organization didn't have an internal auditor. Her sin was having advocated for Wayne's dismissal. When she confronted Oliver North's successor as president, Carolyn Meadows, about how to have Wayne removed as executive vice president, Meadows responded in "a very condescending, ugly manner," Schneider said. Schneider did not suffer fools gladly, and responded with some attitude: "I asked her if she was fucking stupid," she recounted. Later that year Schneider would speak to the New York attorney general about what she had witnessed at the NRA.

Among the attendees at the Women's Leadership Forum event at La Cantera was Wayne himself. Naturally, he continued to play the victim to the crowd, making the laughable statement that he didn't enjoy flying in private jets in the least but that it was necessary because of the harassment and security threats his family faced. Wayne told the well-appointed women in the audience that he was the one who had killed the arrangement for the mansion in Texas and that it was a tremendous burden to be the head of the NRA. They needed to raise money, Wayne said. The left was attacking them; Ollie North was attacking them. Won't you please open up your checkbooks?

The National Rifle Association had been in a financial crisis even before the Indianapolis blowup. But as details about Wayne and Susan's corruption became clearer, NRA membership revenue plummeted to a seven-year low. In 2019 member dues dropped by 34 percent, from $170 million to $113 million. During 2019, a year of acute crisis, Wayne still managed to collect a salary of $1.9 million. And despite all the allegations of financial misconduct that were leveled at him, Wayne kept his NRA-issued credit card.

Following the failed push by some in the NRA grassroots to oust Wayne at the Indianapolis members' meeting, veteran NRA members began speaking out about their experiences. The NRA had long been a black box to outsiders; insiders had been suspicious of the motives of the press and not particularly prone to open dissent. But having been stalled by internal means, rebels began mobilizing and chronicling their views publicly.

Andy Lander, who had worked at the NRA for thirteen years, admonished the NRA leadership in an open letter for treating staff like "indentured servants" and argued that both Ackerman McQueen and the senior leadership at the NRA had to go. "If you're not actively seeking the removal of Mr. LaPierre you are the problem," Lander wrote in one of the first of these public letters.

Former NRA employee Steve Hoback also wrote an open letter condemning the "cult of personality" that seemed to have sprung up around senior NRA officials. "The heedless, unbridled hero worship of many Members and their antipathy toward holding the Old Guard accountable has helped to create the monster that is destroying the Association from within," Hoback wrote.

Lander and Hoback were among the first to speak out, and in June 2019 some dissident NRA members organized into a group determined to push the NRA toward accountability and reform. They called it Save the Second and argued that for their views of the Second Amendment to be properly promoted, they needed an ethical, transparent National Rifle Association. As a group, they urged for a smaller board of directors, term limits, and the NRA to get away from the conservative culture-war messaging and exclusively focus on gun rights. One of its most public supporters was Jeff Knox, the son of Neal Knox, the crusading former NRA official who had been ousted by Wayne in the '90s. The son had picked up his father's cause—and with the same fervor.

Separately, a small group of big-dollar donors to the NRA began rethinking their support for the organization. David Dell'Aquila, who had donated in the six figures to the NRA and had planned to give a substantial portion of his wealth to the organization, led this charge. By the end of 2020, he claimed he had gathered pledges from donors to withhold more than $150 million in contributions to the NRA until it got its financial house in order.

Dell'Aquila, who has something of a pugilistic personality, went even further, bringing a class action lawsuit against the NRA and Wayne LaPierre. The lawsuit, filed on behalf of NRA members, accused Wayne and the NRA of using donor contributions to fraudulently pay for exorbitant legal fees and expenses.

The NRA's strategy with its most generous donors was, as Wayne and Susan had done with the Women's Leadership Forum's elite donors, to play the victim. In a meeting with donors who had given more than $1 million to the NRA, Wayne described how he had been swatted and how security concerns justified the absurd expenses he had directed the nonprofit to pay for.

Other donors were given a different pitch: the NRA was all there was to protect the Second Amendment. The argument, made to large donors who had not quite hit the million-dollar mark, was that their rights were under attack by the socialist left and that the NRA, imperfect as it might be, was the only entity that could stop that.

Both the grassroots and donor revolts were driven by press reporting in the spring and summer of 2019, which laid out for the first time the exorbitant spending the nonprofit had engaged in. After the drama in Indianapolis, investigative reporters began looking more deeply into the group's finances. What followed were story upon story about outrageous expenses, private jets, Susan's hair and makeup, the $6.5 million mansion, and Wayne's salaries. Until the New York attorney general's investigation was completed, press reports built piece by piece the most comprehensive view of the nonprofit's corruption.

Wayne's reputation suffered immensely within the gun owners' community. Those who would never have called him out previously were now expressing their disgust. At a gun industry convention after the events in Indianapolis, Wayne tried to attend a political reception. In previous years, he would have been welcomed with open arms, no questions asked. This time, a former NRA board member stopped him and said Wayne would need to give a personal contribution to attend. It was a humiliating scene, a rebuke of Wayne: this was an event for *paying* attendees, and though Wayne might feel entitled to enter, Wayne hadn't paid. It was a sign of Wayne's diminished standing in this community.

Inside the NRA, the immediate reaction to the growing rebellion was surprise. Some had believed that the NRA being under attack could be good for fundraising; usually when the NRA was criticized in the public, it was good for business. But what they failed to understand was that the rebellion had nothing to do with politics. The NRA wasn't under assault from the left but from Second Amendment supporters. The criticism in this case was based on a nonpartisan, nonideological interest in basic accountability. Those at NRA HQ made the mistake of conflating the NRA with gun rights. They were wrong.

Even before the fracture with Ackerman McQueen, Wayne had become increasingly skeptical of the NRATV project. Driven by Josh Powell's consternation over whether the effort was worth it, the two had begun demanding answers on NRATV metrics in 2017. Unlike many other media organizations, viewership metrics were not readily available inside the organization, even to hosts. And when Wayne and Powell asked for data, they were stonewalled. "We can't tell you—it's impossible to get that information," they were told.

"I have a lot of my people coming to me going, 'Wayne, you're getting snowed. All those numbers are available. You're not being provided accurate information,'" Wayne recalled later.

So the NRA hired an outside consulting firm called Performance Improvement Partners to figure out what kind of viewership the channel had attracted. Ackerman McQueen gave a number of presentations to NRA officials about NRATV, but Ack-Mac repeatedly said it couldn't get the number of "individual viewers" for NRATV. The figures that were available to the public suggested that the millions of dollars used for NRATV were not well spent. A Comscore report suggested that NRATV's website brought in just forty-nine thousand unique visitors in January 2019.

Following the crisis in Indianapolis, the way forward became much more obvious. By June the NRA had cut off all ties with Ackerman McQueen and closed down production of NRATV. Longtime Second Amendment activists were laid off alongside the news division. Dana Loesch, for example, was out.

"We have been evaluating if our investment in NRATV is generating the benefits needed. This consideration included the return on investment and the cost and the direction of the content," Wayne wrote in a statement announcing the move. "Many members expressed concern about the messaging on NRATV becoming too far removed from our core mission: defending the Second Amendment."

By August 2019, the gun rights group's position was clear. After spending tens of millions of dollars on the collaboration, the NRATV project had been an "abject failure," an NRA spokesman said.

CHAPTER 25

Lawfare

Chris Cox initially had not been wrapped up in the so-called coup attempt, and had a long history of hostility toward Ackerman McQueen—an inconvenient fact for the Wayne and Brewer narrative.

After the crisis exploded into public view, Cox went to Wayne and offered to step down from lobbying. He could replace Josh Powell as Wayne's chief of staff, Cox argued, and right the ship after this crisis. Wayne said he would think about it. But as time went on, Wayne and Brewer dragged Cox right into the center of this whole mess.

The NRA's public narrative was not nuanced: Cox had been a coconspirator in the "coup." The only evidence was circumstantial: a series of texts between Cox and Dan Boren form the primary basis for this claim.

The texts show that Boren and Cox arranged to talk by phone. "What a tragic mess," Cox told Boren later by text after they connected. Cox then said that North would call Boren and that "Millie didn't give any details just the ultimatum. Not trustworthy." In another exchange, on the day of North's dramatic and public departure from the NRA, Cox texted an NRA lawyer this vague note: "I fear we are not changing the tides." There is no clear evidence of any plot to oust Wayne—just frantic players in this saga trying to deal with the crisis.

In a later legal filing, Cox said that he never spoke with North about removing Wayne LaPierre and that on their April 24, 2019, phone call, neither of them had expressed an interest in getting Wayne to resign. Wayne wasn't even personally sure if Cox had been a genuine threat to him at any point. "There seemed to be some level of involvement from Chris Cox," Wayne said carefully, later in a private deposition. John Frazer, the NRA's general counsel, seemed to think Cox's involvement was that Cox had conveyed an ultimatum via Oliver North. But the facts don't back that up. Cox had never threatened Wayne—he urged him to withdraw the lawsuit and let cooler heads prevail.

Cox was traveling in California for a work trip when he received a call from an aide at 4:30 A.M. The aide had gotten wind from a reporter that the NRA was about to accuse him of being an "errant fiduciary" who had plotted with North. Cox was put on administrative leave, pending an investigation into his involvement.

"The allegations against me are offensive and patently false. For over 24 years I have been a loyal and effective leader in this organization," Cox said in a statement at the time. "My efforts have always been focused on serving the members of the National Rifle Association, and I will continue to focus all of my energy on carrying out our core mission of defending the Second Amendment."

Cox tried persistently to call Wayne and explain his viewpoint, but Wayne refused to take the call. They would not speak again—although as an old friend, Wayne left Cox a message when Cox's brother passed away.

Facing this investigation, Cox resigned in June 2019, just as NRATV was being shut down. His wife had encouraged him to leave the organization for a long time, and had a dim view of some NRA higher-ups. As he announced his departure, President Donald Trump and Vice President Mike Pence together called Cox to express concern—which highlighted who the strongest conduit between the NRA and the White House was.

Cox's feelings of betrayal seep out even when he reflects on the incident years later. He had always considered himself a loyal friend to Wayne, and had been caught off guard by the accusations the NRA lobbed at him.

"The accusation that led to my suspension was not only false but highly offensive," Cox told me two years after his resignation, calling the NRA's actions "not only outrageous but also unforgivable. I made peace with the decision to close that chapter of my career and I resigned."

Like many senior NRA officials, he had a golden parachute—a post-employment agreement worth $2.4 million. But this agreement was then contested by the NRA. The NRA argued in a confidential arbitration that Cox had not satisfactorily performed as an employee and was not entitled to the payments in the agreement. The bottom line: the NRA claimed Cox was insufficiently loyal to Wayne.

The figures suggest that it became a fight driven by spite: Wayne conceded in April 2021 that the NRA had spent around $7.8 million to stop Cox from receiving around $2 million. The legal fees could reach double that by the time the process runs its course. And in a twist, Cox's previous contract requires the NRA to pay for any legal claims related to his employment. So the NRA is not only paying millions for the lawyers to prevent Cox from receiving his payment, they're also paying millions for the lawyers who are demanding Cox's payment.

Interestingly enough, Cox's lawyer said during public court proceedings that the NRA was no longer contending that Cox was part of a "coup." As of this writing, the fight over Cox's post-employment millions has still not been resolved.

Cox's resignation was part of a torrent of departures from the NRA's lobbying shop in 2019. Cox's chief of staff, Scott Christman, was escorted out of the building by security without warning. ILA spokeswoman Jennifer Baker, who was in Nashville taking care of an ill relative, was asked to fly back—only to be escorted out by security once she arrived. ILA general counsel David Lehman also left. Between the three of them, they had more than forty years of combined experience at the organization.

Cox could have left in 2018, as his instincts and his wife told him to do. But he was persuaded to stay at ILA—a decision he now regrets. "Had I any indication of what might come, I would have left long before," he said.

Josh Powell was also headed to the exits. Accountants inside the organization had found that Powell had charged personal expenses to the NRA. He acknowledged that he had charged some $22,000 in personal expenses to the NRA and tried to pay it back. He felt utterly betrayed by the process: his allies Wayne and Brewer stood by as he was investigated, suspended, and ultimately pushed out.

When the NRA filed its 2019 tax return, it blamed former NRA officials for receiving personal benefits from the nonprofit organization while exculpating Wayne. It admitted that its executives had used the association's funds for private gain, pointing the finger at Josh Powell, David Lehman, Woody Phillips, and Chris Cox.

It reserved special attention for Cox, stating that the NRA was demanding back some $1 million it said Cox had inappropriately obtained in expense reimbursements. Cox responded that the allegation is "both false and offensive." Wayne, the same filing said, had received a mere $300,000 in inappropriate expenses and had "corrected" that by paying that amount back.

As the months passed following the drama at Indianapolis, Wayne renewed his interest in getting out and floating a couple of names for his job, such as former representative Jason Chaffetz and former presidential candidate Mike Huckabee. He had been whining, almost as a tic, for decades about the overwhelming burdens of his job.

He never seemed to have any joy in it. And the job had become progressively more of a nightmare for him. He hated confrontation, and nothing more than *public* confrontation. In the wake of the terrible mass shootings in America over the past decade, he could not so much as walk down the street without being overcome with anxiety. But Wayne was about survival above all else—leaving the reins of power would make him too vulnerable. So he stayed.

·||·

With North's ouster as president, Brewer consolidated his power. He had brought in Wit Davis, who had worked with Brewer on a case related to 3M, to replace Steve Hart as the counsel for the

NRA board of directors. Brewer's firm had been pulling emails from employee accounts, ostensibly to prepare for litigation and a coming battle with the New York attorney general, but that created an atmosphere of fear among staff. By 2020, there were close to a dozen engagement letters between the NRA and the Brewer law firm, outlining the scope of the Brewer firm's work.

Wayne and Brewer oozed vindictiveness with their legal strategy. North had not been reelected as president, but he was still a member of the NRA board, so the NRA initiated legal action to boot him off the board too.

Brewer also used his rapidly accumulating influence to press for additional lawsuits to be launched against Ackerman McQueen. Angus McQueen was hospitalized in mid-May 2019 for his ongoing illness. In keeping with his pattern of striking at a moment of Angus's weakness, Brewer filed the NRA's second lawsuit against Ackerman McQueen while the McQueen family was in transit to visit Angus in the hospital.

The second lawsuit accused Ackerman McQueen of leaking confidential information to the press. As with the previous lawsuit, it was not approved by the board before it was filed. Unlike the previous lawsuit, however, general counsel John Frazer was looped in on it and had signed off on it before it was filed. Grilled by lawyers in a deposition, Frazer could not or would not specify a single piece of evidence that certain letters, which were widely disseminated within the NRA and among its board, were leaked by Ack-Mac.

In May and June, Ackerman issued invoices to the NRA as usual, and the NRA refused to pay. NRATV shut down not long after. Ackerman McQueen, which had been so heavily dependent on the National Rifle Association, was forced to lay off some fifty employees after splitting with the organization. At its peak, Ackerman McQueen had grown to about 250 employees, about a third the size of the NRA's workforce at its largest.

On July 16, 2019, Angus McQueen passed away. Josh Powell received a phone call from Millie with the news. He had been meeting with NRA senior staff at their Fairfax headquarters. He decided to clear the room of everyone except for himself and Wayne.

"Angus died," Powell told Wayne.

Wayne's reaction was muted. He had no time to spare on grief for his supposed friend of several decades, the man he had once affectionately called his "Yoda," the partner whom he had talked to almost every day for much of his life.

"Wow. Really?" Wayne responded.

And that was it. Powell invited the other staff back in, and the meeting continued. Wayne didn't attend Angus's funeral. There was too much acrimony built up by that point.

While he had been sick, Angus had witnessed the collapse of perhaps the most important business relationship of his life. One of the last things he read was a quote from Brewer accusing Ackerman McQueen of breaking the law when it came to its relationship with the NRA. He told his son, Revan, that Brewer was trying to destroy the family.

The NRA filed a third lawsuit against Ackerman McQueen in August 2019. By this point Wayne was almost totally detached from the legal strategy at his association. Asked just one month later in a confidential deposition what he knew about the nature of the third lawsuit, Wayne responded, "Honestly I can't recall what it's about." The lawsuit sought the return of property from Ackerman McQueen after their decades-long relationship.

Throughout the process, throughout Angus's illness, Brewer

sought to use his familial connections for tactical advantage. In a court filing, Angus's son, Revan, accused Brewer of "using family members as channels" as part of the legal maneuvering in these cases.

In the litigation between the NRA and Ackerman McQueen, a mystery remains. Where are the yellow pads? Wayne was frequently seen scribbling notes at critical points, such as when Oliver North committed to cutting his own pay and when Ackerman gave him a presentation on NRATV—but these notes were not produced by the NRA in the discovery phase of its initial lawsuits with Ackerman McQueen. You don't have to be a lawyer to know that if they were improperly destroyed, that could be considered spoliation of evidence. One person familiar with Wayne's notepads said they might have been worthless anyhow—with Wayne's muddled handwriting, "you couldn't read them anyways!"

At different times in his September 2019 deposition, Wayne says that he threw out a large number of notepads several years ago. "It was all dirty and dusty," Wayne said. "Nothing that relevant in any of it." The other notepads he saved were stored in his garage. More recently, he handed notepads encompassing his writing from 2012 onward to the NRA's lawyers. They were considered part of the discovery process in the New York attorney general's investigation. He stopped taking so many notes on legal pads after the subpoena.

CHAPTER 26

The AG Strikes

On the morning of August 6, 2020, I was the first reporter to break the news that New York Attorney General Letitia "Tish" James had filed a lawsuit against the National Rifle Association, seeking to dissolve the organization entirely. The NRA had diverted millions of dollars from the stated mission of the nonprofit, and numerous senior NRA officials had received private gains.

"For nearly three decades, Wayne LaPierre has served as the chief executive officer of the NRA and has exploited the organization for his financial benefit, and the benefit of a close circle of NRA staff, board members, and vendors," the lawsuit states.

The lawsuit was directed at the NRA as an organization but also personally names Wayne, Woody Phillips, Josh Powell, and John Frazer for allegedly breaking the law. The four of them, as well as the NRA as an organization, had contributed to the loss of more than $64 million over three years, the NY AG alleged.

Notably, while Wayne, Woody, and Josh Powell were accused of contributing through financial misconduct, the allegations against Frazer relate to negligent financial filings and a failure to comply with governance requirements.

When Tish James entered office in 2019, she inherited a charities bureau that was already briefed on some of the problems with the NRA. The letter that had been sent to the NY AG's office in September 2015 by Marcus Owens of Loeb & Loeb had been waiting there with a list of the NRA's legal vulnerabilities. They got to work quickly. At least a dozen attorneys began working on the investigation, according to Powell. A number of former senior NRA officials and board members flipped and cooperated with the New York AG's probe into the NRA, exposing the NRA to even deeper peril.

The NRA framed the lawsuit as a politically motivated attack. "The New York Democratic Party political machine seeks to harass, defund, and dismantle the NRA because of what it believes and what it says," the NRA said in its counterclaim against the NY AG. "Only this Court can stop it."

The NRA was already in dire financial straits when James made her move. An audio recording I obtained of a January 2020 board of directors meeting showed Wayne talking about the deep cuts he had to make before and after the Indianapolis fiasco. "The cost that we bore was probably about a hundred-million-dollar hit in lost revenue and real cost to this association in 2018 and 2019," Wayne said. "I mean, we kinda reframed this entire association. We took it down to the studs."

Massive layoffs were initiated: in a 2019 nonprofit filing, the NRA said it had 770 employees. By 2021, that number had dropped to about 490 staff, according to a later legal filing. Those who remained saw substantial pay cuts. The cancellation of the 2020 annual meeting because of the coronavirus also had financial implications: the event usually raises millions for the NRA through sales, rentals of exhibit hall space, and donor contributions.

There were political consequences to this period of austerity: As Trump had feared, the NRA was not the big-money force it had been for him in 2016. Spending to support him nearly halved. ILA spent less than $17 million on the president's reelection campaign, much less than the $30 million it had doled out in his first presidential run. Cox and key members of his team at ILA had been driven out the year before, and were not there to help with the 2020 campaign.

CHAPTER 27

Bankruptcy

In January 2021, the NRA filed for bankruptcy. It was a Hail Mary tactic: it paused both payments to vendors and ongoing litigation. Simultaneously, the NRA announced that it was seeking to use bankruptcy restructuring to move to Texas, and thus away from New York, where Tish James had primary jurisdiction. It was an outcome that had been contemplated and rejected before. "If everything at the NRA was squeaky clean, we would have left long ago. The fact we couldn't is a little-known indictment of the NRA," Powell wrote.

The NRA was not filing for bankruptcy because of financial problems, it said, but instead as a legal strategy. In bankruptcy filings it said that the association had assets of $203 million, compared with liabilities of $153 million.

It turned out not to be a particularly wise strategy. Wayne and other top NRA execs were put under oath and questioned for days about corruption within the organization. It turns out that Wayne had filed for bankruptcy without informing his general counsel, his chief financial officer, his head of General Operations, his top lobbyist, or most of his board. Instead, just over a week before the NRA filed for bankruptcy, NRA board members were presented with a new contract for Wayne, which included the vaguely worded authority for him to "reorganize or restructure the affairs" of the gun rights group. Without specifically mentioning bankruptcy, Wayne and his lawyers took this to mean authorization of a bankruptcy filing, which had the effect of halting all the lawsuits under way—including with Ackerman McQueen and the New York attorney general's attempt to dissolve the organization.

The thrust of the NRA's argument was that they had conducted a top-to-bottom review in 2018, that they were now in compliance with the law, and should be trusted to reorganize in Texas outside the reach of the New York attorney general. As part of this compliance effort, NRA staff were trained on multiple occasions on nonprofit law and how to comply with it. They lasted about an hour. General counsel John Frazer was forced to admit that Wayne never attended one of these sessions.

The testimony in the bankruptcy trial was savage, with some of it coming from some of the NRA's most senior current and former officials. "I believe that the management is corrupted, and I believe the board is corrupted. I don't see anything that is salvageable," said NRA board member Owen Mills, who has spent twelve years on the NRA board. "Mr. LaPierre is not a good business leader."

Phillip Journey, who had previously served on the NRA board from 1995 to 1998, resolved to serve on the board again after witnessing the NRA's Indianapolis fiasco in person. Upon being elected to the board, he was appalled by what he witnessed: "All the safety switches in corporate governance needed to be turned back on . . . they were off," he told the bankruptcy court. He said that he viewed the NRA as "essentially operat[ing] as a kingdom, rather than a corporation . . . Wayne's kingdom." The former CFO, Craig Spray, echoed that, saying that one of the NRA's biggest problems in governance was cultural, and that there was a "'Wayne said' culture" that had run amok in the organization. The chaos that Wayne had cultivated was manipulated by NRA staff at every turn: "There was sometimes a group of people who would get direction from Wayne and then they would propagate that to the rest of the team. It proved problematic because they didn't always interpret Wayne's direction [properly] or would put a twist in it," Spray said.

Other shocking revelations emerged: Carolyn Meadows, the NRA president who replaced Ollie North, said during a deposition for the case that she had typically taken notes of her conversation with NRA officials, but she "destroyed them" in 2019, after she was told they might be subject to a subpoena. "Some, I shredded. Some, I actually burned," she said. After that, she stopped taking notes. You can almost imagine her lawyer's appalled face when she admitted this.

Gayle Stanford was called to testify about her exclusive travel consulting with Wayne. In one instance, a lawyer asked her why certain invoices did not include destination information, as was usual practice. Gayle lay the blame on the NRA's CEO, accusing him of asking her to obfuscate the details:

Lawyer: "The invoices on page 4 and 5 do not include stops to Nebraska or the Bahamas. Why is that?"

Gayle: "I was told how to do the invoices."

Lawyer: "And who told you how to do the invoices?"

Gayle: "Wayne."

But the most notable person to testify was, of course, Wayne himself. Nervous, anxious, and eager to defend himself when challenged by adversarial lawyers—he was a terrible witness by any measure. LaPierre was whiny and argumentative, repeatedly elaborating on answers well beyond the scope of the question and earning the repeated rebuke of the judge. He did not listen to his lawyer, who asked him to respond yes or no to the greatest extent possible. On at least one occasion he started talking about things covered by attorney-client privilege before being stopped by his lawyer.

This was a man without discipline, without competence, and without self-control on display for the whole courtroom, streaming live for the world to see (the trial took place during the COVID pandemic). At one point during a deposition before the trial, Wayne admitted he doesn't even know his own cell phone number.

The bankruptcy judge, who presumably had an eye on Wayne's fitness to continue on as CEO of the NRA, repeatedly told him to stop rambling.

"I'm about to say something I've said for a day and a half now," the judge said. "Can you answer the questions that are asked? . . . Do you understand that I've said that to you more than a dozen times over the last day?"

"Yes, sir, Your Honor. I'm sorry, I'm—I'm doing my best," Wayne responded.

The monthlong trial concluded with the judge dismissing the NRA's attempt to use bankruptcy law to move to Texas. The judge said he was troubled by "the manner and secrecy" in which the NRA sought bankruptcy and said that he did not find that the NRA had filed bankruptcy "in good faith."

This means that the NRA's litigation troubles continue, with a trial in the case between the New York AG and the NRA expected to take place in 2022. Ackerman McQueen, which in the final year of its work with the NRA counted on the gun rights group for some 35 to 40 percent of its revenues, was forced to close its offices in D.C., Dallas, and Colorado Springs. The Brewer firm, on the other hand, was sitting peachy: just before the NRA filed, Wayne authorized $17.5 million to the law firm so that it wouldn't be a creditor during the process. In fact, in less than three years, the NRA paid a whopping $72 million in legal fees to Brewer and his firm—and that's before the costly legal fees associated with representing the NRA during the bankruptcy trial.

The National Rifle Association has traditionally claimed a membership of between 5 and 6 million, up from 2.9 million in 1993. When Wayne was forced to testify under oath as to his organization's actual membership in 2021, he said that it was around 4.9 million, with 2.5 million life members. This puts the NRA's current membership at less than where it was five years ago.

But those numbers don't tell the whole story. The NRA has managed to attract millions more to its culture war. Millions have taken the NRA's firearms courses—and thus identify as members in polls. And still other Americans who are not technically dues-paying members of the organization associate with the association because of its interpretation of the Second Amendment.

It is hard to argue that the NRA, as an organization focused on advocacy, is unsuccessful. After a psychopath murdered children at Sandy Hook Elementary, the group was ruthlessly effective in torpedoing gun reform legislation. Firearms can now be conceal carried in all fifty states. In 1986, when Wayne was a mere lobbyist at the NRA, that number was just nine. Today nearly 13 million people carry concealed handguns—and 3 million people do so on a daily basis. The NRA remains a powerhouse lobbying force on Capitol Hill and a force to be reckoned with in state capitals. Despite the scandals, the NRA and its ideological allies outspent gun control groups like Everytown in the 2020 cycle, reversing the trend from 2018.

It is corruption and financial mismanagement that have threatened the NRA's stability. But to its opponents' chagrin, the whole situation could be turned around with dedicated management. And its core strength—the passion of millions of members—will remain there to be mobilized if and when it does turn around.

Wayne was entitled but not egotistical. In his self-pity he had come to the conclusion that he had earned the gadgets and meals and shiny jets, because the suffering that had come from his anxieties around his job had been such a burden to bear. He was never overly confident, he was never arrogant—if anything, he was too insecure to be an executive of any kind.

You might wonder how many more million members the NRA would have today if it'd had a minimally competent CEO over the past thirty years. When Wayne took over in the early '90s, the NRA had 2.5 million members and a budget of around $87 million. Membership, while down from its peak, has grown, as has its influence.

I've read almost every long-form feature and article about the NRA over the past twenty years, and virtually every one, from the *Washington City Paper* to *Time* to *Vanity Fair*, predicted that the NRA could soon hit its lowest point and might be doomed to destruction: in the late 1990s after the board revolt, in 2000 after

Columbine, and in 2013 post–Sandy Hook. The NRA has not only survived but grown by the millions. To study the NRA is to see its remarkable resilience in the face of near bankruptcy, condemnation, scandal, and internal dissension. Wayne has also shown an unbelievable ability to hang on, to swing from patron to patron—somehow surviving despite his every character flaw.

"I've known Wayne for a long, long time, and he's in such a hole," said NRA board member Phillip Journey. "I don't see how he gets out." So far, he's found a way to endure. As of this writing, Wayne LaPierre remains the EVP and CEO of the National Rifle Association. Meanwhile, *The Wall Street Journal* has reported that the IRS is investigating Wayne for possible tax fraud.

Acknowledgments

The journey that led to this book began with an unusual tip four years ago about a student at American University named Maria Butina. That breakfast meeting had implications beyond my wildest expectations. Both on that day and in the years since, individuals with much to risk have entrusted me with their stories. I am grateful first and foremost for them; this book could not have been written otherwise.

I also want to acknowledge the drill sergeants in my life, both real and figurative. I owe my career to David and Danielle, who over a decade ago took a chance on a recent college graduate with no journalism experience—and for some reason hired me to be a reporter. Their trust, friendship, and mentorship have been key guiding lights for all my adult life. Noah taught me how to craft a story, and how to develop my investigative instincts, which to this day remain the sharpest tools in my journalistic kit.

Over the years-long process of writing this book, my friends have been a constant source of advice and camaraderie. Swin, Byron, and Sahil have listened to my long laments about this project and other outstanding issues—thank you for your patience! Matt and Connor read early drafts and set this book in the right direction. Steve was the best technical adviser a reporter could ever ask for.

I'm very grateful for the efforts of my agents at Javelin, Keith and Matt, who cheered me on despite initial setbacks with the project. Farahn was a perpetual source of laughter and wisdom. Brent, my editor at Dutton, broke land-speed records in order to edit the manuscript on tight deadlines—and never once held it against me for missing the deadlines he had to set for me! I also had an excellent team of researchers assisting me: Ed delved deep into records on my behalf, and Will performed the Herculean task of fact-checking the whole book under arduous time constraints.

There's also no doubt that this telling of the NRA's story benefited from the hard work of other reporters on this beat who churned out incredible reporting, including but not limited to Mike Spies, Mark Maremont, Andrew Jenks, Zak Levitt, and Steve Gutowski.

Finally I want to say thanks to my colleagues at NPR who made this possible. The editors, producers, reporters, and lawyers there are absolutely top-notch, and I learn from them every time we collaborate or review a story for publication.

On every single page of this book, there's evidence of how my colleagues, mentors, and friends have helped shape me personally and professionally. I hope the product is worthy of their efforts and sacrifices.

Notes

The citations below refer to material around the key words displayed.

INTRODUCTION

1   **thanks to his nonprofit organization:** People of the State of New York v. National Rifle Association, Supreme Court of the State of New York, County of New York, "Summons and Complaint," Index No. 451625/2020.

2   **"I'm prepared to do it":** Danny Hakim, "Inside Wayne LaPierre's Battle for the N.R.A.," *New York Times Magazine*, December 18, 2019.

2   **sales rep named Noah:** Wayne LaPierre testimony, United States Bankruptcy Court for the Northern District of Texas Dallas Division, Case 21-30085, April 7, 2021.

3   **"for a number of years":** Wayne LaPierre, confidential deposition, September 24, 2019.

3   **at the age of seventy-five:** Hakim, "Inside Wayne LaPierre's Battle for the N.R.A."

CHAPTER 1: WAYNE

8   **four months prior to this date:** W. LaPierre v. D. LaPierre, Virginia Circuit Court, Alexandria City, CH980109.

9   **called him a brother:** Mildred Hallow, confidential deposition, January 10, 2020.

9   **Oliver North, the Iran-Contra figure:** Wayne LaPierre testimony, United States Bankruptcy Court for the Northern District of Texas Dallas Division, Case 21-30085, April 8, 2021; Oliver Laurence North, confidential deposition, December 18, 2019.

9   **the accused (though never charged) embezzler:** Mike Spies, "The N.R.A.'s Longtime C.F.O. Was Caught Embezzling Before Joining the Organization, Former Colleagues Say," *New Yorker,* June 19, 2019.

10   **firearm-free household:** Gregg Zoroya, "On the Defensive: Amid Both Political and Public Turmoil, NRA Chief Wayne LaPierre Has Stood Fast. But the Strains of Combat—from Within as Well as Without—Are Showing," Sunday Profile, *Los Angeles Times,* June 25, 1995.

10   **father's alma mater:** "Siena Alumni News 1972 Annual Fund Report," *Siena College,* 1972.

10   **New York state legislator:** Zoroya, "On the Defensive."

10   **for this is unknown:** David Emery, "Did NRA Leader Wayne LaPierre Receive a Draft Deferment for a 'Nervous Disorder'?," *Snopes,* February 21, 2018.

10   **developmentally disabled students:** Zoroya, "On the Defensive."

10   **Virginia state legislature:** Joshua L. Powell, *Inside the NRA,* p. 52.

10   **from Boston College:** Zoroya, "On the Defensive."

11   **"backbone of a chocolate eclair":** Michael Powell, "The NRA's Call to Arms," *Washington Post,* August 6, 2000.

11   **was the right decision:** Powell, *Inside the NRA,* p. 88.

11   **"Your life goes by":** Zoroya, "On the Defensive."

11   **nonprofit organization's dime:** People of the State of New York v. National Rifle Association, Supreme Court of the State of New York, County of New York, "Summons and Complaint," Index No. 451625/2020.

12   **House Speaker Tip O'Neill:** Zoroya, "On the Defensive."

12   **across the street:** Wayne LaPierre testimony, United States Bankruptcy Court for the Northern District of Texas Dallas Division, Case 21-30085, April 29, 2021.

12   **his wrinkled suits:** Richard Feldman, *Ricochet: Confessions of a Gun Lobbyist,* p. 64.

12   **lobbying the next year:** "Wayne LaPierre," American Association of Political Consultants, theaapc.org/about-us/board-of-directors/wayne-lapierre/.

13   **LaPierre recalled later in an interview:** Zoroya, "On the Defensive."

13   **two of you were talking:** Powell, *Inside the NRA,* p. 51.

14   **meaning of the notes:** Mildred Hallow, confidential deposition, January 10, 2020.

14   **depending on the topic:** Mildred Hallow, confidential deposition, January 10, 2020.

15   **often organized by year:** Wayne LaPierre, confidential deposition, September 24, 2019.

15   **"with the attorneys now":** Wayne LaPierre, confidential deposition, September 24, 2019.

15   **use computers at all:** Wayne LaPierre deposition, United States Bankruptcy Court for the Northern District of Texas Dallas Division, Case 21-30085, March 22, 2021.

15   **messages that might interest him:** Mildred Hallow, confidential deposition, January 10, 2020.

16 **his rifle around carelessly:** Tim Dickinson, "The NRA vs. America," *Rolling Stone*, June 25, 2018.
16 **"go hunting with Wayne":** Dickinson, "The NRA vs. America."
16 **leaked to *The New Yorker*:** Mike Spies, "The Secret Footage of the N.R.A. Chief's Botched Elephant Hunt," *New Yorker*, April 27, 2021.
17 **with Wayne described him:** Feldman, *Ricochet*, p. 191.

CHAPTER 2: "JUST A VOLUNTEER"

18 **support of Trump's candidacy:** Robert Maguire, "Audit Shows NRA Spending Surged $100 Million Amidst Pro-Trump Push in 2016," OpenSecrets.org, November 15, 2017.
18 **leading pro-Trump super PAC:** Mike Spies and Ashley Balcerzak, "The NRA Placed Big Bets on the 2016 Election, and Won Almost All of Them," OpenSecrets.org, November 9, 2016.
18 **National Park Foundation board instead:** "Susan LaPierre," National Park Foundation, https://www.nationalparks.org/sites/default/files/susan-lapierre.pdf.
18 **leaked video showing:** Spies, "The Secret Footage of the N.R.A. Chief's Botched Elephant Hunt."
19 **stools for the LaPierres:** Spies, "The Secret Footage of the N.R.A. Chief's Botched Elephant Hunt."
19 **"no management style at all":** Josh Powell, *Inside the NRA*, p. 45.
20 **budget came from multiple pots:** People of the State of New York v. National Rifle Association, Supreme Court of the State of New York, County of New York, "Summons and Complaint," Index No. 451625/2020; Wayne LaPierre, confidential deposition, September 24, 2019.
21 **motel in Waukesha County:** Tom Rickert, "Highway 16 Plans Upset Those Whose Homes Are in the Way," *Waukesha Daily Freeman*, December 13, 1973.
21 **Blue Mound Court Motel:** "'Race Track' Unpopular," *Waukesha Daily Freeman*, June 4, 1974.
21 **went off to college:** Wisconsin Death Index, ancestry.com.
21 **joined the Gamma Phi Beta sorority:** *Wisconsin Badger 93* (1980): p. 229.
21 **space shuttle *Columbia* disaster:** Rob Golub, "Clark's Sorority Sisters in Town to Honor Their Friend," *Journal Times*, February 4, 2003.
21 **ultimately earn a degree:** National Student Clearinghouse, https://www.studentclearinghouse.org.
21 **GOP's finance director in Wisconsin:** *State of Wisconsin Blue Book, 1987–1988*, p. 827.
21 **D.C., in the 1980s:** "Newlyweds to Settle in Nation's Capital," *Wisconsin State Journal*, September 6, 1987.
21 **worked in political fundraising:** *National Smokers' Alliance Weekly Report as of March 25, 1994*, Marketing to Youth MSA Collection, University of California, San Francisco, https://www.industrydocuments.ucsf.edu/docs/#id=yjmj0045; Dennis W. Johnson, *No Place for*

Amateurs: How Political Consultants Are Reshaping American Democracy, p. 269.

22   **on hair and makeup:** Betsy Swan, "NRA Spent Tens of Thousands on Hair and Makeup for CEO's Wife," *Daily Beast,* August 16, 2019.

22   **realize the pattern:** Note: Susan LaPierre is not a defendant in the New York attorney general's complaint. However, the complaint does outline allegations of financial impropriety involving Susan LaPierre.

22   **use Brady Wardlaw:** Wayne LaPierre, confidential deposition, September 24, 2019.

22   **and Taylor Swift:** Bradley Wardlaw bio, John David Agency, http://www .johndavidagency.com/brady-wardlaw-bio.

22   **for three events:** People of the State of New York v. National Rifle Association, Supreme Court of the State of New York, County of New York, "Summons and Complaint," Index No. 451625/2020.

23   **"with the Women's Leadership Forum":** People of the State of New York v. National Rifle Association, Supreme Court of the State of New York, County of New York, "Summons and Complaint," Index No. 451625/2020.

23   **that did "special projects":** People of the State of New York v. National Rifle Association, Supreme Court of the State of New York, County of New York, "Summons and Complaint," Index No. 451625/2020.

24   **"overly interested in money":** Richard Feldman, *Ricochet: Confessions of a Gun Lobbyist,* p. 190.

24   **"altogether to flaunt it":** Feldman, *Ricochet: Confessions of a Gun Lobbyist,* p. 190.

25   **assistant and his wife:** Wayne LaPierre, confidential deposition, September 24, 2019.

25   **and send it:** Powell, *Inside the NRA,* p. 205.

25   **with him to the Mayo Clinic:** Tony Makris testimony, United States Bankruptcy Court for the Northern District of Texas Dallas Division, Case 21-30085, April 16, 2021.

25   **$2.2 million in 2018:** Danny Hakim, "Inside Wayne LaPierre's Battle for the N.R.A.," *New York Times Magazine,* December 18, 2019.

25   **by CharityWatch:** "Top Charity Compensation Packages," CharityWatch, https://www.charitywatch.org/top-charity-salaries.

25   **according to the NY AG:** People of the State of New York v. National Rifle Association, Supreme Court of the State of New York County of New York, "Summons and Complaint," Index No. 451625/2020.

26   **Wayne doesn't go to jail:** Tony Makris testimony, United States Bankruptcy Court for the Northern District of Texas Dallas Division, Case 21-30085, April 16, 2021.

CHAPTER 3: THE NRA's FIEFDOMS

27   **Washington, D.C., in 1993:** Maryann Haggerty, "The New Owner of the Old NRA Building Has a Load of Options," *Washington Post,* May 27, 1996.

27   **since opening day:** Daniella Byck, "An Italian Restaurant Is Celebrating Its 40th Anniversary with 1979 Prices," *Washingtonian*, October 28, 2019.

28   **was eight years old:** Tony Makris testimony, United States Bankruptcy Court for the Northern District of Texas Dallas Division, Case 21-30085, April 16, 2021.

28   **NRA president Charlton Heston:** Ed Leibowitz, "Charlton Heston's Last Stand," *Los Angeles*, February 1, 2001.

28   **Wayne's inner circle:** Tony Makris testimony, United States Bankruptcy Court for the Northern District of Texas Dallas Division, Case 21-30085, April 16, 2021.

28   **private room there:** Josh Powell, *Inside the NRA*, p. 43.

29   **future ambiguous reimbursement:** Tony Makris testimony, United States Bankruptcy Court for the Northern District of Texas Dallas Division, Case 21-30085, April 16, 2021.

29   **$140,000 worth of food:** Tony Makris testimony, United States Bankruptcy Court for the Northern District of Texas Dallas Division, Case 21-30085, April 16, 2021.

29   **billed back to the NRA:** Andrew Jenks, "Down to the Studs," *Gangster Capitalism*, May 6, 2020, https://shows.cadence13.com/podcast/gangster -capitalism/episodes/2ef5a2ab-7a5d-4f86-9c60-f509dafea088.

29   **New York AG found:** People of the State of New York v. The National Rifle Association, Supreme Court of the State of New York, County of New York, "Summons and Complaint," Index No. 451625/2020.

29   **through Ackerman McQueen:** People of the State of New York v. The National Rifle Association, Supreme Court of the State of New York, County of New York, "Summons and Complaint," Index No. 451625/ 2020.

31   **"been like this forever":** Powell, *Inside the NRA*, p. 95.

32   **simply as "the Building":** Powell, *Inside the NRA*, p. 45.

32   **to as "the Royals":** Powell, *Inside the NRA*, p. 46.

32   **displayed in plain sight:** Powell, *Inside the NRA*, p. 47.

32   **550 full-time employees:** People of the State of New York v. The National Rifle Association, Supreme Court of the State of New York, County of New York, "Summons and Complaint," Index No. 451625/2020.

32   **HQ on the fifth floor:** Powell, *Inside the NRA*, p. 47.

32   **had seventy-eight staffers:** Powell, *Inside the NRA*, p. 53.

32   **of the group's employees:** Powell, *Inside the NRA*, p. 45; People of the State of New York v. The National Rifle Association, Supreme Court of the State of New York, County of New York, "Summons and Complaint," Index No. 451625/2020.

32   **This division was led from 2002:** Frank Smyth, *The NRA: The Unauthorized History*, p. 159.

33   **John Tanner of Tennessee:** Smyth, *The NRA*, p. 159.

33   **"don't want to upset Chris":** Powell, *Inside the NRA*, p. 54.

33 **own advocacy projects:** John Frazer, confidential deposition, January 16, 2020.

35 **a technical consultant found a device:** Richard Feldman, *Ricochet: Confessions of a Gun Lobby*ist, p. 197.

35 **quipped Neal Knox:** Smyth, *The NRA*, p. 135.

35 **charge expenses to the NRA:** People of the State of New York v. The National Rifle Association, Supreme Court of the State of New York, County of New York, "Summons and Complaint," Index No. 451625/2020.

35 **additional special committees:** John Frazer, confidential deposition, January 16, 2020.

36 **"Chris Cox's lobbying efforts":** Powell, *Inside the NRA*, p. 40.

36 **organization's best interest:** People of the State of New York v. The National Rifle Association, Supreme Court of the State of New York, County of New York, "Summons and Complaint," Index No. 451625/2020.

37 **number of antique firearms:** Danny Hakim, "Inside Wayne LaPierre's Battle for the N.R.A.," *New York Times Magazine*, December 18, 2019.

37 **television hunting program:** Mark Maremont, "Celebrity Board Members Engaged in Big-Ticket Transactions with NRA," *Wall Street Journal*, November 12, 2019.

37 **over a year later:** Maremont, "Celebrity Board Members Engaged in Big-Ticket Transactions."

37 **in recent years:** Beth Reinhard and Katie Zezima, "NRA Money Flowed to Board Members amid Allegedly Lavish Spending by Top Officials and Vendors," *Washington Post*, June 13, 2019.

37 **in the six figures:** Reinhard and Zezima, "NRA Money Flowed to Board Members."

37 **Butz's actual work:** People of the State of New York v. The National Rifle Association, Supreme Court of the State of New York, County of New York, "Summons and Complaint," Index No. 451625/2020.

37 **against New York law:** People of the State of New York v. The National Rifle Association, Supreme Court of the State of New York, County of New York, "Summons and Complaint," Index No. 451625/2020.

37 **sports a bowl haircut:** Andrew Jenks, "Enough Is Enough," *Gangster Capitalism*, April 29, 2020, https://shows.cadence13.com/podcast/gangster -capitalism/episodes/fa40ba46-3e3f-4994-b754-486cb7d4dbc3.

37 **$220,000 a year:** Wayne LaPierre, confidential deposition, September 24, 2019.

37 **without the board's knowledge:** Mark Maremont, "NRA Board Retroactively Approved Transactions Benefiting Insiders," *Wall Street Journal*, September 23, 2019.

38 **he had signed the contract:** Wayne LaPierre, confidential deposition, September 24, 2019.

38 **"She really is":** Wayne LaPierre, confidential deposition, September 24, 2019.

38 **know Angus in 1984:** Wayne LaPierre, confidential deposition, September 24, 2019.

39   **cofounded by his father:** Danny Hakim, "Angus McQueen, the N.R.A.'s Image Maker, Dies at 74," *New York Times*, July 19, 2019.

39   **"genius quality," Wayne explained:** Wayne LaPierre, confidential deposition, September 24, 2019.

39   **Wayne's first call:** Tony Makris testimony, United States Bankruptcy Court for the Northern District of Texas Dallas Division, Case 21-30085, April 16, 2021.

39   **his yellow legal pads:** Tony Makris testimony, United States Bankruptcy Court for the Northern District of Texas Dallas Division, Case 21-30085, April 16, 2021.

39   **Angus once told Wayne:** Powell, *Inside the NRA*, p. 87.

40   **business relationship started:** Bill Winkler testimony, United States Bankruptcy Court for the Northern District of Texas Dallas Division, Case 21-30085, April 16, 2021.

40   **25 employees to 250:** Hakim, "Angus McQueen."

40   **and crisis management:** National Rifle Association v. Ackerman McQueen, United States District Court for the Northern District of Texas, Dallas Division, "Declaration of Revan McQueen," Civil Action No. 3:19-cv-02074-G, March 30, 2020, https://nrawatch.org/filing/declaration -of-revan-mcqueen-appendix-to-ackerman-brief-to-disqualify-nra -attorney-bill-brewer-from-the-case/; McConnell v. Federal Election Commission, United States Supreme Court, 2002.

40   **known as "earned media":** McConnell v. Federal Election Commission, United States Supreme Court, 2002.

42   **"wasn't afraid to show it":** Powell, *Inside the NRA*, p. 81.

CHAPTER 4: THE NRA BEFORE SANDY HOOK

43   **J. Warren Cassidy once said:** Richard Lacayo, "Under Fire," *Time*, June 24, 2001.

43   **or the Boy Scouts:** Frank Smyth, *The NRA: The Unauthorized History*, p. 1.

44   **in their soldiers:** Osha Gray Davidson, *Under Fire*, p. 21.

44   **shotguns and silencers:** Smyth, *The NRA*, p. 50.

44   **sale of handguns:** Michael Powell, "The NRA's Call to Arms," *Washington Post*, August 6, 2000.

44   **loaded weapons in public:** Sarah Ellison, "The Civil War That Could Doom the N.R.A.," *Vanity Fair*, June 27, 2016.

44   **NRA supported him:** Smyth, *The NRA*, p. 74.

44   **"being mentally unsound":** Smyth, *The NRA*, p. 76.

44   **out of the organization's name:** Ellison, "The Civil War That Could Doom the N.R.A."

44   **headquarters to Colorado:** Joel Achenbach, Scott Higham, and Sari Horwitz, "How NRA's True Believers Converted a Marksmanship Group into a Mighty Gun Lobby," *Washington Post*, January 12, 2013.

45   **with walkie-talkies:** Smyth, *The NRA*, p. 98.

45 **bright orange hunting caps:** Ellison, "The Civil War That Could Doom the N.R.A."

45 **until 3:30 A.M.:** Achenbach, Higham, and Horwitz, "How NRA's True Believers Converted a Marksmanship Group."

45 **get them to disperse:** Achenbach, Higham, and Horwitz, "How NRA's True Believers Converted a Marksmanship Group."

45 **changes to the NRA's bylaws:** Achenbach, Higham, and Horwitz, "How NRA's True Believers Converted a Marksmanship Group."

45 **fighting gun control laws:** Achenbach, Higham, and Horwitz, "How NRA's True Believers Converted a Marksmanship Group."

45 **Ackerman McQueen in its stead:** Mary Thornton, "Bloodletting at the Gun Lobby," *Washington Post*, May 20, 1986.

46 **contacts were superior:** Richard Feldman, *Ricochet: Confessions of a Gun Lobbyist*, p. 127.

46 **raise of more than $13,000:** "National Rifle Association Accusations of Race and Sex Discrimination at Bureau of Alcohol, Tobacco, and Firearms 'Lesson in Hypocrisy,'" Violence Policy Center.

46 **him shortly thereafter:** Thornton, "Bloodletting at the Gun Lobby."

46 **public affairs work:** Feldman, *Ricochet*, pp. 128–29.

46 **after a female staffer accused:** Feldman, *Ricochet*, p. 187.

46 **by an interim EVP:** Feldman, *Ricochet*, p. 188.

46 **wanted to stay in ILA:** Wayne LaPierre testimony, United States Bankruptcy Court for the Northern District of Texas Dallas Division, Case 21-30085, April 29, 2021.

46 **"Wayne was bland":** Feldman, *Ricochet*, pp. 189, 191.

46 **"we'll all back you":** Wayne LaPierre testimony, United States Bankruptcy Court for the Northern District of Texas Dallas Division, Case 21-30085, April 29, 2021.

46 **Despite never aspiring to the role:** Gregg Zoroya, "On the Defensive: Amid Both Political and Public Turmoil, NRA Chief Wayne LaPierre Has Stood Fast. But the Strains of Combat—from Within as Well as Without—Are Showing," Sunday Profile, *Los Angeles Times*, June 25, 1995.

46 **gun rights lobbying group:** "Join AAPC," American Association of Political Consultants, theaapc.org/about-us/board-of-directors/wayne-lapierre/.

47 **all without written contracts:** Tom Stabile, "Ready Fire Aim," *Washington City Paper*, August 15, 1997.

47 **following the 1994 elections:** John Mintz, "Ideological War Pits NRA Hard-Liners Against More Moderate Staff," *Washington Post*, May 29, 1995.

47 **long-term investment portfolio:** Stabile, "Ready Fire Aim."

47 **more than $85 million:** Neal Knox, *Gun Rights War* (ebook), p. 919.

47 **the audit stated:** Stabile, "Ready Fire Aim."

47 **written contracts in place:** Knox, *Gun Rights War*, p. 962.

47 **purchase a life membership:** Stabile, "Ready Fire Aim."

47 **Knox wrote at the time:** Knox, *Gun Rights War*, p. 930.

48 **that LaPierre fire Ackerman McQueen:** Powell, "The NRA's Call to Arms."

48   **subsidiary of Ackerman McQueen:** Mike Spies, "Secrecy, Self-Dealing, and Greed at the N.R.A.," *New Yorker*, April 17, 2019.

48   **able to turn back the tide:** Knox, *Gun Rights War*, p. 933.

48   **bribe from the Knox camp:** Powell, "The NRA's Call to Arms."

48   **Knox lost by just four votes:** Knox, *Gun Rights War*, p. 933.

48   **"fewer signs up," she said:** Mildred Hallow, confidential deposition, January 10, 2020.

49   **Regnery's forty-seven-year history:** David Streitfeld, "Writers of the Right," *Washington Post*, December 20, 1994.

49   **making him a conservative:** Julia Ioffe, "How an Obscure Senate Aide Became Trump's Intellectual Architect," *Politico*, June 27, 2016.

49   ***New York Times* bestseller list:** Chantal Da Silva, "This NRA Book Turned a Young Stephen Miller into a Conservative," *Newsweek*, August 14, 2018.

49   **nearly a city a day:** Mildred Hallow, confidential deposition, January 10, 2020.

50   **then never renewed:** Stabile, "Ready Fire Aim."

50   **"Never Reelected Again":** Feldman, *Ricochet*, p. 177.

51   **told *The Washington Post* in 2000:** Powell, "The NRA's Call to Arms."

51   **NRA vendor PM Consulting:** Richard Keil, "The NRA's Mail Bomb," *Mother Jones*, September–October 1995; Mintz, "Ideological War Pits NRA Hard-Liners Against More Moderate Staff."

51   **"attack law-abiding citizens":** "NRA Official Defends Terms Used in Letter," *Washington Post*, May 1, 1995.

51   **Bush wrote in his letter of resignation:** "Letter of Resignation Sent by Bush to Rifle Association," *New York Times*, May 11, 1995.

51   **McCain-Feingold campaign finance reforms:** Kevin Drew, "Campaign Finance Highlights Next Supreme Court Session," CNN, June 29, 2003.

52   **presidential candidates reliably:** Smyth, *The NRA*, p. 174.

52   **Reid was also a gun owner:** Draper, "Inside the Power of the N.R.A."

52   **"Shut the fuck up":** Tim Dickinson, "The NRA vs. America," *Rolling Stone*, June 25, 2018.

52   **quarter of the party's caucus:** Maggie Astor and Weiyi Cai, "The N.R.A. Has Trump. But It Has Lost Allies in Congress," *New York Times*, August 26, 2019.

53   **had dwindled to three:** Astor and Cai, "The N.R.A Has Trump."

CHAPTER 6: SANDY HOOK

57   **In the course of eleven minutes:** "Sandy Hook School Shootings Fast Facts," CNN, June 7, 2013.

57   **rifle and two handguns:** "Sandy Hook School Shootings Fast Facts," CNN, June 7, 2013.

57   **hands and close their eyes:** Mark Memmott, "Tragedy in Connecticut: 20 Children, 6 Adults Killed at Elementary School," NPR, December 14, 2012.

58   **in blood from head to toe:** Matthew Lysiak, *Newtown: An American Tragedy*, p. 121.

58   **first responder crying out for help:** Lysiak, *Newtown*, p. 119.

58   **into contact with the group:** Frank Smyth, *The NRA: The Unauthorized History*, p. 197.

61   **remarks at the Willard InterContinental:** Carol D. Leonnig, Beth Reinhard, and Tom Hamburger, "Newtown Massacre Divided NRA Leaders, Foreshadowing Split to Come," *Washington Post*, July 9, 2019.

62   **"Period," he said:** Jon Greenberg, "Did NRA's LaPierre Once Call for Gun-Free Schools?," PolitiFact, February 23, 2018; Chris Sommerfeldt, "Wayne LaPierre's CPAC Speech Sharply Contradicts His Own 1999 Remarks: 'No Guns in America's Schools, Period,'" New York *Daily News*, April 7, 2018.

62   **police or security guards:** Greenberg, "Did NRA's LaPierre Once Call for Gun-Free Schools?"

63   **covered live on cable TV:** Joel Achenbach, Scott Higham, and Sari Horwitz, "How NRA's True Believers Converted a Marksmanship Group into a Mighty Gun Lobby," *Washington Post*, January 12, 2013.

63   **"call me crazy," he said:** Leonnig, Reinhard, and Hamburger, "Newtown Massacre Divided NRA Leaders."

63   **beaches, was almost $70,000:** Leonnig, Reinhard, and Hamburger, "Newtown Massacre Divided NRA Leaders."

64   **emphasize mental health:** Leonnig, Reinhard, and Hamburger, "Newtown Massacre Divided NRA Leaders."

64   **"mental health system":** Chris Cox, Letter to Congress, National Rifle Association of America Institute for Legislative Action, January 3, 2013, https://www.washingtonpost.com/wp-srv/business/documents/cox-letter.pdf.

65   **wife's interior design business:** Avery Anapol, "NRA Lobbyist Says His Home Has Been Vandalized Twice," The Hill, April 21, 2018.

66   **immediately after the shooting:** Achenbach, Higham, and Horwitz, "How NRA's True Believers Converted a Marksmanship."

66   **discounts for fresh recruits:** Robert Draper, "Inside the Power of the N.R.A.," *New York Times,* December 12, 2013.

Chapter 7: Manchin-Toomey Collapses

68   **They had been swatted:** Calls for Service Report, Fairfax County Police Department, April 4, 2013; Wayne LaPierre, confidential deposition, September 24, 2019.

68   **"almost a year":** Josh Powell, *Inside the NRA*, p. 150.

69   **"another elitist hypocrite":** Phillip Rucker, "NRA's New Ad Calls Obama 'Elitist Hypocrite,'" *Washington Post*, January 15, 2013.

69   **lobbyists about it first:** Mike Spies, "Secrecy, Self-Dealing, and Greed at the N.R.A.," *New Yorker*, April 17, 2019.

69   **had been "ill-advised":** Mario Trujillo, "NRA Official Calls Group's Ad on Obama's Children 'Ill-Advised,'" The Hill, January 25, 2013.

69 **Joe Biden recommended:** Phillip Rucker and Peter Wallsten, "Biden's Gun Task Force Met with All Sides, but Kept Its Eye on the Target," *Washington Post*, January 19, 2013.

70 **to bury the proposal:** Richard Simon, "Senate Votes Down Feinstein's Assault Weapons Ban," *Los Angeles Times*, April 17, 2013.

70 **from a hunting trip:** Robert Draper, "Inside the Power of the N.R.A.," *New York Times*, December 12, 2013.

70 **households own firearms:** Terry L. Schell, Samuel Peterson, Brian G. Vegetabile, Adam Scherling, Rosanna Smart, and Andrew R. Morral, "State-Level Estimates of Household Firearm Ownership," RAND Corporation, 2020.

70 **more than 90 percent:** Eyder Peralta, "Poll: 9 in 10 Americans Support Background Check for All Gun Sales," NPR, February 7, 2013.

70 **whom supported the idea:** W. Gardner Selby, "Lee Leffingwell Says Polls Show 90 Percent of Americans and 74 Percent of NRA Members Support Criminal Background Checks Before All Gun Buys," PolitiFact, April 4, 2013.

70 **ask about universal background checks:** Draper, "Inside the Power of the N.R.A."

70 **in part to NRA opposition:** Draper, "Inside the Power of the N.R.A."

71 **sparked an amicable conversation:** Colby Itkowitz, "How Pat Toomey Brokered Gun Control Deal," *Morning Call*, April 13, 2013.

71 **on gun legislation:** Itkowitz, "How Pat Toomey Brokered Gun Control Deal."

71 **of a gun reform bill:** Itkowitz, "How Pat Toomey Brokered Gun Control Deal."

71 **chain founded by two Pennsylvanians:** Itkowitz, "How Pat Toomey Brokered Gun Control Deal."

72 **in-person meetings in March:** Draper, "Inside the Power of the N.R.A."

73 **decade prior had the NRA's support:** Tom Hamburger and Ed O'Keefe, "Gun Rights Group Endorses Manchin-Toomey," *Washington Post*, April 14, 2013.

73 **had told Congress in 1999:** Frank Smyth, *The NRA: The Unauthorized History*, p. 159.

74 **found its way to the press:** Itkowitz, "How Pat Toomey Brokered Gun Control Deal."

74 **formally announced to the public:** Itkowitz, "How Pat Toomey Brokered Gun Control Deal."

74 **portion of the bill:** Heidi Przybyla, "How the NRA Undercut the Last Big Gun Reform Effort," NBC News, March 1, 2018.

74 **included allowing interstate handgun sales:** Molly Moorhead, "A Summary of the Manchin-Toomey Gun Proposal," PolitiFact, April 30, 2013.

75 **background check system:** Moorhead, "A Summary of the Manchin-Toomey Gun Proposal."

75 **they are hunting in:** Hamburger and O'Keefe, "Gun Rights Group Endorses Manchin-Toomey."

75 **prohibiting a national gun registry:** Hamburger and O'Keefe, "Gun Rights Group Endorses Manchin-Toomey."

75 **talks over background checks:** Manu Raju and John Bresnahan, "Manchin, NRA Talking," *Politico*, March 23, 2013.

76 **to voice their opinion:** Draper, "Inside the Power of the N.R.A."

76 **NRA had stopped negotiating with Manchin's office:** Draper, "Inside the Power of the N.R.A."

76 **"not keep our kids safe in schools":** "Statement from the National Rifle Association Regarding Toomey-Manchin Background Check Proposal," National Rifle Association of America Institute for Legislative Action, April 10, 2013.

76 **from the gun rights group:** Carol D. Leonnig, Beth Reinhard, and Tom Hamburger, "Newtown Massacre Divided NRA Leaders, Foreshadowing Split to Come," *Washington Post*, July 9, 2019.

76 **He never got a straight answer:** Draper, "Inside the Power of the N.R.A."

77 **states joined Republicans to oppose:** U.S. Senate, "Roll Call Vote, 113th Congress in 1st Session: On the Amendment (Manchin Amdt. No. 715)," April 17, 2013, https://www.senate.gov/legislative/LIS/roll_call_lists/roll_call_vote_cfm.cfm?congress=113&session=1&vote=00097.

77 **Gottlieb said at the time:** "CCRKBA Pulls Support of Manchin-Toomey Alternative Over Rights Restoration," Citizens Committee for the Right to Keep and Bear Arms, April 17, 2013.

77 **Biden presiding over the chamber:** Jonathan Tamari, "Senate Rejects Toomey-Manchin Gun Bill; 'Shameful Day,' Says Obama," *Philadelphia Inquirer,* April 18, 2013.

77 **54 votes for to 46 opposed:** U.S. Senate, "Roll Call Vote 113th Congress in 1st Session."

77 **Sandy Hook Elementary School:** Tamari, "Senate Rejects Toomey-Manchin Gun Bill."

78 **rewarded for his *no* vote:** U.S. Senate, "Roll Call Vote 113th Congress in 1st Session."

78 **Pryor's opponent, Senator Tom Cotton:** "NRA Endorses Tom Cotton for U.S. Senate in Arkansas," National Rifle Association of America Political Victory Fund, September 9, 2014.

78 **$100,000 in ads criticizing him:** Przybyla, "How the NRA Undercut the Last Big Gun Reform Effort."

78 **they gave him a D:** Jamie Green and Liz Newton, "Does Joe Manchin Have a D Rating from the National Rifle Association?," PolitiFact, September 28, 2018.

78 **C the next time he was graded:** Laura Olson, "Pat Toomey Draws Lower Grade in New NRA Ratings," *Morning Call*, October 5, 2016.

80 **"federal nightmare bureaucracy":** Liz Halloran, "LaPierre Fights to Stop the 'Nightmare' of Background Checks," NPR, January 30, 2013.

80 **with very few people:** Mildred Hallow, confidential deposition, January 10, 2020.

80   **began flying on private jets:** Mildred Hallow, confidential deposition, January 10, 2020.

81   **broader "culture war":** Sarah Ellison, "The Civil War That Could Doom the N.R.A.," *Vanity Fair,* June 27, 2016.

CHAPTER 8: THE RISE OF EVERYTOWN

83   **demonstration in America's capital:** Mark Follman, "These Women Are the NRA's Worst Nightmare," *Mother Jones*, September–October 2014.

85   **narrowly defeated in 2000:** "Hillary Clinton vs. the NRA," *Chicago Tribune*, March 17, 2016.

85   **2004, it was not renewed:** Ron Elving, "The U.S. Once Had a Ban on Assault Weapons—Why Did It Expire?," NPR, August 13, 2019.

85   **received A ratings from the NRA:** Kara Voght, "How Michael Bloomberg Bought the Gun Control Movement," *Mother Jones*, March 3, 2020.

85   **lay off staff to stay afloat:** Kara Voght, "How Michael Bloomberg Bought the Gun Control Movement," *Mother Jones*, March 3, 2020.

86   **some consensus on gun reform:** Sewell Chan, "Mayors Discuss Efforts on Gun Crimes," *New York Times*, April 25, 2006.

87   **said on NBC's *Meet the Press*:** "December 16: Dannel Malloy, Michael Bloomberg, Dianne Feinstein, Bill Bennett, David Brooks, Randi Weingarten, Tom Ridge, Michael Eric Dyson, Pete Williams," *Meet the Press*, transcript, NBC News, December 16, 2012.

88   **brought in $347 million in 2013:** Alex Yablon, "NRA Membership Revenues Dropped by $47 Million After Sandy Hook Surge," *The Trace*, January 23, 2016.

90   **get the group off the ground:** Jeremy W. Peters, "Bloomberg Plans a $50 Million Challenge to the N.R.A.," *New York Times*, April 15, 2014.

91   **"members' fight is won or lost":** Richard Feldman, *Ricochet: Confessions of a Gun Lobbyist*, p. 60.

91   **when the new group started:** Leigh Ann Caldwell, Kevin Bohn, and Ed Payne, "Bloomberg to Spend $50 Million to Challenge NRA on Gun Safety," CNN, April 16, 2014.

91   **who supported gun control measures:** Mara Gay, "Bloomberg's 'Data Guy' Leads His Gun-Control Campaign," *Wall Street Journal*, January 9, 2015.

91   **NRA in the congressional midterms:** Danny Hakim and Rachel Shorey, "Gun Control Groups Eclipse N.R.A. in Election Spending," *New York Times*, November 16, 2018.

CHAPTER 9: WAYNE'S POSSE AND NRA HQ

93   **rising to $32,000 per year:** Tim Mak, "As Leaks Show Lavish NRA Spending, Former Staff Detail Poor Conditions at Nonprofit," NPR, May 15, 2019.

94   **"were horribly underpaid":** Mak, "As Leaks Show Lavish NRA Spending, Former Staff Detail Poor Conditions at Nonprofit."

94 **"comparable position elsewhere":** Mak, "As Leaks Show Lavish NRA Spending, Former Staff Detail Poor Conditions at Nonprofit."

95 **internal travel guidelines read:** People of the State of New York v. The National Rifle Association, Supreme Court of the State of New York, County of New York, "Summons and Complaint," Index No. 451625/2020.

97 **"management by chaos":** Tony Makris testimony, United States Bankruptcy Court for the Northern District of Texas Dallas Division, Case 21-30085, April 16, 2021.

97 **"'this information to me'":** Tony Makris testimony, United States Bankruptcy Court for the Northern District of Texas Dallas Division, Case 21-30085, April 16, 2021.

97 **"decisions," Powell would later recall:** Josh Powell, *Inside the NRA*, pp. 132–33.

98 **appropriate approval from his board:** People of the State of New York v. The National Rifle Association, Supreme Court of the State of New York, County of New York, "Summons and Complaint," Index No. 451625/2020.

98 **whether he actually worked:** Mike Spies, "Secrecy, Self-Dealing, and Greed at the N.R.A.," *New Yorker*, April 17, 2019.

98 **fundraising, the New York AG found:** People of the State of New York v. The National Rifle Association, Supreme Court of the State of New York, County of New York, "Summons and Complaint," Index No. 451625/2020.

98 **international hunting excursions:** People of the State of New York v. The National Rifle Association, Supreme Court of the State of New York, County of New York, "Summons and Complaint," Index No. 451625/2020.

98 **$150,000 lump sum:** Spies, "Secrecy, Self-Dealing, and Greed at the N.R.A."

98 **fired to $1.8 million:** People of the State of New York v. The National Rifle Association, Supreme Court of the State of New York, County of New York, "Summons and Complaint," Index No. 451625/2020.

98 **"Confidentiality and Non-Disparagement":** People of the State of New York v. The National Rifle Association, Supreme Court of the State of New York, County of New York, "Summons and Complaint," Index No. 451625/2020.

98 **"he did or didn't":** People of the State of New York v. The National Rifle Association, Supreme Court of the State of New York, County of New York, "Summons and Complaint," Index No. 451625/2020.

98 **entailed by the payments:** People of the State of New York v. The National Rifle Association, Supreme Court of the State of New York, County of New York, "Summons and Complaint," Index No. 451625/2020.

98 **work under the agreement:** People of the State of New York v. The National Rifle Association, Supreme Court of the State of New York, County of New York, "Summons and Complaint," Index No. 451625/2020.

99 **"NRA income for life":** People of the State of New York v. The National Rifle Association, Supreme Court of the State of New York, County of New York, "Summons and Complaint," Index No. 451625/2020.

99   **Managing Director, Operations Outreach:** Powell, *Inside the NRA*, p. 49.

99   **but never got a degree:** Mildred Hallow, confidential deposition, January 10, 2020.

99   **Wayne's "special assistant":** Mildred Hallow, confidential deposition, January 10, 2020.

99   **quarter million dollars per year:** People of the State of New York v. The National Rifle Association, Supreme Court of the State of New York, County of New York, "Summons and Complaint," Index No. 451625/2020.

100 **Wayne and Chris Cox:** Powell, *Inside the NRA*, p. 49; deposition of John Frazer, January 16, 2020.

100 **St. Pius X Catholic school in Maryland:** Mildred Hallow, confidential deposition, January 10, 2020.

100 **grades one through eight:** Mildred Hallow, confidential deposition, January 10, 2020.

100 **in the summer of 1994:** Mildred Hallow, confidential deposition, January 10, 2020.

100 **no background in gun issues:** Mildred Hallow, confidential deposition, January 10, 2020.

100 **Her salary more than doubled:** Mildred Hallow, confidential deposition, January 10, 2020.

100 **Nowadays she can't remember:** Mildred Hallow, confidential deposition, January 10, 2020.

100 **the theft of $23,691:** Sandra Evans, "Former Arts Official Named Guilty," *Washington Post*, June 6, 1984.

100 **eighteen months in 1982 and 1983:** Evans, "Former Arts Official Named Guilty."

100 **unauthorized bank account to disburse the funds:** Ed Bruske, "Bautista Receives Probation," *Washington Post*, August 18, 1984.

101 **she had falsified her résumé:** Bruske, "Bautista Receives Probation"; Jacqueline Trescott, "After Bautista: Money and the Arts," *Washington Post*, March 25, 1984.

101 **"have placed their faith in me":** Trescott, "After Bautista."

101 **on probation for three years:** Bruske, "Bautista Receives Probation."

101 **"It was an awful and humiliating time":** Mildred Hallow, confidential deposition, January 10, 2020.

101 **charge for more than a decade:** Carolyn Meadows deposition read into evidence, United States Bankruptcy Court for the Northern District of Texas Dallas Division, Case 21-30085, April 20, 2021.

101 **mostly for personal clothing and travel:** Mildred Hallow, confidential deposition, January 10, 2020.

101 **confiscation of her credit card:** Mildred Hallow, confidential deposition, January 10, 2020; People of the State of New York v. The National Rifle Association, Supreme Court of the State of New York, County of New York, "Summons and Complaint," Index No. 451625/20.

101 **she was asked to pay back:** Mildred Hallow, confidential deposition, January 10, 2020.

102 **travel expenses and events:** People of the State of New York v. The National Rifle Association, Supreme Court of the State of New York, County of New York, "Summons and Complaint," Index No. 451625/2020.

102 **to approve her expenses:** People of the State of New York v. The National Rifle Association, Supreme Court of the State of New York, County of New York, "Summons and Complaint," Index No. 451625/2020.

102 **wedding in Elk River, Minnesota:** People of the State of New York v. The National Rifle Association, Supreme Court of the State of New York, County of New York, "Summons and Complaint," Index No. 451625/2020.

102 **Wayne, Susan, and Chris Cox:** Mildred Hallow, confidential deposition, January 10, 2020.

102 **were submitted to the NRA:** Mildred Hallow, confidential deposition, January 10, 2020.

102 **son's wedding expenses:** Mildred Hallow, confidential deposition, January 10, 2020.

102 **affiliated ACU Foundation:** "Meet the Team," American Conservative Union, https://www.conservative.org/about/staff.

102 **"That's completely untrue":** "Wayne LaPierre deposition, United States Bankruptcy Court for the Northern District of Texas Dallas Division, Case 21-30085, March 22, 2021.

102 **chauffeured black cars:** People of the State of New York v. The National Rifle Association, Supreme Court of the State of New York, County of New York, "Summons and Complaint," Index No. 451625/2020.

103 **fundraising trip in France:** People of the State of New York v. The National Rifle Association, Supreme Court of the State of New York, County of New York, "Summons and Complaint," Index No. 451625/2020.

103 **she later acknowledged:** Mildred Hallow, confidential deposition, January 10, 2020.

103 **to perform music:** People of the State of New York v. The National Rifle Association, Supreme Court of the State of New York, County of New York, "Summons and Complaint," Index No. 451625/2020.

103 **diverted $40,000 from the NRA:** John Frazer testimony, United States Bankruptcy Court for the Northern District of Texas Dallas Division, Case 21-30085, April 6, 2021.

103 **forced to pay it all:** John Frazer deposition, United States Bankruptcy Court for the Northern District of Texas Dallas Division, Case 21-30085, March 15, 2021.

103 **wrote in an email:** Mildred Hallow, confidential deposition, January 10, 2020.

103 **"my brain," she testified:** Mildred Hallow, confidential deposition, January 10, 2020.

104 **NRA to check on it:** Wayne LaPierre, confidential deposition, September 24, 2019.

104 **money from his organization:** Wayne LaPierre, confidential deposition, September 24, 2019.

104 **as treasurer and CFO:** People of the State of New York v. The National Rifle Association, Supreme Court of the State of New York, County of New York, "Summons and Complaint," Index No. 451625/2020.

105 **at least $1 million:** Mike Spies, "The N.R.A.'s Longtime C.F.O. Was Caught Embezzling Before Joining the Organization, Former Colleagues Say," *New Yorker*, June 19, 2019.

105 **hadn't received the funds:** Andrew Jenks, "A Clear Crisis," *Gangster Capitalism*, March 25, 2020, https://shows.cadence13.com/podcast/gangster-capitalism/episodes/21414f17-5229-4b7c-919a-223e25fba333.

105 **through fraudulent invoices:** Jenks, "A Clear Crisis"; Spies, "The N.R.A.'s Longtime C.F.O. Was Caught Embezzling."

105 **"Mary, who else knows about this?"** Jenks, "A Clear Crisis."

105 **business if it came out:** Spies, "The N.R.A.'s Longtime C.F.O. Was Caught Embezzling."

105 **also the CFO at Memberdrive:** Spies, "The N.R.A.'s Longtime C.F.O. Was Caught Embezzling."

105 **Susan, worked as an executive:** Vanessa O'Connell, "Marketing Initiative for the NRA Buckles Under Antigun Pressure," *Wall Street Journal*, March 26, 2002.

106 **"'rights—we're doing okay'":** Powell, *Inside the NRA*, p. 59.

106 **most important vendor:** John Frazer, confidential deposition, January 16, 2020.

106 **woman named Nancy Richards:** Mark Maremont, "NRA Board Retroactively Approved Transactions Benefiting Insiders," *Wall Street Journal*, September 23, 2019.

106 **they did not have authority over:** People of the State of New York v. The National Rifle Association, Supreme Court of the State of New York, County of New York, "Summons and Complaint," Index No. 451625/2020.

107 **this kind of misconduct:** People of the State of New York v. The National Rifle Association, Supreme Court of the State of New York, County of New York, "Summons and Complaint," Index No. 451625/2020.

107 **convince him to stay:** Wayne LaPierre, confidential deposition, September 24, 2019.

107 **services for the NRA:** People of the State of New York v. The National Rifle Association, Supreme Court of the State of New York, County of New York, "Summons and Complaint," Index No. 451625/2020.

107 **1994 book tour:** Mildred Hallow, confidential deposition, January 10, 2020.

107 **Charlton Heston had been a client:** Gayle Stanford testimony, United States Bankruptcy Court for the Northern District of Texas Dallas Division, Case 21-30085, April 8, 2021.

107 **she was in her late seventies:** Gayle Stanford testimony, United States Bankruptcy Court for the Northern District of Texas Dallas Division, Case 21-30085, April 8, 2021.

107 **as a travel agent:** Mark Maremont, "NRA's Unusual Travel Setup Spotlights Governance Gaps," *Wall Street Journal*, November 4, 2019.

107 **the lawsuit claimed:** Maremont, "NRA's Unusual Travel Setup Spotlights Governance Gaps."

107 **while denying the allegations:** Maremont, "NRA's Unusual Travel Setup Spotlights Governance Gaps."

108 **investment fraud scheme:** Maremont, "NRA's Unusual Travel Setup Spotlights Governance Gaps."

108 **its internal travel bookings:** Mildred Hallow, confidential deposition, January 10, 2020.

108 **it was for security reasons:** Mildred Hallow, confidential deposition, January 10, 2020.

108 **booked through Gayle's operation:** Mildred Hallow, confidential deposition, January 10, 2020.

108 **fundraising division later testified:** "NRA On Trial: Day 9 Summary of Bankruptcy Trial," NRAWatch, April 22, 2021, https://nrawatch.org/filing/nra-on-trial-day-9-summary-of-bankruptcy-trial/.

108 **never provided a policy:** Gayle Stanford testimony, United States Bankruptcy Court for the Northern District of Texas Dallas Division, Case 21-30085, April 8, 2021.

108 **Wayne about confidentiality:** Gayle Stanford testimony, United States Bankruptcy Court for the Northern District of Texas Dallas Division, Case 21-30085, April 8, 2021.

108 **August 2016 ($11,435):** People of the State of New York v. The National Rifle Association, Supreme Court of the State of New York, County of New York, "Summons and Complaint," Index No. 451625/2020.

108 **Dallas to Orlando ($26,995):** People of the State of New York v. The National Rifle Association, Supreme Court of the State of New York, County of New York, "Summons and Complaint," Index No. 451625/2020.

108 **Kearney, Nebraska ($8,800):** People of the State of New York v. The National Rifle Association, Supreme Court of the State of New York, County of New York, "Summons and Complaint," Index No. 451625/2020.

109 **where Wayne's niece lives:** People of the State of New York v. The National Rifle Association, Supreme Court of the State of New York, County of New York, "Summons and Complaint," Index No. 451625/2020.

109 **"Wayne," his former chief of staff said:** Powell, *Inside the NRA*, pp. 170–71.

109 **no other clients:** Gayle Stanford testimony, United States Bankruptcy Court for the Northern District of Texas Dallas Division, Case 21-30085, April 8, 2021.

109 **as a travel consultant:** People of the State of New York v. The National Rifle Association, Supreme Court of the State of New York, County of New York, "Summons and Complaint," Index No. 451625/2020.

109 **or hotel rooms:** Wayne LaPierre, confidential deposition, September 24, 2019.

109 **$19,000 per month:** People of the State of New York v. The National Rifle Association, Supreme Court of the State of New York, County of New York, "Summons and Complaint," Index No. 451625/2020.

109 **or $318,000 per year:** People of the State of New York v. The National Rifle Association, Supreme Court of the State of New York, County of New York, "Summons and Complaint," Index No. 451625/2020.

109 **would add 10 percent:** Wayne LaPierre testimony, United States Bankruptcy Court for the Northern District of Texas Dallas Division, Case 21-30085, April 8, 2021.

109 **NRA's own rules:** People of the State of New York v. The National Rifle Association, Supreme Court of the State of New York, County of New York, "Summons and Complaint," Index No. 451625/2020.

109 **$13.5 million:** People of the State of New York v. The National Rifle Association, Supreme Court of the State of New York, County of New York, "Summons and Complaint," Index No. 451625/2020.

109 **$1 million for her services:** People of the State of New York v. The National Rifle Association, Supreme Court of the State of New York, County of New York, "Summons and Complaint," Index No. 451625/2020.

110 **required expense documentation:** Maremont, "NRA's Unusual Travel Setup."

110 **kept in Woody's office:** Maremont, "NRA's Unusual Travel Setup."

110 **she operates her businesses:** Maremont, "NRA's Unusual Travel Setup."

CHAPTER 10: MARIA BUTINA AND THE ROOTS OF NRA-RUSSIA

111 **Rhode Island Avenue, pre-1993:** Michael D. Shear, "NRA Makes Move to Fair Oaks," *Washington Post*, March 18, 1993.

113 **"almost certainly" approved them:** U.S. Senate Select Committee on Intelligence, *Counterintelligence Threats and Vulnerabilities*, vol. 5 of *Russian Active Measures Campaigns and Interference in the 2016 U.S. Election*, p. 568.

113 **"Russian intelligence services":** U.S. Senate Select Committee on Intelligence, *Counterintelligence Threats and Vulnerabilities*, p. 575.

114 **"the godfather":** Sebastian Rotella, "Russian Politician Who Reportedly Sent Millions to NRA Has Long History in Spain," ProPublica, January 19, 2018.

114 **United States and Russia in 2010:** Josh Meyer, "Putin Ally Wooed Young Americans Visiting Moscow," *Politico Europe*, August 14, 2018.

114 **high-ranking national security officials:** Tim Mak, "Depth of Russian Politician's Cultivation of NRA Ties Revealed," NPR, March 1, 2018.

114 **awarded him a medal in 2016:** Tim Dickinson, "Inside the Decade-Long Russian Campaign to Infiltrate the NRA and Help Elect Trump," *Rolling Stone*, April 2, 2018.

114 **"the boss" and "godfather":** Rotella, "Russian Politician Who Reportedly Sent Millions to NRA."

114 **bank accounts in Spain:** Esteban Duarte, Henry Meyer, and Evgenia Pismennaya, "Mobster or Central Banker? Spanish Cops Allege This Russian Both," Bloomberg, August 8, 2016.

114 **having been tipped off:** Rotella, "Russian Politician Who Reportedly Sent Millions to NRA."

114 **told the Spanish newspaper *El Pais*:** José María Irujo and John Carlin, "The Spanish connection with Trump's Russia Scandal," *El Pais*, April 3, 2017.

115 **infamous AK-47 rifle:** Rosalind S. Helderman and Tom Hamburger, "Guns and Religion: How American Conservatives Grew Closer to Putin's Russia," *Washington Post*, April 30, 2017.

115 **National Rifle Association in 2010:** Dickinson, "Inside the Decade-Long Russian Campaign."

115 **Russian pamphlet promoting the concept:** Helderman and Hamburger, "Guns and Religion."

115 **known visit was in 2004:** Meyer, "Putin Ally Wooed Young Americans Visiting Moscow."

115 **settle for the lieutenant governor:** Tim Mak, "Documents Reveal How Russian Official Courted Conservatives in U.S. Since 2009," NPR, May 11, 2018.

115 **president David Keene in 2011:** Helderman and Hamburger, "Guns and Religion."

116 **Keene's naked money grab:** Mike Allen, "Exclusive: Conservative Group Offers Support for $2m," *Politico*, July 17, 2009.

116 **sentenced to ten years in prison:** Associated Press, "Former Manager at ACU Pleads Guilty to Embezzling," June 6, 2011.

116 **missed the other driver's head:** "Crime," *Washington Post*, December 18, 2002.

117 **was acting as its bookkeeper:** Brian Fitzpatrick, "CPAC Host Hit with Scandal," WND, December 14, 2010.

117 **discovered in May 2010:** Fitzpatrick, "CPAC Host Hit with Scandal."

117 **Carr was sentenced to one year in jail:** Jonathan Wilson, "Former ACU Employee Sentenced to a Year," WAMU, American University Radio, September 16, 2011.

117 **Keene left the ACU:** Byron Tau, "Keene to Leave ACU," *Politico*, January 26, 2011.

117 **phone number on the form:** U.S. Senate Select Committee on Intelligence, *Counterintelligence Threats and Vulnerabilities*, p. 578.

117 **"please don't hesitate to let us know":** Dickinson, "Inside the Decade-Long Russian Campaign."

117 **Torshin bragged brazenly at the time:** Mak, "Depth of Russian Politician's Cultivation of NRA Ties Revealed."

117 **affairs committee:** James Bamford, "The Spy Who Wasn't," *New Republic*, February 11, 2019.

117 **meeting from 2012 to 2016:** Mak, "Depth of Russian Politician's Cultivation of NRA Ties Revealed."

118 **was a needlepoint enthusiast:** Helderman and Hamburger, "Guns and Religion."

118 **Cors's favorite topic:** Mak, "Depth of Russian Politician's Cultivation of NRA Ties Revealed."

118 **at Altai State University:** United States v. Maria Butina, United States District Court for the District of Columbia, "Sentencing Memorandum On Behalf Of Maria Butina," Case 1:18-cr-00218-TSC (2019).

119 **nod to the Second Amendment:** United States v. Maria Butina, United States District Court for the District of Columbia, "Sentencing Memorandum On Behalf Of Maria Butina," Case 1:18-cr-00218-TSC (2019).

119 **provocatively handles firearms:** Егор Мостовщиков, "How to Create a Weapon Lobby and Not Burn Out," *GQ Russia*, July 18, 2018.

119 **During her first year in Moscow:** U.S. Senate Select Committee on Intelligence, *Counterintelligence Threats and Vulnerabilities*, p. 571.

119 **then Russian prime minister said in 2011:** Carl Schreck, "Gun Play: The Rise and Fall of Maria Butina's Wannabe Russian NRA," *Radio Free Europe*, July 26, 2018.

119 **Konstantin Nikolaev, a Russian billionaire:** Rosalind S. Helderman, "Russian Billionaire with U.S. Investments Backed Alleged Agent Maria Butina, According to a Person Familiar with Her Senate Testimony," *Washington Post*, July 22, 2018.

119 **Russian military and FSB:** Mike McIntire, "Billionaire Backer of Maria Butina Had Russian Security Ties," *New York Times*, September 21, 2018.

119 **stores in the Moscow region:** U.S. Senate Select Committee on Intelligence, *Counterintelligence Threats and Vulnerabilities*, p. 572.

119 **severely restricted in Russia:** U.S. Senate Select Committee on Intelligence, *Counterintelligence Threats and Vulnerabilities*, p. 570.

120 **some ten thousand members:** U.S. Senate Select Committee on Intelligence, *Counterintelligence Threats and Vulnerabilities*, p. 57.

120 **Paul Erickson along for the trip:** United States v. Maria Butina, United States District Court for the District of Columbia, "Sentencing Memorandum On Behalf Of Maria Butina," Case 1:18-cr-00218-TSC (2019).

120 **NRA paid for his trip:** U.S. Senate Select Committee on Intelligence, *Counterintelligence Threats and Vulnerabilities*, p. 580.

120 **been to Russia before:** U.S. Senate Select Committee on Intelligence, *Counterintelligence Threats and Vulnerabilities*, p. 580.

120 **featured a fashion show:** Tim Mak, "John Bolton's Curious Appearance in a Russian Gun Rights Video," NPR, March 22, 2018.

120 **belts that also worked as holsters:** Dickinson, "Inside the Decade-Long Russian Campaign."

120 **"We need to work together":** Dickinson, "Inside the Decade-Long Russian Campaign."

121 **Vice President Spiro Agnew:** John Bolton, *Surrender Is Not an Option: Defending America at the United Nations and Abroad*, p. 13.

121 **"advice to your great people":** Mak, "John Bolton's Curious Appearance."

121 **dating the following year:** United States v. Maria Butina, United States District Court for the District of Columbia, "Sentencing Memorandum On Behalf Of Maria Butina," Case 1:18-cr-00218-TSC (2019).

121 **attendee at her son's wedding:** Mildred Hallow, confidential deposition, January 10, 2020.

121 **broke his own nose:** Tim Stanley, *The Crusader: The Life and Tumultuous Times of Pat Buchanan*, p. 166.

122 **played a role in the introduction:** Seth Tupper, "Trump, Putin . . . and Erickson? Russian Probe Just Another Chapter in South Dakotan's Unusual Life," *Rapid City Journal*, February 11, 2018.

122 **Zairean president Mobutu Sese Seko:** Tupper, "Trump, Putin . . . and Erickson?"

122 **also represented the dictator in the past:** Betsy Swan and Tim Mak, "Top Trump Aide Led the 'Torturers' Lobby," *Daily Beast*, November 6, 2017.

122 **over a years-long scam:** Jonathan Ellis, "Former Political Operative Paul Erickson Sentenced to Federal Prison," *Sioux Falls Argus Leader*, July 6, 2020.

122 **U.S. visa in years prior:** Josh Meyer, "Accused Russian Agent Says She Was Twice Denied Visas to Travel to U.S.," *Politico*, July 20, 2018.

122 **visa to the United States:** U.S. Senate Select Committee on Intelligence, *Counterintelligence Threats and Vulnerabilities*, p. 582.

122 **National Rifle Association annual meeting:** United States v. Maria Butina, United States District Court for the District of Columbia, "Sentencing Memorandum On Behalf Of Maria Butina," Case 1:18-cr-00218-TSC (2019).

122 **handle the visa interview:** U.S. Senate Select Committee on Intelligence, *Counterintelligence Threats and Vulnerabilities*, p. 584.

122 **Committee chairman Ed Royce:** U.S. Senate Select Committee on Intelligence, *Counterintelligence Threats and Vulnerabilities*, p. 585.

122 **including a work visa:** United States v. Maria Butina, United States District Court for the District of Columbia, "Sentencing Memorandum On Behalf Of Maria Butina," Case 1:18-cr-00218-TSC (2019).

CHAPTER 11: THE OBAMA YEARS

126 **included hiring her own niece:** People of the State of New York v. The National Rifle Association, Supreme Court of the State of New York, County of New York, "Summons and Complaint," Index No. 451625/2020.

127 **its board of trustees:** People of the State of New York v. The National Rifle Association, Supreme Court of the State of New York, County of New York, "Summons and Complaint," Index No. 451625/2020.

127 **disclosing these contributions:** Mike Spies, "The NRA Made Unreported Donations to a Charity Led by Wayne LaPierre's Wife," *The Trace*, May 30, 2019.

128 **"to travel and hotels":** Josh Powell, *Inside the NRA*, p. 83.

128 **according to a leaked memo:** Letter from William Winkler, "RE: Documentation of expenses incurred by Ackerman McQueen (AMc) and billed to the National Rifle Association (NRA)," Ackerman McQueen, April 22, 2019, https://s.wsj.net/public/resources/documents/NRAletters .pdf.

129 **CastaDiva Resort in Como, Italy:** Winkler, "RE: Documentation of expenses incurred."

129 **which was $17,550:** Winkler, "RE: Documentation of expenses incurred."

129 **question him about it:** Wayne LaPierre, confidential deposition, September 24, 2019.

129 **cost nearly $50,000:** Winkler, "RE: Documentation of expenses incurred."

129 **"credit cards were being hacked":** Wayne LaPierre, confidential deposition, September 24, 2019.

129 **$39,000 in a single day in 2015:** Letter from William Winkler, "RE: Clothing purchases by Ackerman McQueen (AMc) on your behalf," Ackerman McQueen, April 22, 2019. https://s.wsj.net/public/resources /documents/NRAletters.pdf.

130 **shipped to Wayne's address:** Wayne LaPierre, confidential deposition, September 24, 2019.

130 **suits, shirts, and ties cost:** Wayne LaPierre, confidential deposition, September 24, 2019.

130 **repeatedly in a deposition:** Wayne LaPierre, confidential deposition, September 24, 2019.

130 **fire chief of Great Falls, Virginia:** Wayne LaPierre deposition, United States Bankruptcy Court for the Northern District of Texas Dallas Division, Case 21-30085, March 22, 2021.

130 **looking for an internship:** Wayne LaPierre, confidential deposition, September 24, 2019.

131 **total of $13,804.84:** Winkler, "RE: Documentation of expenses incurred."

131 **through this invoicing:** "Studio, 1, 2 & 3-Bedroom Apartments," Ridgewood by Winsor, https://www.ridgewoodbywindsor.com/floor plans.

131 **"There is no relationship":** Wayne LaPierre, confidential deposition, September 24, 2019.

131 **with Susan's Women's Leadership Forum:** Megan Allen, LinkedIn page, https://www.linkedin.com/in/megan-allen-2a9999154/.

131 **at about $70,000 per year:** Mark Maremont, "Private Jets Ferried Relatives of NRA Chief Executive," *Wall Street Journal*, August 26, 2019.

131 **and Colleen's daughter:** Maremont, "Private Jets Ferried Relatives of NRA Chief Executive."

131   **Wayne traveling with them:** People of the State of New York v.
      The National Rifle Association, Supreme Court of the State of New
      York, County of New York, "Summons and Complaint," Index No. 451625/
      2020.

131   **Wayne was not a passenger:** People of the State of New York v. The
      National Rifle Association, Supreme Court of the State of New
      York, County of New York, "Summons and Complaint," Index No. 451625/
      2020.

132   **at $1,350 a night:** People of the State of New York v. The National Rifle
      Association, Supreme Court of the State of New York, County of New York,
      "Summons and Complaint," Index No. 451625/2020.

132   **half a million dollars:** People of the State of New York v. The National
      Rifle Association, Supreme Court of the State of New York, County of New
      York, "Summons and Complaint," Index No. 451625/2020.

132   **visiting a man:** People of the State of New York v. The National Rifle
      Association, Supreme Court of the State of New York, County of New York,
      "Summons and Complaint," Index No. 451625/2020.

132   **mailing and PR services:** Mark Maremont, "Hollywood Producer Emerges
      as Key Figure in Alleged NRA Financial Abuses," *Wall Street Journal*,
      August 14, 2020.

132   **boat, and two Jet Skis:** People of the State of New York v.
      The National Rifle Association, Supreme Court of the State of
      New York, County of New York, "Summons and Complaint," Index No.
      451625/2020.

133   **New York attorney general reported:** People of the State of
      New York v. The National Rifle Association, Supreme Court of
      the State of New York, County of New York, "Summons and Complaint,"
      Index No. 451625/2020.

133   **2013 to 2018 he visited:** Wayne LaPierre deposition, United States
      Bankruptcy Court for the Northern District of Texas Dallas Division, Case
      21-30085, March 23, 2021.

133   **"'nobody can get me here'":** Wayne LaPierre deposition, United States
      Bankruptcy Court for the Northern District of Texas Dallas Division, Case
      21-30085, March 23, 2021.

133   **"security retreat":** Wayne LaPierre testimony, United States Bankruptcy
      Court for the Northern District of Texas Dallas Division, Case 21-30085,
      April 7, 2021.

133   **unvetted staff:** Wayne LaPierre deposition, United States Bankruptcy
      Court for the Northern District of Texas Dallas Division, Case 21-30085,
      March 23, 2021.

133   **his niece Colleen there:** Wayne LaPierre deposition, United States
      Bankruptcy Court for the Northern District of Texas Dallas Division, Case
      21-30085, March 23, 2021.

133   **"was private," he stammered:** Wayne LaPierre testimony, United States
      Bankruptcy Court for the Northern District of Texas Dallas Division, Case
      21-30085, April 7, 2021.

133 **"I've dealt with them":** Wayne LaPierre deposition, United States Bankruptcy Court for the Northern District of Texas Dallas Division, Case 21-30085, March 23, 2021.

134 **same time period for its services:** "Nonprofit Explorer: National Rifle Association of America," ProPublica, https://projects.propublica.org /nonprofits/organizations/530116130.

136 **revenue of the gun group:** Danny Hakim, "Inside Wayne LaPierre's Battle for the N.R.A.," *New York Times Magazine*, December 18, 2019.

136 **$1.2 million in expenses:** People of the State of New York v. The National Rifle Association, Supreme Court of the State of New York, County of New York, "Summons and Complaint," Index No. 451625/2020.

136 **gifts on the NRA's dime:** People of the State of New York v. The National Rifle Association, Supreme Court of the State of New York, County of New York, "Summons and Complaint," Index No. 451625/2020.

136 **armored vehicle for Wayne:** People of the State of New York v. The National Rifle Association, Supreme Court of the State of New York, County of New York, "Summons and Complaint," Index No. 451625/2020.

136 **near the nation's capital:** People of the State of New York v. The National Rifle Association, Supreme Court of the State of New York, County of New York, "Summons and Complaint," Index No. 451625/2020.

136 **approving his expenses:** People of the State of New York v. The National Rifle Association, Supreme Court of the State of New York, County of New York, "Summons and Complaint," Index No. 451625/2020.

Chapter 12: Operation Second Pozner

138 **Central Bank of Russia:** U.S. Senate Committee on Finance, *The NRA and Russia* (2019), p. 4.

138 **"only in person":** U.S. Senate Committee on Finance, *The NRA and Russia*, p. 5.

138 **Millie Hallow with the request:** U.S. Senate Committee on Finance, *The NRA and Russia*, p. 5.

138 **ties with the Republican Party:** U.S. Senate Select Committee on Intelligence, *Counterintelligence Threats and Vulnerabilities*, vol. 5 of *Russian Active Measures Campaigns and Interference in the 2016 U.S. Election*, p. 587.

138 **disinformation department of the KGB:** U.S. Senate Select Committee on Intelligence, *Counterintelligence Threats and Vulnerabilities*, pp. 587–88; United States v. Maria Butina, United States District Court for the District of Columbia, "Affidavit in Support of an Application for a Criminal Complaint," Case 1:18-cr-00218-TSC (2019).

139 **opportunity to change that:** U.S. Senate Select Committee on Intelligence, *Counterintelligence Threats and Vulnerabilities*, pp. 587–88; United States v. Maria Butina, United States District Court for the District of Columbia, "Affidavit in Support of an Application for a Criminal Complaint," Case 1:18-cr-00218-TSC (2019).

139 **their interests lay:** United States v. Maria Butina, United States District Court for the District of Columbia, "Document 99-3," Case 1:18-cr-00218-TSC (April 19, 2019).

139 **prosecutors would later argue:** United States v. Maria Butina, United States District Court for the District of Columbia, "Document 99-3," Case 1:18-cr-00218-TSC (April 19, 2019).

140 **"damage to the United States":** United States v. Maria Butina, United States District Court for the District of Columbia, "Document 99-3," Case 1:18-cr-00218-TSC (April 19, 2019).

140 **Butina was later arrested:** Lesley Stahl, "Maria Butina: The Russian Accused of Trying to Influence U.S. Policies for the Kremlin," CBS News, November 3, 2019.

141 **entering their offices:** U.S. Senate Select Committee on Intelligence, *Counterintelligence Threats and Vulnerabilities*, p. 590.

141 **"the SVR," she wrote:** U.S. Senate Select Committee on Intelligence, *Counterintelligence Threats and Vulnerabilities*, p. 590.

141 **the summer of 2015:** U.S. Senate Select Committee on Intelligence, *Counterintelligence Threats and Vulnerabilities*, p. 589.

141 **education and living expenses:** U.S. Senate Select Committee on Intelligence, *Counterintelligence Threats and Vulnerabilities*, p. 573.

141 **Nick Perrine, Keene's assistant:** U.S. Senate Select Committee on Intelligence, *Counterintelligence Threats and Vulnerabilities*, p. 589.

142 **pair—back to the NRA:** U.S. Senate Committee on Finance, *The NRA and Russia*, p. 59.

142 **Torshin declined to do so:** U.S. Senate Select Committee on Intelligence, *Counterintelligence Threats and Vulnerabilities*, p. 591.

142 **presidential ticket:** U.S. Senate Committee on Finance, *The NRA and Russia*, p. 59.

142 **governor Scott Walker at the venue:** U.S. Senate Select Committee on Intelligence, *Counterintelligence Threats and Vulnerabilities*, p. 592.

142 **wanted to travel to Moscow:** U.S. Senate Select Committee on Intelligence, *Counterintelligence Threats and Vulnerabilities*, p. 594.

143 **lied about them to the FBI:** James Gordon Meek, "What You Need to Know About the Indictment Against Michael Flynn," ABC News, February 20, 2019.

143 **special counsel Robert Mueller's probe:** Mark Landler and Eric Lichtblau, "Jeff Sessions Recuses Himself from Russia Inquiry," *New York Times*, March 2, 2017.

143 **lasted for about three hours:** U.S. Senate Committee on Intelligence, *Counterintelligence Threats and Vulnerabilities*, p. 593; U.S. Senate Committee on Finance, *The NRA and Russia*, p. 33.

143 **attended his farewell party in D.C.:** U.S. Senate Committee on Finance, *The NRA and Russia*, p. 33.

144 **name of a Walker adviser:** U.S. Senate Select Committee on Intelligence, *Counterintelligence Threats and Vulnerabilities*, p. 594.

144 **between Russia and the United States:** U.S. Senate Select Committee on Intelligence, *Counterintelligence Threats and Vulnerabilities*, p. 594.

144 **with a data analysis firm:** Tim Mak, "Russia's Pro-Gun Influence Accounts Copied the NRA—and Sometimes, Vice Versa," NPR, September 21, 2018; Tim Mak, "Russia's Divisive Twitter Campaign Took a Rare Consistent Stance: Pro-Gun," NPR, September 21, 2018.

145 **"o'er the steppe by a cruel gale":** Mak, "Russia's Pro-Gun Influence Accounts Copied the NRA—and Sometimes, Vice Versa"; Mak, "Russia's Divisive Twitter Campaign Took a Rare Consistent Stance: Pro-Gun."

146 **"during the 2016 U.S. election":** U.S. Senate Select Committee on Intelligence, *Counterintelligence Threats and Vulnerabilities*, p. 635.

146 **Council for National Policy:** U.S. Senate Committee on Finance, *The NRA and Russia*, p. 61.

146 **Russia as a presidential candidate:** Rosalind S. Helderman and Tom Hamburger, "Guns and Religion: How American Conservatives Grew Closer to Putin's Russia," *Washington Post*, April 30, 2017.

147 **report on the exchange:** U.S. Senate Select Committee on Intelligence, *Counterintelligence Threats and Vulnerabilities*, p. 595.

147 **adviser to Senator Rand Paul:** John Biggs, "Rand Paul Appoints Bitcoin-Friendly Overstock CEO to Tech Counsel, TechCrunch, May 11, 2015.

147 **Russian gun rights group:** Sheelah Kolhatkar, "A Tycoon's Deep-State Conspiracy Dive," *New Yorker*, December 7, 2020.

147 **Anton Chekhov, and John Locke:** Michael Corkery, "Overstock C.E.O. Takes Aim at 'Deep State' After Romance with Russian Agent," *New York Times*, August 15, 2019.

147 **Byrne agreed to lunch:** Kolhatkar, "A Tycoon's Deep-State Conspiracy Dive."

147 **"with women in burkas":** U.S. Senate Select Committee on Intelligence, *Counterintelligence Threats and Vulnerabilities*, p. 596.

148 **"between our two nations":** U.S. Senate Select Committee on Intelligence, *Counterintelligence Threats and Vulnerabilities*, p. 627.

148 **Byrne said on a podcast:** Celia Aniskovich, "Truth Is in the Eye of the Beholder," *Spy Affair* podcast, April 26, 2021.

148 **romantic, off and on:** Corkery, "Overstock C.E.O. Takes Aim at 'Deep State.'"

148 **"Overstock.com CEO Comments on Deep State":** Patrick M. Byrne, "Overstock.com CEO Comments on Deep State, Withholds Further Comment," Overstock.com, August 12, 2019, http://investors.overstock .com/news-releases/news-release-details/overstockcom-ceo-comments -deep-state-withholds-further-comment.

148 **30 percent over two days:** Corkery, "Overstock C.E.O. Takes Aim at 'Deep State.'"

148 **with Butina, Byrne resigned:** Cade Metz and Julie Creswell, "Patrick Byrne, Overstock C.E.O., Resigns After Disclosing Romance with Russian Agent," *New York Times*, August 22, 2019.

148 **former top FBI officials deny:** David Shortell and Caroline Kelly, "Former Officials Deny Ex-CEO's Claim FBI Asked Him to Pursue Maria Butina," CNN, August 23, 2019.

148 **theories about voter fraud:** Kolhatkar, "A Tycoon's Deep-State Conspiracy Dive."

Chapter 13: Ackerman McQueen Power Grows

150 **O'Leary's handiwork:** Richard Keil, "The NRA's Mail Bomb," *Mother Jones*, September–October 1995.

150 **"major league ballplayer blush":** Keil, "The NRA's Mail Bomb."

152 **National Rifle Association with its services:** Danny Hakim, "Angus McQueen, the N.R.A.'s Image Maker, Dies at 74," *New York Times*, July 19, 2019.

152 **"distract the eye from tragedy":** Danny Hakim, "Inside Wayne LaPierre's Battle for the N.R.A.," *New York Times Magazine*, December 18, 2019.

152 **CEO from 1987 to 2019:** National Rifle Association v. Ackerman McQueen, United States District Court for the Northern District of Texas, Dallas Division, "Declaration of Revan McQueen," Civil Action No. 3:19-cv-02074-G, March 30, 2020.

154 **rather than the other way around:** Josh Powell, *Inside the NRA*, p. 87.

155 **a hundred people working:** Powell, *Inside the NRA*, p. 83.

155 **approve projects and bills verbally:** Powell, *Inside the NRA*, p. 91.

155 **"Out of Pocket" project:** People of the State of New York v. The National Rifle Association, Supreme Court of the State of New York, County of New York, "Summons and Complaint," Index No. 451625/2020.

155 **through American Express cards:** Andrew Jenks, "Down to the Studs," *Gangster Capitalism*, May 6, 2020, https://shows.cadence13.com/podcast/gangster-capitalism/episodes/2ef5a2ab-7a5d-4f86-9c60-f509dafea088.

156 **no knowledge of this practice:** Wayne LaPierre, confidential deposition, September 24, 2019.

156 **send invoices to the NRA:** Bill Winkler testimony, United States Bankruptcy Court for the Northern District of Texas Dallas Division, Case 21-30085, April 16, 2021.

156 **since at least the 1990s:** Bill Winkler testimony, United States Bankruptcy Court for the Northern District of Texas Dallas Division, Case 21-30085, April 16, 2021.

156 **exceeded $560,000 in 2016:** Tony Makris testimony, United States Bankruptcy Court for the Northern District of Texas Dallas Division, Case 21-30085, April 16, 2021.

157 **Makris later recalled:** Tony Makris testimony, United States Bankruptcy Court for the Northern District of Texas Dallas Division, Case 21-30085, April 16, 2021.

157 **redirect the private jet:** Tony Makris testimony, United States Bankruptcy Court for the Northern District of Texas Dallas Division, Case 21-30085, April 16, 2021.

157   **lodging ran $9,550:** People of the State of New York v. The National Rifle Association, Supreme Court of the State of New York, County of New York, "Summons and Complaint," Index No. 451625/2020.

157   **for by the gun group:** People of the State of New York v. The National Rifle Association, Supreme Court of the State of New York, County of New York, "Summons and Complaint," Index No. 451625/2020.

157   **twice to the Mayo Clinic:** Tony Makris testimony, United States Bankruptcy Court for the Northern District of Texas Dallas Division, Case 21-30085, April 16, 2021.

157   **"backasswards work-around":** Powell, *Inside the NRA*, p. 186.

157   **$7,500 in gratuities:** Tony Makris testimony, United States Bankruptcy Court for the Northern District of Texas Dallas Division, Case 21-30085, April 16, 2021.

157   **especially in L.A. and Las Vegas:** Tony Makris testimony, United States Bankruptcy Court for the Northern District of Texas Dallas Division, Case 21-30085, April 16, 2021.

158   **law called McCain-Feingold:** Wayne LaPierre, confidential deposition, September 24, 2019.

158   **when it launched in 2004:** Associated Press, "NRA to Launch News Company," April 16, 2004.

158   **pirate radio station:** Jesse Walker, "Offshore Gun Talk," Reason, December 18, 2003.

158   **to reach this audience:** Wayne LaPierre, confidential deposition, September 24, 2019.

158   **formally launched in 2016:** James Parker, "Live-Streaming the Apocalypse with NRATV," *The Atlantic*, June 2018.

158   **NRA through the project:** Wayne LaPierre, confidential deposition, September 24, 2019.

158   **be Angus's girlfriend:** Nolan Clay, "Ackerman McQueen CEO Sued by Ex-Employee," *The Oklahoman*, July 19, 2020.

158   **rants on race wars:** Danny Hakim, "Incendiary N.R.A. Videos Find New Critics: N.R.A. Leaders," *New York Times*, March 11, 2019.

158   **sharia law:** Alfred Joyner, "NRATV Canceled: Five Controversial Remarks Dana Loesch Made Hosting the Gun Rights Channel," *Newsweek*, June 26, 2019.

159   **"Want to make a socialist cry?":** "Make a Socialist Cry," Official NRA Store, http://graphics.nra.org/online_store/CustClub/3-5-18CC.html.

159   **with Ku Klux Klan hoods:** Chloe Melas, "NRA TV Depicts 'Thomas & Friends' Characters in KKK Hoods," CNN, September 14, 2018.

159   **"them curb-stomped":** Joyner, "NRATV Canceled."

159   **"return on investment":** Hakim, "Incendiary N.R.A. Videos Find New Critics."

160   **discipline anyone for it:** Powell, *Inside the NRA*, p. 101.

160   **$25 million a year by 2018:** Powell, *Inside the NRA*, p. 99.

160   **NRATV in January 2019:** Hakim, "Incendiary N.R.A. Videos Find New Critics."

160   **not provide internal metrics:** Powell, *Inside the NRA*, p. 99.

160   **"anything to NRATV!":** Powell, *Inside the NRA*, p. 102.

Chapter 14: Moscow Bound

162   **dinner with Russian president:** Tim Mak, "Top Trump Ally Met with
      Putin's Deputy in Moscow," *Daily Beast*, March 7, 2017.

162   **On December 8:** Maria Butina, "THE PROGRAM of the visit of the
      delegation from The National Rifle Association of America (The NRA) to
      Moscow 8–3 December 2015."

162   **Russian equivalent, the Right to Bear Arms:** "Ex-Sheriff David Clarke's
      2015 Trip Expenses Paid by Alleged Russian Agent's Group," *Fox 6 Now
      Milwaukee*, July 17, 2018.

162   **"(The NRA) to Moscow":** Butina, "THE PROGRAM of the visit of the
      delegation from The National Rifle Association of America."

163   **meet along the way:** U.S. Senate Committee on Finance, *The NRA and
      Russia* (2019), p. 21.

163   **might have with the trip:** U.S. Senate Committee on Finance, *The NRA
      and Russia*, p. 21.

163   **in American politics:** U.S. Senate Committee on Finance, *The NRA and
      Russia*, p. 26.

163   **NRA trip to Moscow:** Betsy Swan, "Kremlin Blessed Russia's NRA
      Operation, U.S. Intel Report Says," *Daily Beast,* January 13, 2019.

163   **trip was being organized:** U.S. Senate Committee on Finance, *The NRA
      and Russia*, p. 28.

164   **"they are in the USA politics":** U.S. Senate Select Committee on
      Intelligence, *Counterintelligence Threats and Vulnerabilities*, vol. 5 of
      *Russian Active Measures Campaigns and Interference in the 2016 U.S.
      Election*, p. 599.

164   **Goldschlager and his daughter:** Jennifer Mascia, "Alleged Russian Spy
      Maria Butina and the NRA: A Photographic History," *The Trace*, July 16,
      2018.

164   **$1 million to the NRA:** U.S. Senate Committee on Finance, *The NRA and
      Russia*, p. 17.

164   **"argument with my doctors":** U.S. Senate Committee on Finance, *The
      NRA and Russia*, p. 18.

164   **"the NRA and of me":** U.S. Senate Committee on Finance, *The NRA and
      Russia*, p. 19.

164   **Bolshoi Theatre:** Butina, "THE PROGRAM of the visit of the delegation
      from The National Rifle Association of America."

165   **opportunities in Russia all year:** U.S. Senate Committee on Finance, *The
      NRA and Russia*, p. 46.

165   **broader Brownells brand:** U.S. Senate Committee on Finance, *The NRA
      and Russia*, p. 47.

165   **to convince him to go:** U.S. Senate Committee on Finance, *The NRA and
      Russia*, p. 49.

165 **business in Russia:** U.S. Senate Committee on Finance, *The NRA and Russia*, pp. 47–48.

165 **while he was in Russia:** U.S. Senate Committee on Finance, *The NRA and Russia*, p. 51.

165 **explained to his staff:** U.S. Senate Committee on Finance, *The NRA and Russia*, p. 53.

165 **accompanied by Butina:** U.S. Senate Committee on Finance, *The NRA and Russia*, p. 8.

165 **"export and import deals":** U.S. Senate Committee on Finance, *The NRA and Russia*, p. 48.

165 **"heaven & earth":** U.S. Senate Committee on Finance, *The NRA and Russia*, p. 51.

166 **close contacts with Putin's office:** U.S. Senate Select Committee on Intelligence, *Counterintelligence Threats and Vulnerabilities*, pp. 607–608.

166 **was interested in helping:** U.S. Senate Select Committee on Intelligence, *Counterintelligence Threats and Vulnerabilities*, p. 607.

166 **Torshin to get one:** U.S. Senate Select Committee on Intelligence, *Counterintelligence Threats and Vulnerabilities*, p. 602.

166 **"outlet's home country":** U.S. Senate Select Committee on Intelligence, *Counterintelligence Threats and Vulnerabilities*, p. 602.

166 **international trips like this:** U.S. Senate Committee on Finance, *The NRA and Russia*, p. 56.

167 **join the delegation to Moscow :** U.S. Senate Committee on Finance, *The NRA and Russia*, p. 30.

167 **minister Sergei Lavrov:** U.S. Senate Select Committee on Intelligence, *Counterintelligence Threats and Vulnerabilities*, p. 604.

167 **Putin's presidential campaigns:** U.S. Senate Select Committee on Intelligence, *Counterintelligence Threats and Vulnerabilities*, p. 600.

167 **after the sanctions were imposed:** Mak, "Top Trump Ally Met with Putin's Deputy."

167 **keep the meeting secret:** U.S. Senate Select Committee on Intelligence, *Counterintelligence Threats and Vulnerabilities*, p. 605.

167 **for the delegation:** U.S. Senate Select Committee on Intelligence, *Counterintelligence Threats and Vulnerabilities*, p. 605.

168 **Russian Shooting Federation:** Mak, "Top Trump Ally Met with Putin's Deputy."

168 **talked about gun rights:** U.S. Senate Select Committee on Intelligence, *Counterintelligence Threats and Vulnerabilities*, p. 606.

168 **was a chance encounter:** U.S. Senate Committee on Finance, *The NRA and Russia*, p. 34.

168 **by former sheriff David Clarke:** David A. Clarke Jr. (@SheriffClarke), Twitter, December 11, 2015, https://twitter.com/SheriffClarke/status/675442397044711424.

168 **Goldschlager recalled later:** Peter Stone and Greg Gordon, "FBI Investigating Whether Russian Money Went to NRA to Help Trump," McClatchy DC Bureau, January 18, 2018.

168　**had left Moscow:** U.S. Senate Committee on Finance, *The NRA and Russia*, p. 6.

168　**Moscow hunting club:** Danny Hakim, "N.R.A. Seeks Distance from Russia as Investigations Heat Up," *New York Times*, January 28, 2019.

168　**Trophy House:** Butina, "THE PROGRAM of the visit of the delegation from The National Rifle Association of America."

169　**Liberatore and his wife:** U.S. Senate Committee on Finance, *The NRA and Russia*, p. 22.

169　**"U.S. domestic shell company":** U.S. Senate Committee on Finance, *The NRA and Russia*, p. 24.

169　**"would be seen very badly":** U.S. Senate Select Committee on Intelligence, *Counterintelligence Threats and Vulnerabilities*, p. 607.

169　**"avoid international economic sanction problems":** U.S. Senate Committee on Finance, *The NRA and Russia*, p. 23.

169　**NRA president's office budget:** U.S. Senate Committee on Finance, *The NRA and Russia*, p. 23.

170　**"NRA special project, $6,000":** Mildred Hallow, confidential deposition, January 10, 2020.

170　**investigation eventually concluded:** U.S. Senate Committee on Finance, *The NRA and Russia*, p. 24.

170　**"the trip off the NRA's books":** U.S. Senate Committee on Finance, *The NRA and Russia*, p. 24.

170　**"Brownell has done":** Mildred Hallow, confidential deposition, January 10, 2020.

170　**"fogged in my brain," she said:** Mildred Hallow, confidential deposition, January 10, 2020.

170　**"about [the Russia] invoice":** Mildred Hallow, confidential deposition, January 10, 2020.

170　**punished in any way:** Mildred Hallow, confidential deposition, January 10, 2020.

171　**would meet on this trip:** U.S. Senate Committee on Finance, *The NRA and Russia*, p. 6.

171　**Wayne opposed the trip:** Hakim, "N.R.A. Seeks Distance from Russia."

171　**in their personal capacities:** U.S. Senate Committee on Finance, *The NRA and Russia*, p. 18.

171　**on the NRA's letterhead:** U.S. Senate Committee on Finance, *The NRA and Russia*, p. 18.

171　**D.C., to meet with Torshin:** U.S. Senate Committee on Finance, *The NRA and Russia*, p. 63.

171　**for their lodging:** U.S. Senate Select Committee on Intelligence, *Counterintelligence Threats and Vulnerabilities*, p. 610.

172　**a total of $520:** U.S. Senate Committee on Finance, *The NRA and Russia*, p. 65.

172　**National Prayer Breakfast:** U.S. Senate Select Committee on Intelligence, *Counterintelligence Threats and Vulnerabilities*, p. 609.

172 **next year's breakfast:** U.S. Senate Select Committee on Intelligence, *Counterintelligence Threats and Vulnerabilities*, p. 610.

172 **"desire and authority to listen":** United States v. Maria Butina, United States District Court for the District of Columbia, "Government's Opposition to Defendant's Motion for Bond Review," Case 1:18-cr-00218-TSC (2019).

172 **start in the fall of 2016:** U.S. Senate Select Committee on Intelligence, *Counterintelligence Threats and Vulnerabilities*, p. 611.

172 **with the Rockefeller heir:** U.S. Senate Select Committee on Intelligence, *Counterintelligence Threats and Vulnerabilities*, p. 610.

172 **"pro-Russian sentiment in the USA":** U.S. Senate Select Committee on Intelligence, *Counterintelligence Threats and Vulnerabilities*, p. 611.

173 **"building this communication channel":** U.S. Senate Select Committee on Intelligence, *Counterintelligence Threats and Vulnerabilities*, p. 611.

173 **"The rest is easier":** United States v. Maria Butina, United States District Court for the District of Columbia, "Affidavit in Support of an Application for a Criminal Complaint" and "Criminal Complaint," Case 1:18-cr-00218-TSC (2019).

173 **"into any [Republican] administration":** United States v. Maria Butina, United States District Court for the District of Columbia, "Affidavit in Support of an Application for a Criminal Complaint" and "Criminal Complaint," Case 1:18-cr-00218-TSC (2019).

CHAPTER 15: BUTINA'S BACK CHANNEL

174 **one of her priorities:** U.S. Senate Committee on Finance, *The NRA and Russia* (2019), p. 67.

174 **itinerary for Butina and Torshin:** U.S. Senate Committee on Finance, *The NRA and Russia*, pp. 67–68.

175 **"for the Republican Party":** U.S. Senate Select Committee on Intelligence, *Counterintelligence Threats and Vulnerabilities*, vol. 5 of *Russian Active Measures Campaigns and Interference in the 2016 U.S. Election*, p. 615.

175 **approved the trip:** U.S. Senate Select Committee on Intelligence, *Counterintelligence Threats and Vulnerabilities*, p. 615.

175 **"certainly prove useful":** U.S. Senate Select Committee on Intelligence, *Counterintelligence Threats and Vulnerabilities*, p. 615.

176 **"with a new Republican White House":** U.S. Senate Select Committee on Intelligence, *Counterintelligence Threats and Vulnerabilities*, p. 616.

176 **"before the election":** U.S. Senate Select Committee on Intelligence, *Counterintelligence Threats and Vulnerabilities*, p. 617.

176 **Butina and Torshin had been designated:** U.S. Senate Select Committee on Intelligence, *Counterintelligence Threats and Vulnerabilities*, pp. 618–19.

176 **ultimately rejected this effort:** U.S. Senate Select Committee on Intelligence, *Counterintelligence Threats and Vulnerabilities*, p. 619.

177 **and they took photos:** U.S. Senate Select Committee on Intelligence, *Counterintelligence Threats and Vulnerabilities*, p. 622.

177 **"insight into this meeting"**: U.S. Senate Select Committee on Intelligence, *Counterintelligence Threats and Vulnerabilities*, p. 624.

177 **Cox later lamented:** Email from Christopher Cox to Millie Hallow, Jennifer Baker, and David Lehman, "Fox News Query," November 22, 2017.

177 **"Niet! Dude":** Email from Millie Hallow to Christopher Cox, Jennifer Baker, and David Lehman, "Fox News Query," November 22, 2017.

178 **"She's probably with the FSB":** Josh Powell, *Inside the NRA*, p. 155.

179 **"doing the right thing":** United States v. Maria Butina, United States District Court for the District of Columbia, "Government's Opposition to Defendant's Motion for Bond Review," Case 1:18-cr-00218-TSC (2019).

CHAPTER 16: THE NRA AND THE 2016 CAMPAIGN

180 **defining component of Manchin-Toomey:** Tom Kertscher, "Lena Taylor: Most NRA Members Back Background Checks on All Gun Purchases," PolitiFact, March 18, 2015.

181 **up from 4.5 million in 2013:** Alex Yablon, "New NRA Tax Filing Shows Membership Revenues Dropped by $47 Million Following Sandy Hook Surge," *The Trace*, January 23, 2016.

182 **owned at least two handguns:** Emily Miller, "Donald Trump's Guns," *Washington Times*, November 14, 2012.

182 **Trump Jr. was a lifetime NRA member:** Phil Taylor, "Trump's Son Woos Sportsmen, Covets Top Job at Interior," *E&E News*, May 12, 2016.

182 **training on nonprofit law:** "AG James Secures Court Order Against Donald J. Trump, Trump Children, and Trump Foundation," New York State Office of the Attorney General, November 7, 2019, https://ag.ny.gov/press-release /2019/ag-james-secures-court-order-against-donald-j-trump-trump -children-and-trump.

183 **endorsing presidential candidates at all:** Frank Smyth, *The NRA: The Unauthorized History*, p. 217.

184 **the case for Mitt Romney:** Jonathan Easley, "NRA Endorses Romney as 'Only Hope' for Firearms Freedom," *The Hill*, October 4, 2012.

184 **he said at the time:** Louis Jacobson, "Did Mitt Romney Flip-Flop on Gun Control?," PolitiFact, May 18, 2012.

184 **that category of firearms:** Jacobson, "Did Mitt Romney Flip-Flop on Gun Control?"

184 **"enemies of the Second Amendment":** Jonathan Stein, "The Long Saga of John McCain and the NRA," *Mother Jones*, October 8, 2018.

184 **gun show loophole:** Stein, "The Long Saga of John McCain and the NRA."

184 **NRA members during the campaign:** Marc Ambinder, "McCain, at NRA, Acknowledges Disagreement, but Speaks of 'Real Differences' with Democrats," *The Atlantic*, May 16, 2008.

184 **respective election years:** Vaughn Ververs, "McCain Gets NRA Backing," CBS News, October 9, 2008.

185 **"it's time to get over it":** John Santucci and Meghan Keneally, "NRA
     Endorses Donald Trump for President," ABC News, May 20, 2016.

185 **candidates in the 2016 elections:** Mike Spies, "Secrecy, Self-Dealing, and
     Greed at the N.R.A.," *New Yorker*, April 17, 2019.

185 **99 percent of that on Republicans:** Kurtis Lee and Maloy Moore, "The
     NRA Used to Donate to Democrats' Campaigns, Too. Why Did It Stop?,"
     Governing, March 5, 2018.

185 **paltry $20.3 million:** Mike Spies and Ashley Balcerzak, "The NRA Placed
     Big Bets on the 2016 Election, and Won Almost All of Them," OpenSecrets
     .org, November 9, 2016.

186 **"the score with . . . Trump voters":** Theodore Schleifer, "NRA Returns to
     Trump's Defense with $5 Million Ad Buy," CNN, September 20, 2016.

187 **"Vote Donald Trump for president":** National Rifle Association of
     America Institute for Legislative Action, "NRA's Largest Trump Ad
     Launched in Key Battleground States," October 5, 2016.

187 **advertising buy of the cycle:** National Rifle Association of America
     Institute for Legislative Action, "NRA's Largest Trump Ad Launched in Key
     Battleground States."

187 **on national cable:** Sarah Wheaton, "NRA Out with Biggest Ad Buy Yet to
     Boost Trump," *Politico*, October 5, 2016.

187 **him over Clinton:** Brad Todd and Salena Zito, *The Great Revolt: Inside the
     Populist Coalition Reshaping American Politics*, p. 130.

187 **"their TV ads":** Fred Barnes, "Gunning for Hillary," *Washington Examiner*,
     February 24, 2017.

187 **"just bought a Supreme Court seat":** Todd and Zito, *The Great Revolt*,
     p. 108.

188 **racked up in 2016:** Anna Massoglia, Kaitlin Washburn, and Karl Evers-
     Hillstrom, "NRA Spends Second Straight Year in the Red with $18 Million
     Deficit," OpenSecrets.org, November 27, 2018.

188 **catastrophe a "Trump slump":** Danny Hakim, "Inside Wayne LaPierre's
     Battle for the N.R.A.," *New York Times Magazine*, December 18, 2019.

188 **"threat to people's rights":** Hakim, "Inside Wayne LaPierre's Battle for the
     N.R.A."

189 **"'I need gasoline'":** Tony Makris testimony, United States Bankruptcy
     Court for the Northern District of Texas Dallas Division, Case 21-30085,
     April 16, 2021.

Chapter 17: Butina's Downfall

190 **Soviet hammer and sickle:** Tim Mak, "The Kremlin and GOP Have a New
     Friend—and Boy, Does She Love Guns," *Daily Beast*, February 23, 2017;
     Rosalind S. Helderman, Moriah Balingit, Shane Harris, and Tom
     Hamburger, "Before Her Arrest as an Alleged Russian Agent, Maria
     Butina's Proud Defense of Her Homeland Drew Notice at American
     University," *Washington Post*, July 25, 2018.

190 *The Great Gatsby* **in the other:** Tim Dickinson, "Inside the Decade-Long Russian Campaign to Infiltrate the NRA and Help Elect Trump," *Rolling Stone*, April 2, 2018.

191 **responsive to her entreaties:** Mak, "The Kremlin and GOP Have a New Friend"; Helderman, Balingit, Harris, and Hamburger, "Maria Butina's Proud Defense of Her Homeland."

191 **Russia's Ministry of Foreign Affairs:** U.S. Senate Select Committee on Intelligence, *Counterintelligence Threats and Vulnerabilities*, vol. 5 of *Russian Active Measures Campaigns and Interference in the 2016 U.S. Election*, p. 630.

191 **"vis-a-vis the United States":** U.S. Senate Select Committee on Intelligence, *Counterintelligence Threats and Vulnerabilities*, p. 631.

191 **without official government involvement:** .S. Senate Select Committee on Intelligence, *Counterintelligence Threats and Vulnerabilities*, p. 631.

191 **center of one of them:** Mak, "The Kremlin and GOP Have a New Friend."

192 **she told him at the time:** United States v. Maria Butina, United States District Court for the District of Columbia, "Government's Opposition to Defendant's Motion for Bond Review," Case 1:18-cr-00218-TSC (2019).

192 **"For some time," she told Torshin:** United States v. Maria Butina, United States District Court for the District of Columbia, "Government's Opposition to Defendant's Motion for Bond Review," Case 1:18-cr-00218-TSC (2019).

192 **going to the press:** Sheelah Kolhatkar, "A Tycoon's Deep-State Conspiracy Dive," *New Yorker*, December 7, 2020.

193 **Russian intelligence officer:** United States v. Maria Butina, United States District Court for the District of Columbia, "Government's Memorandum in Support of Pretrial Detention," Case 1:18-cr-00218-TSC (2019).

193 **the NRA's 2015 trip:** United States v. Maria Butina, United States District Court for the District of Columbia, "Transcript of Detention Hearing and Arraignment Before the Honorable Deborah A. Robinson, United States Magistrate Judge," Case 1:18-cr-00218-TSC (2019).

193 **NRA and its Russian ties:** U.S. Senate Committee on Finance, *The NRA and Russia* (2019), p. 3.

193 **interfere in the 2016 election:** United States v. Maria Butina, United States District Court for the District of Columbia, "Transcript of Detention Hearing and Arraignment Before the Honorable Deborah A. Robinson, United States Magistrate Judge," Case 1:18-cr-00218-TSC (2019).

193 **"frequently incomplete and misleading":** U.S. Senate Select Committee on Intelligence, *Counterintelligence Threats and Vulnerabilities*, p. 568.

194 **what was clearly his jurisdiction:** Oliver Laurence North, confidential deposition, December 18, 2019.

194 **member Oliver North said:** Oliver Laurence North, confidential deposition, December 18, 2019.

194 **Committee's ultimate report noted:** U.S. Senate Select Committee on Intelligence, *Counterintelligence Threats and Vulnerabilities*, p. 568.

194 **"International Man of Mystery":** Betsy Swan and Spencer Ackerman, "Boyfriend's Email: Butina 'Manipulated' Russian Spy Agency for NRA Trip," *Daily Beast*, February 14, 2019.

194 **"Weapons King":** U.S. Senate Committee on Finance, *The NRA and Russia*, p. 61.

194 **evidence of criminal activity:** United States v. Maria Butina, United States District Court for the District of Columbia, "Transcript of Detention Hearing and Arraignment Before the Honorable Deborah A. Robinson, United States Magistrate Judge," Case 1:18-cr-00218-TSC (2019).

195 **"FSB offer of employment?":** United States v. Maria Butina, United States District Court for the District of Columbia, "Government's Memorandum in Support of Pretrial Detention," Case 1:18-cr-00218-TSC (2019).

195 **FSB on her contact list:** United States v. Maria Butina, United States District Court for the District of Columbia, "Government's Memorandum in Support of Pretrial Detention," Case 1:18-cr-00218-TSC (2019).

195 **Wimbledon men's final:** James Bamford, "The Spy Who Wasn't," *New Republic*, February 11, 2019.

195 **apartment 208:** Bamford, "The Spy Who Wasn't."

195 **her under arrest:** Bamford, "The Spy Who Wasn't."

195 **"espionage lite":** Office of the Inspector General, U.S. Department of Justice, "Audit of the National Security Division's Enforcement and Administration of the Foreign Agents Registration Act," September 2016.

196 **in cell 2FO2:** Bamford, "The Spy Who Wasn't."

197 **country's "malign activities":** "Treasury Designates Russian Oligarchs, Officials, and Entities in Response to Worldwide Malign Activity," U.S. Department of the Treasury, April 6, 2018.

197 **Taganskaya organized crime group:** Tim Mak, "Exclusive: Documents Detail Meetings of Russians with Treasury, Federal Reserve," NPR, May 10, 2018.

197 **to global financial institutions:** Tim Mak, "Documents Reveal How Russian Official Courted Conservatives in U.S. Since 2009," NPR, May 11, 2018.

197 **started scrutinizing his businesses:** Jonathan Ellis, "Former Political Operative Paul Erickson Sentenced to Federal Prison," *Sioux Falls Argus Leader*, July 6, 2020.

197 **for more than a decade:** Danielle Ferguson, "Paul Erickson, Former Boyfriend of Indicted Russian Agent Maria Butina, Pleads Guilty to Wire Fraud," *Sioux Falls Argus Leader*, November 26, 2019.

197 **Butina eventually served:** Ellis, "Former Political Operative Paul Erickson Sentenced."

197 **Trump called Erickson's crimes "minor":** Seth Tupper, "Trump Pardon Wipes Out $3 Million for Erickson Victims," SDPB Radio, January 20, 2021.

198 **North wrote in a memo:** Letter from Oliver North to Wayne LaPierre, "Personal and Confidential," National Rifle Association of America Office of the President, April 8, 2019.

198 **hired Elaine Lammert:** John Frazer, confidential deposition, January 16, 2020.

198 **principal deputy general counsel:** "Elaine Lammert," George Washington University College of Professional Studies, https://www.cps .gwu.edu/elaine-lammert.

198 **"We did nothing":** Email, Scott Christman to Jason Ouimet and Jennifer Baker, September 2, 2018.

198 **"team player Jen Baker":** Email, from Andrew Arulanandam to Anthony Makris and Josh Powell, January 19, 2018.

199 **reportedly, by the FBI:** Peter Stone and Greg Gordon, "FBI Investigating Whether Russian Money Went to NRA to Help Trump," McClatchy DC Bureau, January 18, 2018.

199 **was just over $2,500:** Tim Mak, "NRA, in New Document, Acknowledges More Than 20 Russian-Linked Contributors," NPR, April 11, 2018.

199 **NRA membership dues in 2012:** Matthew H. Bower, "Letter to Federal Election Commission Re: MUR 7314," National Rifle Association of America Office of the General Counsel, March 19, 2019, https://www.fec .gov/files/legal/murs/7314/19044473559.pdf.

199 **moment of self-reflection:** Matthew Rosenberg, Michael LaForgia, and Andrew E. Kramer, "Wife of Former N.R.A President Tapped Accused Russian Agent in Pursuit of Jet Fuel Payday," *New York Times*, September 2, 2018.

CHAPTER 18: THE START OF THE END

200 **332 incidents of gunfire:** "Gunfire on School Grounds in the United States," Everytown Research & Policy, accessed May 22, 2021, https:// everytownresearch.org/maps/gunfire-on-school-grounds/.

200 **for changes in gun laws:** Peter Jamison, Joe Heim, Lori Aratini, and Marissa J. Lang, "'Never Again!' Students Demand Action Against Gun Violence in Nation's Capital," *Washington Post*, March 24, 2018.

201 **do business with it:** Josh Powell, *Inside the NRA*, p. 164.

201 **against the NRA's servers:** Powell, *Inside the NRA*, p. 165.

201 **full-time security guard to two:** Powell, *Inside the NRA*, p. 167.

201 **ball cap, jeans, and sunglasses:** Wayne LaPierre, confidential deposition, September 24, 2019.

201 **wore a bulletproof vest:** Powell, *Inside the NRA*, p. 170.

202 **"somebody starts yelling at me":** Wayne LaPierre, confidential deposition, September 24, 2019.

202 **"leaving or quitting":** Powell, *Inside the NRA*, p. 167.

202 **meeting in a disguise:** Bill Winkler testimony, United States Bankruptcy Court for the Northern District of Texas Dallas Division, Case 21-30085, April 16, 2021.

202 **Officers Compensation Committee:** People of the State of New York v. The National Rifle Association, Supreme Court of the State of New York, County of New York, "Summons and Complaint," Index No. 451625/2020, p. 50.

202 **guarded, gated homes:** Wayne LaPierre, confidential deposition, September 24, 2019.

202 **ten-thousand-square-foot mansion:** Carol D. Leonnig and Beth Reinhard, "NRA Chief Sought Purchase of $6 Million Mansion in Wake of Parkland Shooting," *Washington Post*, August 7, 2019.

202 **exclusive golf community** Mark Maremont, "NRA Chief Sought Help of Group's Ad Agency in Trying to Buy $5 Million Mansion," *Wall Street Journal*, August 6, 2019.

202 **called "WBB Investments":** People of the State of New York v. The National Rifle Association, Supreme Court of the State of New York, County of New York, "Summons and Complaint," Index No. 451625/2020, p. 51.

203 **French-style country estate:** Leonnig and Reinhard, "NRA Chief Sought Purchase of $6 Million Mansion."

203 **faced after Parkland:** Wayne LaPierre, confidential deposition, September 24, 2019.

203 **the home's cabinetry:** People of the State of New York v. The National Rifle Association, Supreme Court of the State of New York, County of New York, "Summons and Complaint," Index No. 451625/2020, p. 51.

203 **to a nearby golf club:** People of the State of New York v. The National Rifle Association, Supreme Court of the State of New York, County of New York, "Summons and Complaint," Index No. 451625/2020, p. 51.

203 **money was returned:** People of the State of New York v. The National Rifle Association, Supreme Court of the State of New York, County of New York, "Summons and Complaint," Index No. 451625/2020, p. 52.

203 **version of the story:** Maremont, "NRA Chief Sought Help of Group's Ad Agency."

203 **"just wasn't correct":** Bill Winkler testimony, United States Bankruptcy Court for the Northern District of Texas Dallas Division, Case 21-30085, April 16, 2021.

203 **"I killed it":** Wayne LaPierre, confidential deposition, September 24, 2019.

204 **that the NRA was running:** Carol D. Leonnig and Tom Hamburger, "How a Hard-Charging Lawyer Helped Fuel a Civil War Inside the NRA," *Washington Post*, September 18, 2019.

205 **his ten-year anniversary:** Alex Yablon, "NRA's TV Operation Lays Off Several Employees," *The Trace*, November 28, 2018.

205 **less than a year:** Lachlan Markay, "Dan Bongino out at NRATV," *Daily Beast*, December 10, 2018.

205 **bring down expenses:** People of the State of New York v. The National Rifle Association, Supreme Court of the State of New York, County of New York, "Summons and Complaint," Index No. 451625/2020, p. 39.

205 **includes organizing volunteers:** Beth Reinhard, "NRA Boosted Executive Pay While Cutting Funding to Key Programs, Filing Shows," *Washington Post*, November 26, 2019.

205 **NRA posted a $2.7 million deficit:** Mark Maremont and James V. Grimaldi, "NRA Paid Wayne LaPierre $2.2 Million in 2018, a 55% Increase," *Wall Street Journal*, November 15, 2019.

206 **according to the NY AG probe:** People of the State of New York v. The National Rifle Association, Supreme Court of the State of New York, County of New York, "Summons and Complaint," Index No. 451625/2020, pp. 94–95.

206 **Wayne told lawyers in a deposition:** Wayne LaPierre, confidential deposition, September 24, 2019.

206 **making up the difference:** Reinhard, "NRA Chief Wayne LaPierre Received a 57 Percent Pay Raise."

206 **justify the extra money:** People of the State of New York v. The National Rifle Association, Supreme Court of the State of New York, County of New York, "Summons and Complaint," Index No. 451625/2020, p. 96.

206 **"security concerns" Wayne faced:** People of the State of New York v. The National Rifle Association, Supreme Court of the State of New York, County of New York, "Summons and Complaint," Index No. 451625/ 2020, p. 96.

206 **bonuses over twelve years:** People of the State of New York v. The National Rifle Association, Supreme Court of the State of New York, County of New York, "Summons and Complaint," Index No. 451625/2020, p. 100.

207 **"I stayed on as EVP":** People of the State of New York v. The National Rifle Association, Supreme Court of the State of New York, County of New York, "Summons and Complaint," Index No. 451625/2020, p. 99.

207 **"NRA as a charitable institution":** "Protecting New Yorkers from Gun Violence," Tish James for Attorney General: The People's Lawyer, https:// www.tishjames2018.com/protecting-new-yorkers-from-gun-violence/.

207 **"organization," James said:** Teddy Grant, "Letitia 'Tish' James on Becoming New York's Next Attorney General," *Ebony*, October 31, 2018.

208 **compliance with the law:** Wayne LaPierre, confidential deposition, September 24, 2019.

209 **to themselves or others:** Martin Kaste, "NRA Signals Openness to Gun Removal Laws—with Conditions," NPR, March 19, 2018.

209 **"guns, thank you":** Josh Hafner, "National Walkout Day: NRA Posts Photo of AR-15 One Month After Parkland Shooter Used AR-15," *USA Today*, March 14, 2018.

209 **in the Parkland shootings:** Josh Bowden, "NRA Tweets During Student Gun-Control Protests: 'I'll Control My Own Guns, Thank You,'" *The Hill*, March 14, 2018.

210 **site of a demonstration:** Danny Hakim, "Inside Wayne LaPierre's Battle for the N.R.A.," *New York Times Magazine*, December 18, 2019.

210 **Cox to threaten to quit:** Oliver Laurence North, confidential deposition, December 18, 2019.

210 **Wayne if he were to leave:** Oliver Laurence North, confidential deposition, December 18, 2019.

210   **"What do you want?":** Oliver Laurence North, confidential deposition, December 18, 2019.

210   **outspend the NRA:** Karl Evers-Hillstrom, "Midterms: Gun Control Groups Outspend NRA and Other Gun Rights Rivals," OpenSecrets.org, October 26, 2018.

210   **"I don't need any help," Wayne insisted:** Oliver Laurence North, confidential deposition, December 18, 2019.

211   **nearly $1.4 million:** Reinhard, "NRA Boosted Executive Pay While Cutting Funding to Key Programs."

211   **drama that followed:** Hakim, "Inside Wayne LaPierre's Battle for the N.R.A."

211   **Cox hard not to leave:** Oliver Laurence North, confidential deposition, December 18, 2019.

211   **"everybody wanted":** Oliver Laurence North, confidential deposition, December 18, 2019.

211   **be Wayne's successor:** Oliver Laurence North, confidential deposition, December 18, 2019.

CHAPTER 19: WHISTLEBLOWERS AND AN ANGRY MOTHER

212   **vibrant contrast to her husband:** Jacqui Shine, "How Civil Must America Be?," *New York Times*, August 11, 2018; Rekha Basu, "Grinnell Anti-gun Violence Activists Hope to Meet with Their Neighbor: the NRA President," *Des Moines Register*, November 18, 2017.

212   **east of Des Moines:** Stav Ziv, "Five Years After Sandy Hook, the NRA President's Neighbors Plead for Real Talk on Gun Violence," *Newsweek*, December 4, 2017.

212   **local students to the school:** Shine, "How Civil Must America Be?"

213   **spot in the Golden Ring of Freedom:** Basu, "Grinnell Anti-gun violence Activists Hope to Meet with Their Neighbor."

213   **at Sandy Hook Elementary School:** Basu, "Grinnell Anti-gun violence Activists Hope to Meet with Their Neighbor."

213   **"shootings are good for business":** Shine, "How Civil Must America Be?"

214   **"[on] family reasons":** Wayne LaPierre, confidential deposition, September 24, 2019.

214   **to his leaving:** Oliver Laurence North, confidential deposition, December 18, 2019.

214   **"this," North recalled:** Oliver Laurence North, confidential deposition, December 18, 2019.

215   **firearms-related issues:** People of the State of New York v. The National Rifle Association, Supreme Court of the State of New York, County of New York, "Summons and Complaint," Index No. 451625/2020, p. 65.

215   **working at the gun rights group:** John Frazer, confidential deposition, January 16, 2020.

215   **while working at the NRA:** John Frazer, confidential deposition, January 16, 2020.

215 **general counsel of the NRA:** John Frazer, confidential deposition, January 16, 2020.

216 **he led a team of five:** John Frazer, confidential deposition, January 16, 2020.

216 **with the New York laws:** People of the State of New York v. The National Rifle Association, Supreme Court of the State of New York, County of New York, "Summons and Complaint," Index No. 451625/2020, p. 3.

216 **"facilitate his misuse of charitable assets":** People of the State of New York v. The National Rifle Association, Supreme Court of the State of New York, County of New York, "Summons and Complaint," Index No. 451625/2020, p. 3.

216 **Frazer's history and background:** People of the State of New York v. The National Rifle Association, Supreme Court of the State of New York, County of New York, "Summons and Complaint," Index No. 451625/2020, p. 66.

217 **audit committee's role:** People of the State of New York v. The National Rifle Association, Supreme Court of the State of New York, County of New York, "Summons and Complaint," Index No. 451625/2020, p. 115.

217 **internal auditing at the NRA:** People of the State of New York v. The National Rifle Association, Supreme Court of the State of New York, County of New York, "Summons and Complaint," Index No. 451625/2020, p. 115.

217 **collects AK-47s:** Gregory J. Millman, "Gunning for Risk at the NRA," *Wall Street Journal*, May 19, 2015.

217 **as a risk manager:** David Katz, "Managing Risks at the National Rifle Association." *CFO*, April 22, 2016.

217 ***CFO* magazine in 2016:** Katz, "Managing Risks at the National Rifle Association."

218 **one whistleblower later said:** Sonya Rowling deposition, United States Bankruptcy Court for the Northern District of Texas Dallas Division, Case 21-30085, March 19, 2021.

218 **course of this year:** People of the State of New York v. The National Rifle Association, Supreme Court of the State of New York, County of New York, "Summons and Complaint," Index No. 451625/2020, p. 117.

218 **At least five staffers:** Sonya Rowling deposition, United States Bankruptcy Court for the Northern District of Texas Dallas Division, Case 21-30085, March 19, 2021; Josh Powell, *Inside the NRA*, p. 185.

218 **one-and-a-half-page:** Mike Spies, "NRA Memo Reveals New Details About Leadership's Conflicts and Unexplained Spending," *The Trace*, May 7, 2019.

218 **on July 30, 2018:** People of the State of New York v. The National Rifle Association, Supreme Court of the State of New York, County of New York, "Summons and Complaint," Index No. 451625/2020, p. 117.

218 **before the presentation began:** People of the State of New York v. The National Rifle Association, Supreme Court of the State of New York, County of New York, "Summons and Complaint," Index No. 451625/2020, p. 117.

218 **he claimed later:** Charles Cotton testimony, United States Bankruptcy Court for the Northern District of Texas Dallas Division, Case 21-30085, April 5, 2021.

218 **in particular Ackerman McQueen:** Mike Spies, "Secrecy, Self-Dealing, and Greed at the N.R.A.," *New Yorker*, April 17, 2019.

218 **to former NRA employees:** Spies, "Secrecy, Self-Dealing, and Greed at the N.R.A."

218 **all these arrangements:** Spies, "Secrecy, Self-Dealing, and Greed at the N.R.A."

218 **"step up + fulfill its duties!":** Spies, "Secrecy, Self-Dealing, and Greed at the N.R.A."

218 **the meeting that day:** People of the State of New York v. The National Rifle Association, Supreme Court of the State of New York, County of New York, "Summons and Complaint," Index No. 451625/2020, p. 118.

219 **whistleblowers' complaints:** People of the State of New York v. The National Rifle Association, Supreme Court of the State of New York, County of New York, "Summons and Complaint," Index No. 451625/2020, p. 118.

219 **that story, in November 2018:** Mike Maremont, "NRA Awarded Contracts to Firms with Ties to Top Officials," *Wall Street Journal*, November 30, 2018.

219 **resigned in November 2018:** Martin Levine, "Another Voice Says Something Is Rotten at the NRA," *Nonprofit Quarterly*, August 2, 2019.

219 **changed her phone number:** John Frazer deposition, United States Bankruptcy Court for the Northern District of Texas Dallas Division, Case 21-30085, March 15, 2021.

219 **"You're not leaving!" Angus said:** Powell, *Inside the NRA*, p. 183.

219 **$1.8 million "consulting" package:** People of the State of New York v. The National Rifle Association, Supreme Court of the State of New York, County of New York, "Summons and Complaint," Index No. 451625/2020, pp. 56–57.

219 **investigate the complaints:** People of the State of New York v. The National Rifle Association, Supreme Court of the State of New York, County of New York, "Summons and Complaint," Index No. 451625/2020, p. 118.

CHAPTER 20: BREWER REPLACES ACKERMAN McQUEEN

220 **Lieutenant Colonel Oliver L. North (Ret.):** Oliver Laurence North, confidential deposition, December 18, 2019.

221 **Comerica Bank Tower in Dallas:** Jeanne Prejean, "My Office: William 'Bill' Brewer," *D Magazine*, October 2016.

221 **whose "Rambo tactics":** Mark Donald, "Rambo Justice," *Dallas Observer*, March 19, 1998.

221 **Brewer, Attorney & Counselors—in 1984:** Prejean, "My Office."

221 **"the bad boys of the Dallas Bar":** Donald, "Rambo Justice."

222 **jerk to other lawyers:** Donald, "Rambo Justice."

222 **"where" and "when":** Donald, "Rambo Justice."

223 **resulting in a mistrial:** Donald, "Rambo Justice."

223 **tainted a jury pool:** Carol D. Leonnig and Tom Hamburger, "How a Hard-Charging Lawyer Helped Fuel a Civil War Inside the NRA," *Washington Post*, September 18, 2019.

223 **working with the NRA:** Wayne LaPierre, confidential deposition, September 24, 2019.

223 **intern at Brewer's firm:** Danny Hakim, "Inside Wayne LaPierre's Battle for the N.R.A.," *New York Times Magazine*, December 18, 2019.

223 **of the Second Amendment:** National Rifle Association v. Ackerman McQueen, United States District Court for the Northern District of Texas, Dallas Division, "Brief in Support of Defendants' Motion to Disqualify Plaintiff's Counsel," Civil Action No. 3:19-cv-02074-G-BK, April 15, 2020.

223 **Second Amendment case:** Leonnig and Hamburger, "How a Hard-Charging Lawyer Helped Fuel a Civil War."

223 **and Beto O'Rourke:** Hakim, "Inside Wayne LaPierre's Battle for the N.R.A."

223 **$1,400 an hour, of course:** John Frazer, confidential deposition, January 16, 2020.

223 **"bills were hefty":** Mike Spies, "New Documents Raise Ethical and Billing Concerns About the NRA's Outside Counsel," ProPublica, July 30, 2019.

223 **Brewer's no-bid contract:** People of the State of New York v. The National Rifle Association, Supreme Court of the State of New York, County of New York, "Summons and Complaint," Index No. 451625/2020, p. 109.

224 **John Frazer said later:** John Frazer, confidential deposition, January 16, 2020.

224 **in early 2018:** National Rifle Association v. Ackerman McQueen, United States District Court for the Northern District of Texas, Dallas Division, "Brief in Support of Defendants' Motion to Disqualify Plaintiff's Counsel," Civil Action No. 3:19-cv-02074-G-BK, April 15, 2020.

224 **"issues at the NRA":** Josh Powell, *Inside the NRA*, p. 180.

224 **them the "Vampires":** Powell, *Inside the NRA*, p. 180.

224 **existed for decades:** National Rifle Association v. Ackerman McQueen, United States District Court for the Northern District of Texas, Dallas Division, "Brief in Support of Defendants' Motion to Disqualify Plaintiff's Counsel," Civil Action No. 3:19-cv-02074-G-BK, April 15, 2020.

224 **twenty years her senior:** Andrew Jenks, "Family Business," *Gangster Capitalism*, April 22, 2020, https://shows.cadence13.com/podcast/gangster-capitalism/episodes/4594b033-ab09-454c-ae57-afa20f0b0f6a.

224 **Brewer's fourth marriage:** Hakim, "Inside Wayne LaPierre's Battle for the N.R.A."

225 **Revan, in a later declaration:** National Rifle Association v. Ackerman McQueen, United States District Court for the Northern District of Texas, Dallas Division, "Declaration of Revan McQueen," Civil Action No. 3:19-cv-02074-G, March 30, 2020.

225 **for its relationship with the NRA:** National Rifle Association v. Ackerman McQueen, United States District Court for the Northern District of Texas, Dallas Division, "Brief in Support of Defendants' Motion to Disqualify Plaintiff's Counsel," Civil Action No. 3:19-cv-02074-G-BK, April 15, 2020.

225   **to overthrow Angus:** National Rifle Association v. Ackerman McQueen, United States District Court for the Northern District of Texas, Dallas Division, "Declaration of Revan McQueen," Civil Action No. 3:19-cv-02074-G, March 30, 2020.

225   **bills with Brewer's firm:** National Rifle Association v. Ackerman McQueen, United States District Court for the Northern District of Texas, Dallas Division, "Brief in Support of Defendants' Motion to Disqualify Plaintiff's Counsel," Civil Action No. 3:19-cv-02074-G-BK, April 15, 2020.

226   **saw at the organization:** Wayne LaPierre, confidential deposition, September 24, 2019.

226   **that drove up expenses:** Wayne LaPierre, confidential deposition, September 24, 2019.

226   **she wrote in her memo:** Wayne LaPierre, confidential deposition, September 24, 2019.

226   **key NRA personnel:** Powell, *Inside the NRA*, p. 200.

226   **for this purpose:** "Our Story," Brewer, Attorneys & Counselors, https://www.brewerattorneys.com/story.

226   **claimed in her memo:** Wayne LaPierre, confidential deposition, September 24, 2019.

226   **Brewer told him, for example:** Mildred Hallow, confidential deposition, January 10, 2020.

226   **heard of these burn books:** Wayne LaPierre, confidential deposition, September 24, 2019.

227   **on June 1, 2018:** National Rifle Association v. Ackerman McQueen, United States District Court for the Northern District of Texas, Dallas Division, "Declaration of Revan McQueen," Civil Action No. 3:19-cv-02074-G, March 30, 2020.

227   **$19 million in legal fees:** People of the State of New York v. The National Rifle Association, Supreme Court of the State of New York, County of New York, "Summons and Complaint," Index No. 451625/2020, p. 109.

227   **outline his work with the NRA:** John Frazer, confidential deposition, January 16, 2020.

227   **his legal invoices:** John Frazer, confidential deposition, January 16, 2020.

227   **"I did not . . . that's not my job":** Wayne LaPierre, confidential deposition, September 24, 2019.

228   **Conservative Political Action Conference in 2018:** National Rifle Association v. Ackerman McQueen, United States District Court for the Northern District of Texas, Dallas Division, "Declaration of Revan McQueen," Civil Action No. 3:19-cv-02074-G, March 30, 2020.

228   **as Angus became sicker:** National Rifle Association v. Ackerman McQueen, United States District Court for the Northern District of Texas, Dallas Division, "Declaration of Revan McQueen," Civil Action No. 3:19-cv-02074-G, March 30, 2020.

228   **keep Wayne out of jail:** National Rifle Association v. Ackerman McQueen, United States District Court for the Northern District of Texas, Dallas

Division, "Brief in Support of Defendants' Motion to Disqualify Plaintiff's Counsel," Civil Action No. 3:19-cv-02074-G-BK, April 15, 2020.

228 **become convinced this was the case:** National Rifle Association v. Ackerman McQueen, United States District Court for the Northern District of Texas, Dallas Division, "Declaration of Revan McQueen," Civil Action No. 3:19-cv-02074-G, March 30, 2020.

228 **new expense-reimbursement procedures:** Wayne LaPierre, confidential deposition, September 24, 2019.

228 **this letter on his behalf:** National Rifle Association v. Ackerman McQueen, United States District Court for the Northern District of Texas, Dallas Division, "Declaration of Revan McQueen," Civil Action No. 3:19-cv-02074-G, March 30, 2020.

229 **sworn court filing:** National Rifle Association v. Ackerman McQueen, United States District Court for the Northern District of Texas, Dallas Division, "Declaration of Revan McQueen," Civil Action No. 3:19-cv-02074-G, March 30, 2020.

229 **41 percent of its gross revenue:** Danny Hakim, "N.R.A. Shuts Down Production of NRATV, and Its No. 2 Official Resigns," *New York Times*, June 25, 2019.

229 **what their objective was:** National Rifle Association v. Ackerman McQueen, United States District Court for the Northern District of Texas, Dallas Division, "Declaration of Revan McQueen," Civil Action No. 3:19-cv-02074-G, March 30, 2020.

229 **Over two days:** John Frazer, confidential deposition, January 16, 2020.

229 **expenses through Ackerman McQueen:** John Frazer, confidential deposition, January 16, 2020.

229 **"just a pawn on Brewer's chess board":** National Rifle Association v. Ackerman McQueen, United States District Court for the Northern District of Texas, Dallas Division, "Declaration of Revan McQueen," Civil Action No. 3:19-cv-02074-G, March 30, 2020.

229 **to around $100,000 a day:** National Rifle Association v. Ackerman McQueen, United States District Court for the Northern District of Texas, Dallas Division, "Brief in Support of Defendants' Motion to Disqualify Plaintiff's Counsel," Civil Action No. 3:19-cv-02074-G-BK, April 15, 2020; Mike Spies, "Former NRA Executive Says Top NRA Lawyer Stymied Internal Financial Probes While Racking Up Fees, *The Trace*, July 30, 2019.

CHAPTER 21: THE COLONEL

230 **"It's almost like a volcano":** Oliver Laurence North, confidential deposition, December 18, 2019.

230 **the original suggestion:** Oliver Laurence North, confidential deposition, December 18, 2019.

230 **pair met on April 22, 2018:** Oliver Laurence North, confidential deposition, December 18, 2019.

230   **didn't take part in the meeting:** Oliver Laurence North, confidential
        deposition, December 18, 2019.

230   **"new Charlton Heston":** Oliver Laurence North, confidential deposition,
        December 18, 2019.

230   **build the NRA membership:** Oliver Laurence North, confidential
        deposition, December 18, 2019.

230   **NRA leader taking the reins:** Wayne LaPierre, confidential deposition,
        September 24, 2019.

231   **the organization's board:** Oliver Laurence North, confidential deposition,
        December 18, 2019.

231   **their personal friendship:** Oliver Laurence North, confidential deposition,
        December 18, 2019.

231   **at least a quarter century:** Wayne LaPierre, confidential deposition,
        September 24, 2019.

231   **NRA board in 1998:** Brendan V. Sullivan Jr., Steven M. Cady, and
        Alexander S. Zolan, "Defense of LtCol Oliver North to the NRA's Baseless
        and Illegal Attempt to Expel Him," *LtCol North Submission*, Index No.
        903843-20, https://nrawatch.org/wp-content/uploads/2020/07/2020.07.22
        _North-Answer-Ex-2.pdf.

231   **in part by Wayne:** Wayne LaPierre, confidential deposition, September 24,
        2019.

231   **"the NRA," he recalled:** Oliver Laurence North, confidential deposition,
        December 18, 2019.

231   **Meanwhile, his wife, Betsy:** Oliver Laurence North, confidential
        deposition, December 18, 2019.

231   **his gig at Fox News:** Oliver Laurence North, confidential deposition,
        December 18, 2019.

231   **"I knew it," North said:** Oliver Laurence North, confidential deposition,
        December 18, 2019.

231   **him a stable income:** Oliver Laurence North, confidential deposition,
        December 18, 2019.

232   **"out," Wayne promised:** Oliver Laurence North, confidential deposition,
        December 18, 2019.

232   **making both pitches at once:** Wayne LaPierre, confidential deposition,
        September 24, 2019.

232   **salary back to the NRA:** Wayne LaPierre, confidential deposition,
        September 24, 2019.

232   **"strategic direction of NRA":** Oliver Laurence North, confidential
        deposition, December 18, 2019.

232   **"president of the NRA":** Oliver Laurence North, confidential deposition,
        December 18, 2019.

233   **"and a dry face":** Oliver Laurence North, confidential deposition,
        December 18, 2019.

233   **confusion about the arrangement:** Oliver Laurence North, confidential
        deposition, December 18, 2019.

233 **Fox—by year three:** Oliver Laurence North, confidential deposition, December 18, 2019.

233 **NRA presidency in September:** Oliver Laurence North, confidential deposition, December 18, 2019.

234 **His father was:** Edward Power, "Oliver North Seen As 'A Tremendously Complex Man,'" *Roanoke Times*, October 26, 1994.

234 **"I just stopped killing things":** Oliver Laurence North, confidential deposition, December 18, 2019.

234 **in guns and hunting again:** Oliver Laurence North, confidential deposition, December 18, 2019.

234 **to the National Rifle Association:** Sullivan, Cady, and Zolan, "Defense of LtCol Oliver North."

234 **He was posted to:** "Oliver North," *Encyclopedia Britannica*, https://www .britannica.com/biography/Oliver-North.

234 **took part in a scheme:** "The Iran-Contra Affair," PBS, https://www.pbs.org /wgbh/americanexperience/features/reagan-iran.

234 **indicted in 1988:** "Understanding the Iran-Contra Affairs—The Legal Aftermath," Brown University, https://www.brown.edu/Research /Understanding_the_Iran_Contra_Affair/profile-north.php.

234 **He was charged with:** "Understanding the Iran-Contra Affairs—The Legal Aftermath," Brown University.

235 **vacated on appeal:** Annys Shin, "When Oliver North Avoided Prison Time for His Role in the Iran-Contra Scandal," *Washington Post*, June 28, 2018.

235 **and other documents:** Oliver Laurence North, confidential deposition, December 18, 2019.

235 **them for the letter:** Oliver North, "National Rifle Association of America Report of the Audit Committee," *LtCol North Submission 006*, September 8–9, 2018, Index No. 903843-20, https://nrawatch.org/wp-content/uploads /2020/07/2020.07.22_North-Answer-Ex-2.pdf.

235 **serving as NRA president:** Oliver Laurence North, confidential deposition, December 18, 2019.

236 **six million to fourteen million:** Zachary Warmbrodt, "Oliver North Looks to Recruit Millions to NRA, *Politico*, May 20, 2018.

236 **"I took over as president":** Oliver Laurence North, confidential deposition, December 18, 2019.

236 **"My Marines kept me alive":** Oliver Laurence North, confidential deposition, December 18, 2019.

236 **signature yellow pads:** Oliver Laurence North, confidential deposition, December 18, 2019.

236 **North shot back:** Oliver Laurence North, confidential deposition, December 18, 2019.

236 **his "kitchen cabinet":** Oliver Laurence North, confidential deposition, December 18, 2019.

236 **president of the board:** Oliver Laurence North, confidential deposition, December 18, 2019.

237 **didn't need any help:** Oliver Laurence North, confidential deposition, December 18, 2019.

237 **"thousand years," North said:** Oliver Laurence North, confidential deposition, December 18, 2019.

238 **interfering with his work:** Wayne LaPierre, confidential deposition, September 24, 2019.

238 **"we expected," North later testified:** Oliver Laurence North, confidential deposition, December 18, 2019.

239 **thing was a mess:** Oliver Laurence North, confidential deposition, December 18, 2019.

239 **Wayne had changed his mind:** Oliver Laurence North, confidential deposition, December 18, 2019.

239 **"investigations," North pleaded:** Oliver Laurence North, confidential deposition, December 18, 2019.

239 **Brewer's overall compensation was:** Oliver Laurence North, confidential deposition, December 18, 2019.

239 **the abbreviation "WTF?":** Oliver Laurence North, confidential deposition, December 18, 2019.

240 **including the Brewer invoices:** Oliver Laurence North, confidential deposition, December 18, 2019.

240 **North wrote in one such letter:** Oliver North, "Letter to John Frazer and Charles Cotton," *LtCol North Submission 041*, Index No. 903843-20, April 18, 2019, https://nrawatch.org/wp-content/uploads/2020/07/2020.07.22 _North-Answer-Ex-2.pdf.

240 **day around early 2019:** North, "Letter to John Frazer and Charles Cotton."

240 **$2.9 million per month:** North, "Letter to John Frazer and Charles Cotton."

240 **Brewer firm's invoices:** North, "Letter to John Frazer and Charles Cotton."

240 **"Well, you need help":** Oliver Laurence North, confidential deposition, December 18, 2019.

240 **and losing his job:** John Frazer, confidential deposition, January 16, 2020.

241 **Wayne's travel agent:** John Frazer, confidential deposition, January 16, 2020.

241 **North later fumed:** Oliver Laurence North, confidential deposition, December 18, 2019.

241 **for him to inquire:** Oliver Laurence North, confidential deposition, December 18, 2019.

241 **read one such letter:** Oliver Laurence North, confidential deposition, December 18, 2019.

241 **"audit," North later said:** Oliver Laurence North, confidential deposition, December 18, 2019.

242 **Wayne would say:** Wayne LaPierre, confidential deposition, September 24, 2019.

242 **"like this waterboarding of me":** Danny Hakim, "Inside Wayne LaPierre's Battle for the N.R.A.," *New York Times Magazine*, December 18, 2019.

242 **"maybe your wife, Susan":** Oliver Laurence North, confidential deposition, December 18, 2019.

242 **North later recounted:** Oliver Laurence North, confidential deposition, December 18, 2019.

242 **"Mercury Group," he said:** Oliver Laurence North, confidential deposition, December 18, 2019.

243 **to secure health insurance:** Oliver Laurence North, confidential deposition, December 18, 2019.

243 **"benefit," North later said:** Oliver Laurence North, confidential deposition, December 18, 2019.

243 **Lawyer: "Okay":** Wayne LaPierre, confidential deposition, September 24, 2019.

243 **"ever being explored":** Oliver Laurence North, confidential deposition, December 18, 2019.

243 **"in a pool of sharks":** Oliver Laurence North, confidential deposition, December 18, 2019.

244 **Hart later testified:** National Rifle Association v. Ackerman McQueen, United States District Court for the Northern District of Texas, Dallas Division, "Brief in Support of Defendants' Motion to Disqualify Plaintiff's Counsel," Civil Action No. 3:19-cv-02074-G-BK, April 15, 2020.

244 **"Brewer's bill for [the] day":** Oliver Laurence North, confidential deposition, December 18, 2019.

244 **hands on Brewer's invoices:** Oliver Laurence North, confidential deposition, December 18, 2019.

244 **examined them either:** Wayne LaPierre, confidential deposition, September 24, 2019.

245 **he told Wayne:** Wayne LaPierre, confidential deposition, September 24, 2019.

245 **"yelled at," he said:** Wayne LaPierre, confidential deposition, September 24, 2019.

245 **"million cuss words":** Wayne LaPierre, confidential deposition, September 24, 2019.

245 **"the truth," Wayne recalled:** Wayne LaPierre, confidential deposition, September 24, 2019.

245 **Wayne: "No":** Wayne LaPierre, confidential deposition, September 24, 2019.

246 **"pressure from the board":** Josh Powell, *Inside the NRA*, p. 201.

246 **review Ackerman McQueen's financial records:** National Rifle Association v. Ackerman McQueen, United States District Court for the Northern District of Texas, Dallas Division, "Declaration of Revan McQueen," Civil Action No. 3:19-cv-02074-G, March 30, 2020.

246 **assist in the effort:** Powell, *Inside the NRA*, p. 187.

246 **"we went," observed Powell:** Powell, *Inside the NRA*, p. 187.

246 **"an emotional meeting":** Bill Winkler testimony, United States Bankruptcy Court for the Northern District of Texas Dallas Division, Case 21-30085, April 16, 2021.

246 **threatened and harassed:** Tony Makris testimony, United States Bankruptcy Court for the Northern District of Texas Dallas Division, Case 21-30085, April 16, 2021.
246 **Angus was especially affronted:** Bill Winkler testimony, United States Bankruptcy Court for the Northern District of Texas Dallas Division, Case 21-30085, April 16, 2021.
246 **"You're dead to me":** Wayne LaPierre deposition, United States Bankruptcy Court for the Northern District of Texas Dallas Division, Case 21-30085, March 23, 2021.
246 **"He begged us":** Tony Makris testimony, United States Bankruptcy Court for the Northern District of Texas Dallas Division, Case 21-30085, April 16, 2021.
247 **including about its other clients:** National Rifle Association v. Ackerman McQueen, United States District Court for the Northern District of Texas, Dallas Division, "Declaration of Revan McQueen," Civil Action No. 3:19-cv-02074-G, March 30, 2020.
247 **"it's palpable":** Tony Makris testimony, United States Bankruptcy Court for the Northern District of Texas Dallas Division, Case 21-30085, April 16, 2021.
247 **conducted by Ackerman McQueen:** Powell, *Inside the NRA*, p. 205.
247 **for Wayne the previous year:** National Rifle Association v. Ackerman McQueen, United States District Court for the Northern District of Texas, Dallas Division, "Declaration of Revan McQueen," Civil Action No. 3:19-cv-02074-G, March 30, 2020.
247 **nephew pick out an apartment:** Tony Makris testimony, United States Bankruptcy Court for the Northern District of Texas Dallas Division, Case 21-30085, April 16, 2021.
247 **"What has you so scared?":** Tony Makris testimony, United States Bankruptcy Court for the Northern District of Texas Dallas Division, Case 21-30085, April 16, 2021.
248 **admitting his great fear:** Tony Makris testimony, United States Bankruptcy Court for the Northern District of Texas Dallas Division, Case 21-30085, April 16, 2021.
248 **Wayne has denied:** Wayne LaPierre deposition, United States Bankruptcy Court for the Northern District of Texas Dallas Division, Case 21-30085, March 23, 2021.
248 **Forensic Risk Alliance:** John Frazer, confidential deposition, January 16, 2020.
248 **behalf of the gun group:** John Frazer, confidential deposition, January 16, 2020.
248 **gave it the code O-N:** John Frazer, confidential deposition, January 16, 2020.
248 **had originally planned:** John Frazer, confidential deposition, January 16, 2020.
248 **to see the records:** Wayne LaPierre, confidential deposition, September 24, 2019.

248 **gave it the green light:** Wayne LaPierre, confidential deposition, September 24, 2019.

248 **his medical condition was improving:** National Rifle Association v. Ackerman McQueen, United States District Court for the Northern District of Texas Dallas Division, "Declaration of Revan McQueen," Civil Action No. 3:19-cv-02074-G, March 30, 2020.

249 **election that year:** Oliver Laurence North, confidential deposition, December 18, 2019.

249 **he takes a pay cut:** Oliver Laurence North, confidential deposition, December 18, 2019.

249 **committee chairman Charles Cotton:** Oliver Laurence North, confidential deposition, December 18, 2019.

249 **"expenses for the last 30 years":** Hakim, "Inside Wayne LaPierre's Battle for the N.R.A."

249 **he said at a deposition:** Wayne LaPierre, confidential deposition, September 24, 2019.

249 **"I knew they were doing it":** Wayne LaPierre, confidential deposition, September 24, 2019.

250 **general counsel, John Frazer:** John Frazer, confidential deposition, January 16, 2020.

250 **a chance to vote on it:** Wayne LaPierre, confidential deposition, September 24, 2019.

250 **from public news reports:** Oliver Laurence North, confidential deposition, December 18, 2019.

250 **North said about this time:** Oliver Laurence North, confidential deposition, December 18, 2019.

CHAPTER 22: WEDNESDAY, APRIL 24, 2019

251 **catastrophic financial situation:** Mike Spies, "Secrecy, Self-Dealing, and Greed at the N.R.A.," *New Yorker*, April 17, 2019.

252 **"inconsistent with industry standards":** Oliver Laurence North, confidential deposition, December 18, 2019.

252 **leak to *The Wall Street Journal*:** Mark Maremont, "Leaked Letters Reveal Details of NRA Chief's Alleged Spending," *Wall Street Journal*, May 11, 2019.

253 **He left it unsigned:** Oliver Laurence North, confidential deposition, December 18, 2019.

253 **NRA for more than a decade:** John Frazer, confidential deposition, January 16, 2020.

253 **"crazy," Wayne responded:** Wayne LaPierre, confidential deposition, September 24, 2019.

253 **Hart as he pleased:** John Frazer, confidential deposition, January 16, 2020.

254 **Wayne LaPierre never writes emails:** Wayne LaPierre, confidential deposition, September 24, 2019.

254 **in front of Wayne to sign:** Oliver Laurence North, confidential deposition, December 18, 2019.
254 **were demanding to talk to him:** Mildred Hallow, confidential deposition, January 10, 2020.
254 **held in North's suite:** Mildred Hallow, confidential deposition, January 10, 2020.
254 **allies in his own suite:** Mildred Hallow, confidential deposition, January 10, 2020.
254 **now was arriving late:** Oliver Laurence North, confidential deposition, December 18, 2019.
254 **he had entered the room:** Oliver Laurence North, confidential deposition, December 18, 2019.
254 **"the colonel and me!":** Oliver Laurence North, confidential deposition, December 18, 2019.
254 **claimed not to know anything:** Oliver Laurence North, confidential deposition, December 18, 2019.
255 **Cotton told Wayne:** Wayne LaPierre, confidential deposition, September 24, 2019.
255 **how he wanted them to act:** Oliver Laurence North, confidential deposition, December 18, 2019.
255 **directly into North's eyes:** Wayne LaPierre, confidential deposition, September 24, 2019.
255 **Millie's phone rang:** Wayne LaPierre, confidential deposition, September 24, 2019.
256 **who needed to talk to her:** Mildred Hallow, confidential deposition, January 10, 2020.
256 **members at the convention:** Oliver Laurence North, confidential deposition, December 18, 2019.
256 **punched in the stomach:** Mildred Hallow, confidential deposition, January 10, 2020.
256 **unless Wayne resigned:** Mildred Hallow, confidential deposition, January 10, 2020.
256 **"Wayne," Boren said:** Mildred Hallow, confidential deposition, January 10, 2020.
256 **information to Wayne immediately:** Mildred Hallow, confidential deposition, January 10, 2020.
256 **"couple hours," Boren said:** Mildred Hallow, confidential deposition, January 10, 2020.
256 **them by a sliding wall:** Mildred Hallow, confidential deposition, January 10, 2020.
256 **Wayne absolutely erupted:** Mildred Hallow, confidential deposition, January 10, 2020.
256 **not prone to swearing:** Mildred Hallow, confidential deposition, January 10, 2020.
256 **before storming out of the room:** Mildred Hallow, confidential deposition, January 10, 2020.

256 **"This is not right":** Richard Childress, "To the NRA Hearing Board," *LtCol North Submission 111,* Index No. 903843-20, May 28, 2020, https://nrawatch.org/wp-content/uploads/2020/07/2020.07.22_North-Answer-Ex-2.pdf.

256 **answer from Childress:** Mildred Hallow, confidential deposition, January 10, 2020.

257 **"Not today," North responded:**   Mildred Hallow, confidential deposition, January 10, 2020.

257 **plane to talk to Angus:** Oliver Laurence North, confidential deposition, December 18, 2019.

257 **"ameliorate the hostility":** Oliver Laurence North, confidential deposition, December 18, 2019.

257 **"shooting at each other":** Oliver Laurence North, confidential deposition, December 18, 2019.

257 **"corrupt," North recalled:** Oliver Laurence North, confidential deposition, December 18, 2019.

258 **he later said:** Oliver Laurence North, confidential deposition, December 18, 2019.

258 **course of the day, dozens:** Wayne LaPierre, confidential deposition, September 24, 2019.

258 **support to stay on:** Mildred Hallow, confidential deposition, January 10, 2020.

258 **at around 4 P.M.:** Carolyn Meadows deposition read into evidence, United States Bankruptcy Court for the Northern District of Texas Dallas Division, Case 21-30085, April 20, 2021.

258 **McQueen had on Wayne:** Chris Cox, "To the NRA Hearing Board," *LtCol North Submission 116,* Index No. 903843-20, May 28, 2020, https://nrawatch.org/wp-content/uploads/2020/07/2020.07.22_North-Answer-Ex-2.pdf.

258 **"walk down the street":** Wayne LaPierre, confidential deposition, September 24, 2019.

259 **"That's what they're going to do":** Wayne LaPierre, confidential deposition, September 24, 2019.

259 **but couldn't reach him:** Oliver Laurence North, confidential deposition, December 18, 2019.

259 **points during the day:** Oliver Laurence North, confidential deposition, December 18, 2019.

259 **close to Wayne and Susan:** Mildred Hallow, confidential deposition, January 10, 2020.

259 **the window was short:** Mildred Hallow, confidential deposition, January 10, 2020.

259 **by a comfortable retirement:** Mildred Hallow, confidential deposition, January 10, 2020.

259 **had bonded over it:** Mildred Hallow, confidential deposition, January 10, 2020.

259 **Betsy, his wife:** Oliver Laurence North, confidential deposition, December 18, 2019.

259 **warm and straightforward:** Oliver Laurence North, confidential deposition, December 18, 2019.

260 **North would later say:** Oliver Laurence North, confidential deposition, December 18, 2019.

260 **staying on at the NRA:** Mildred Hallow, confidential deposition, January 10, 2020.

260 **aloud from her notes:** Mildred Hallow, confidential deposition, January 10, 2020.

260 **woman told Josh Powell:** Josh Powell, *Inside the NRA*, p. 215.

260 **North later said in a deposition:** Oliver Laurence North, confidential deposition, December 18, 2019.

260 **"I ran a few, right":** Oliver Laurence North, confidential deposition, December 18, 2019.

260 **Marine Corps officer responded:** Oliver Laurence North, confidential deposition, December 18, 2019.

Chapter 23: The Weekend from Hell

262 **"yet it happened":** Oliver Laurence North, confidential deposition, December 18, 2019.

262 **NRA for some thirty years:** John Frazer, confidential deposition, January 16, 2020.

262 **the same day as Cooper:** John Frazer, confidential deposition, January 16, 2020.

263 **"DO NOT HESITATE TO CALL WITH ANY QUESTIONS":** Oliver North, "Email to John Frazer and William 'Wit' Davis," *LtCol North Submission 50*, Index No. 903843-20, April 25, 2020, https://nrawatch.org/wp-content/uploads/2020/07/2020.07.22_North-Answer-Ex-2.pdf.

263 **members of the audit committee:** Wayne LaPierre, confidential deposition, September 24, 2019.

263 **Millie but blessed by Wayne:** Oliver Laurence North, confidential deposition, December 18, 2019.

263 **the email read:** Danny Hakim, "How Wayne LaPierre Survived a Revolt at the N.R.A.," *New York Times*, August 22, 2019.

263 **North, but she refused:** Mildred Hallow, confidential deposition, January 10, 2020.

263 **which she did reluctantly:** Mildred Hallow, confidential deposition, January 10, 2020.

263 **"I'm not going to stay for this":** Oliver Laurence North, confidential deposition, December 18, 2019.

264 **investigation could be started:** Oliver Laurence North, confidential deposition, December 18, 2019.

264 **money from Ackerman McQueen:** Wayne LaPierre, "Letter to Members of the Board," National Rifle Association of America, April 25, 2019.

264 **"backroom retirement deal":** LaPierre, "Letter to Members of the Board."

265 **address the NRA's annual conference:** Andrew Jenks, "Let Loose the Dogs of War," *Gangster Capitalism*, March 25, 2020, https://shows.cadence13.com /podcast/gangster-capitalism/episodes/986fb1de-ce23-4d73-a40e -7903cca52fab.

265 **"the Second Amendment":** Dwight Adams, "Read Donald Trump's Speech from the NRA Convention in Indianapolis," *IndyStar*, April 26, 2019.

265 **not be able to support him:** Maggie Haberman and Annie Karni, "N.R.A.'s LaPierre Asks Trump to 'Stop the Games' Over Gun Legislation in Discussion About Its Support," *New York Times*, September 27, 2019.

265 **legal team was "lousy":** Betsy Swan and Asawin Suebsaeng, "Trump to NRA Bigwigs: Get Better Lawyers," *Daily Beast*, August 8, 2019.

266 **"get back to GREATNESS—FAST!":** Allan Smith, "Trump Says NRA 'Must Get Its Act Together Quickly' Amid Internal Strife, New York Probe," NBC News, April 29, 2019.

266 **Childress told the crowd:** Shannon Watts (@shannonrwatts), "BREAKING: @NRA Board member reads a letter from Oliver North saying he has been forced out of the organization . . . ," Twitter, April 27, 2019, https://twitter.com/shannonrwatts/status/1122144959526768647.

266 **NRA's alleged financial misconduct:** Oliver North, "Statement of LtCol Oliver North to the NRA Board," *LtCol North Submission 94*, Index No. 903843-20, April 27, 2020, https://nrawatch.org/wp-content/uploads/2020 /07/2020.07.22_North-Answer-Ex-2.pdf.

267 **"I will come":** North, "Statement of LtCol Oliver North to the NRA Board."

267 **crowd sat in stunned silence:** Tim Mak, "As NRA Leadership Fight Spills into Public, N.Y. Attorney General Opens Investigation," NPR, April 17, 2019.

267 **sat silently onstage:** Tim Mak reporting notes, April 27, 2019; Tim Mak (@timkmak), "Oliver North and Wayne LaPierre slated to sit next to each other at the NRA annual meeting," Twitter, April 27, 2019, https://twitter .com/timkmak/status/1122138599133196290.

267 **audit, finance, and executive committees:** Russ McQuaid, "NRA's 'Dirty Laundry' Aired at Indy Convention; Oliver North Ousted," *Fox 59 News*, April 27, 2019.

268 **his cane on the ground:** *Washington Free Beacon*, "Turmoil at the 2019 NRA Annual Meeting: Range Time with Stephen Gutowski," YouTube, April 28, 2019.

268 **details from being revealed:** Stephen Gutowski (@StephenGutowski), "Here's an example of how heated debate [is] inside the NRA members meeting . . . ," Twitter, April 27, 2019, https://twitter.com/StephenGutowski /status/1122281294786904065.

268 **"attack from within":** McQuaid, "NRA's 'Dirty Laundry' Aired at Indy Convention."

268 **document preservation requests:** Tim Mak (@timkmak), "Spokesperson for New York AG Letitia James to me just now . . . ," Twitter, April 27, 2019, https://twitter.com/timkmak/status/1122249185435234305.

269 **"to good governance":** Tim Mak (@timkmak), "Spokesperson for New York AG Letitia James to me just now . . ."

269 **nine-and-a-half-hour board meeting:** Stephen Gutowski, "Marathon NRA Board Meeting Ends with Few Publicly Announced Changes," *Washington Free Beacon*, April 30, 2019.

269 **meeting to the public:** Gutowski, "Marathon NRA Board Meeting Ends with Few Publicly Announced Changes."

269 **eye contact with Wayne:** Josh Powell, *Inside the NRA*, p. 233.

269 **statement of great betrayal:** Powell, *Inside the NRA*, p. 233.

269 **Wayne's financial improprieties:** *Washington Free Beacon*, "Allen West on NRA Leadership Fight: 'We Have to Investigate This,' 'Come Up with Reforms,'" YouTube, April 27, 2019.

269 **reporters that weekend:** Tim Mak, "Wayne LaPierre Re-Elected as NRA Leader Amid Internal Turmoil and Outside Probe," NPR, April 29, 2019.

269 **There was a rumor:** Powell, *Inside the NRA*, p. 233.

270 **was reelected by acclamation:** Stephen Gutowski, "Allen West Says NRA Board Voted for LaPierre, Others in Voice Vote," *Washington Free Beacon*, May 1, 2019.

270 **private, closed-door session:** Gutowski, "Marathon NRA Board Meeting Ends."

270 **"vision for the future":** NRA Staff, "NRA EVP Wayne LaPierre and Other Officers Elected Unanimously," *American Rifleman*, April 29, 2019.

CHAPTER 24: REBELLION

271 **LaPierre, to *The New York Times*:** Danny Hakim, "Inside Wayne LaPierre's Battle for the N.R.A.," *New York Times Magazine*, December 18, 2019.

271 **"by force and violence":** Frank Smyth, *The NRA: The Unauthorized History*, p. 159.

272 **La Cantera Resort in Texas:** "2019 WLP Summit," NRA Women's Leadership Forum, https://www.nrawlf.org/events/2019/2019-summit/.

272 **But he received no response:** Deposition of Robert Pincus, June 28, 2019.

272 **representation of the NRA:** People of the State of New York v. The National Rifle Association, Supreme Court of the State of New York, County of New York, "Summons and Complaint," Index No. 451625/2020, pp. 113–14.

273 **needed his full attention:** Tom Hamburger, "Pete Brownell, Who Heads Major Supplier of Firearms Accessories, Resigns from NRA Board," *Washington Post*, May 30, 2019.

273 **Dan Boren resigned in November:** "Former Oklahoma Congressman Dan Boren Resigns from NRA Board," News 9, November 2, 2019.

273 **twelve board members:** Will Van Sant and Daniel Ness, "The NRA Exodus: Who Left the Organization During a Year of Upheaval," *The Trace*, March 2, 2020.

273 **one nasty Facebook post:** Esther Schneider testimony, United States Bankruptcy Court for the Northern District of Texas Dallas Division, Case 21-30085, April 20, 2021.

274 **personally recruited to the board:** Esther Schneider testimony, United States Bankruptcy Court for the Northern District of Texas Dallas Division, Case 21-30085, April 20, 2021.

274 **"condescending, ugly manner":** Esther Schneider testimony, United States Bankruptcy Court for the Northern District of Texas Dallas Division, Case 21-30085, April 20, 2021.

274 **speak to the New York:** Esther Schneider testimony, United States Bankruptcy Court for the Northern District of Texas Dallas Division, Case 21-30085, April 20, 2021.

275 **$170 million to $113 million:** Will Van Sant, "NRA Membership Revenue Fell 34% in 2019, Tumbling to a 7-Year Low," *The Trace*, August 26, 2020.

275 **salary of $1.9 million:** Will Van Sant, "NRA Tax Documents Reveal the Gun Group Is in the Red—Again," *The Trace*, November 25, 2020.

275 **NRA-issued credit card:** John Frazer, confidential deposition, January 16, 2020.

275 **first of these public letters:** Andy Lander, "Post in Military Arms Channel Facebook Page," Facebook, April 28, 2019.

275 **"within," Hoback wrote:** Dan Zimmerman, "Open Letter to NRA Members from Former Staffer Steve Hoback," Truth About Guns, April 29, 2019.

276 **in June 2019:** Jeff Knox, "Save the Second Amendment—by Reforming the NRA," AmmoLand, June 20, 2019.

276 **focus on gun rights:** "Our Five Goals," Save the Second, https://www .savethe2a.org/our-5-goals/.

276 **led this charge:** Danny Hakim, "N.R.A. Donor Directs a Revolt Against a 'Radioactive' Leader," *New York Times*, June 2, 2019.

276 **legal fees and expenses:** David Dell'Aquila et al. v. Wayne LaPierre et al., United States District Court for the Middle District of Tennessee, "Second Amended Complaint," Case No. 3:19-cv-00679, January 22, 2020.

276 **nonprofit to pay for:** Beth Reinhard, "NRA Boosted Executive Pay While Cutting Funding to Key Programs, Filing Shows," *Washington Post*, November 26, 2019.

278 **Wayne and Powell were told:** Wayne LaPierre, confidential deposition, September 24, 2019.

278 **Wayne recalled later:** Wayne LaPierre, confidential deposition, September 24, 2019.

278 **officials about NRATV:** Wayne LaPierre, confidential deposition, September 24, 2019.

278 **"individual viewers" for NRATV:** Wayne LaPierre, confidential deposition, September 24, 2019.

279 **in January 2019:** Danny Hakim, "N.R.A. Shuts Down Production of NRATV, and Its No. 2 Official Resigns," *New York Times*, June 25, 2019.

279 **"defending the Second Amendment":** Wayne LaPierre, "A Statement by NRA Executive Vice President and CEO Wayne LaPierre," National Rifle Association of America, https://home.nra.org/statements/nra-members/.

279 **an NRA spokesman said:** Betsy Swan, "NRATV Creator Laid Off Dozens After Split from Gun Group: Lawyer," *Daily Beast*, August 28, 2019.

CHAPTER 25: LAWFARE

280 **after this crisis:** Wayne LaPierre, confidential deposition, September 24, 2019.

280 **would think about it:** John Frazer, confidential deposition, January 16, 2020.

280 **basis for this claim:** John Frazer, confidential deposition, January 16, 2020.

280 **"Not trustworthy":** Tim Dickinson, "Read the Texts That Got the NRA's Top Lobbyist Suspended," *Rolling Stone*, July 21, 2019.

281 **"not changing the tides":** Danny Hakim, "How Wayne LaPierre Survived a Revolt at the N.R.A.," *New York Times*, August 22, 2019.

281 **getting Wayne to resign:** Chris Cox, "To the NRA Hearing Board," *LtCol North Submission 116*, Index No. 903843-20, May 28, 2020, https://nrawatch.org/wp-content/uploads/2020/07/2020.07.22_North-Answer-Ex-2.pdf.

281 **later in a private deposition:** Wayne LaPierre, confidential deposition, September 24, 2019.

281 **ultimatum via Oliver North:** John Frazer, confidential deposition, January 16, 2020.

281 **"defending the Second Amendment":** Danny Hakim, "N.R.A. Suspends Second-in-Command, Implicating Him in Coup Attempt," *New York Times*, June 20, 2019.

282 **Wayne refused to take the call:** Josh Powell, *Inside the NRA*, p. 243.

282 **Cox's brother passed away:** Wayne LaPierre, confidential deposition, September 24, 2019.

282 **agreement worth $2.4 million:** Christopher W. Cox Proof of Claim Official Form 410, United States Bankruptcy Court for the Northern District of Texas Dallas Division, Case 21-30085, April 8, 2021.

282 **Wayne conceded in April 2021:** Wayne LaPierre testimony, United States Bankruptcy Court for the Northern District of Texas Dallas Division, Case 21-30085, April 8, 2021.

283 **lawyers who are demanding Cox's payment:** Christopher W. Cox Proof of Claim Official Form 410, United States Bankruptcy Court for the Northern District of Texas Dallas Division, Case 21-30085, April 8, 2021.

283 **Cox's chief of staff, Scott Christman:** Scott Christman, LinkedIn page, https://www.linkedin.com/in/scotttchristman/.

283 **ILA spokeswoman Jennifer Baker:** Alex Isenstadt, "Another Top NRA Staffer Departs amid Upheaval," *Politico*, July 17, 2019.

283 **general counsel David Lehman:** Sara Murray, Michael Warren, and Veronica Stracqualursi, "First on CNN: More NRA Leaders Step Down Amid Spending Controversy," CNN, August 20, 2019.

283 **ultimately pushed out:** Powell, *Inside the NRA*, p. 260.

284 **obtained in expense reimbursements:** Beth Reinhard and Carol D. Leonnig, "NRA Reports Alleged Misspending by Current and Former Executives to IRS," *Washington Post*, November 25, 2020.

284 **paying that amount back:** Reinhard and Leonnig, "NRA Reports Alleged Misspending."

284 **presidential candidate Mike Huckabee:** Powell, *Inside the NRA*, p. 247.

285 **Brewer firm's work:** John Frazer, confidential deposition, January 16, 2020.

285 **him off the board too:** National Rifle Association v. Oliver North, Supreme Court of the State of New York, County of Albany, "Complaint," Index No. 903843-20, July 12, 2020.

285 **his ongoing illness:** National Rifle Association v. Ackerman McQueen, United States District Court for the Northern District of Texas, Dallas Division, "Declaration of Revan McQueen," Civil Action No. 3:19-cv-02074-G, March 30, 2020.

285 **Angus in the hospital:** National Rifle Association v. Ackerman McQueen, United States District Court for the Northern District of Texas, Dallas Division, "Declaration of Revan McQueen," Civil Action No. 3:19-cv-02074-G, March 30, 2020.

285 **board before it was filed:** Wayne LaPierre, confidential deposition, September 24, 2019; deposition of John Frazer, January 16, 2020.

285 **were leaked by Ack-Mac:** John Frazer, confidential deposition, January 16, 2020.

286 **splitting with the organization:** Betsy Swan, "NRATV Creator Laid Off Dozens After Split from Gun Group: Lawyer," *Daily Beast*, August 28, 2019.

286 **grown to about 250 employees:** Danny Hakim, "Angus McQueen, the N.R.A.'s Image Maker, Dies at 74," *New York Times*, July 19, 2019.

286 **NRA's workforce at its largest:** National Rifle Association of America and Sea Girt LLC, United States Bankruptcy Court for the Northern District of Texas Dallas Division, "Debtors' Informational Brief in Connection with Voluntary Chapter 11 Petitions," Case 21-30085, January 20, 2021.

286 **to destroy the family:** National Rifle Association v. Ackerman McQueen, United States District Court for the Northern District of Texas, Dallas Division, "Declaration of Revan McQueen," Civil Action No. 3:19-cv-02074-G, March 30, 2020.

287 **cutting his own pay:** Oliver Laurence North, confidential deposition, December 18, 2019.

287 **New York attorney general's investigation:** Wayne LaPierre, confidential deposition, September 24, 2019.

287 **stopped taking so many notes:** Wayne LaPierre deposition, United States Bankruptcy Court for the Northern District of Texas Dallas Division, Case 21-30085, March 22, 2021.

CHAPTER 26: THE AG STRIKES

288 **the lawsuit states:** People of the State of New York v. The National Rifle Association, Supreme Court of the State of New York, County of New York, "Summons and Complaint," Index No. 451625/2020, p. 1.

289 **with governance requirements:** People of the State of New York v. The National Rifle Association, Supreme Court of the State of New York, County of New York, "Summons and Complaint," Index No. 451625/2020, pp. 65–66.

289 **according to Powell:** Josh Powell, *Inside the NRA*, p. 209.

289 **"down to the studs":** Tim Mak, "Secret Recording Reveals NRA's Legal Troubles Have Cost the Organization $100 Million," NPR, August 21, 2020.

289 **saw substantial pay cuts:** National Rifle Association of America and Sea Girt LLC, United States Bankruptcy Court for the Northern District of Texas Dallas Division, "Debtors' Informational Brief in Connection with Voluntary Chapter 11 Petitions," Case 21-30085, January 20, 2021.

290 **his first presidential run:** Beth Reinhard and Carol D. Leonnig, "NRA Reports Alleged Misspending by Current and Former Executives to IRS," *Washington Post*, November 25, 2020.

CHAPTER 27: BANKRUPTCY

291 **"NRA," Powell wrote:** Josh Powell, *Inside the NRA*, p. 208.

291 **liabilities of $153 million:** National Rifle Association of America and Sea Girt LLC, United States Bankruptcy Court for the Northern District of Texas Dallas Division, "Debtors' Informational Brief in Connection with Voluntary Chapter 11 Petitions," Case 21-30085, January 20, 2021.

291 **without informing his general counsel:** Wayne LaPierre testimony, United States Bankruptcy Court for the Northern District of Texas Dallas Division, Case 21-30085, April 7, 2021.

292 **Wayne never attended:** John Frazer testimony, United States Bankruptcy Court for the Northern District of Texas Dallas Division, Case 21-30085, April 7, 2021.

292 **"management is corrupted":** Owen Mills testimony, United States Bankruptcy Court for the Northern District of Texas Dallas Division, Case 21-30085, April 20, 2021.

292 **resolved to serve:** Phillip Journey testimony, United States Bankruptcy Court for the Northern District of Texas Dallas Division, Case 21-30085, April 13, 2021.

293 **"Wayne's kingdom":** Phillip Journey testimony, United States Bankruptcy Court for the Northern District of Texas Dallas Division, Case 21-30085, April 13, 2021.

293 **"'Wayne said' culture":** Craig Spray testimony, United States Bankruptcy Court for the Northern District of Texas Dallas Division, Case 21-30085, April 13, 2021.

293 **"twist in it":** Craig Spray testimony, United States Bankruptcy Court for the Northern District of Texas Dallas Division, Case 21-30085, April 13, 2021.

293 **"destroyed them":** Carolyn Meadows deposition read into evidence, United States Bankruptcy Court for the Northern District of Texas Dallas Division, Case 21-30085, April 20, 2021.

293 **Gayle lay the blame:** Gayle Stanford testimony, United States Bankruptcy Court for the Northern District of Texas Dallas Division, Case 21-30085, April 8, 2021.

294 **his own cell phone number:** Wayne LaPierre deposition, United States Bankruptcy Court for the Northern District of Texas Dallas Division, Case 21-30085, March 22, 2021.

294 **"I'm doing my best":** Wayne LaPierre testimony, United States Bankruptcy Court for the Northern District of Texas Dallas Division, Case 21-30085, April 8, 2021.

295 **35 to 40 percent:** Bill Winkler testimony, United States Bankruptcy Court for the Northern District of Texas Dallas Division, Case 21-30085, April 16, 2021.

295 **authorized $17.5 million:** Wayne LaPierre testimony, United States Bankruptcy Court for the Northern District of Texas Dallas Division, Case 21-30085, April 7, 2021.

295 **whopping $72 million:** Tim Mak, "Judge Dismisses NRA Bankruptcy Case, Heightening Risk For Dissolution Of Group," NPR, May 11, 2021.

295 **up from 2.9 million in 1993:** Dave Gilson, "The NRA Says It Has 5 Million Members. Its Magazines Tell Another Story," *Mother Jones*, March 7, 2018.

295 **around 4.9 million:** Wayne LaPierre testimony, United States Bankruptcy Court for the Northern District of Texas Dallas Division, Case 21-30085, April 29, 2021.

295 **identify as members in polls:** Robert Draper, "Inside the Power of the N.R.A.," *New York Times*, December 12, 2013.

296 **was just nine:** Sarah Ellison, "The Civil War That Could Doom the N.R.A.," *Vanity Fair,* June 27, 2016.

296 **so on a daily basis:** Frank Smyth, *The NRA: The Unauthorized History*, p. 164.

296 **in the 2020 cycle:** Anna Massoglia and Alyce McFadden, "NRA Bankruptcy Follows Years of Declining Political Spending," Center for Responsive Politics, January 27, 2021.

297 **"I don't see how he gets out":** Phillip Journey deposition, United States Bankruptcy Court for the Northern District of Texas Dallas Division, Case 21-30085, March 23, 2021.

297 **possible tax fraud:** Mark Maremont and Aruna Viswanatha, "IRS Investigating NRA's Wayne LaPierre for Possible Tax Fraud," *Wall Street Journal*, October 5, 2020.

Index

Access Hollywood tapes, 186–187
Ackerman McQueen (Ack-Mac). *See also* McQueen, Angus
after Sandy Hook, 61
auditing of, 228–229
Brewer and, 225, 241, 242, 244–248
closing offices of, 295
corrupt financial practices and, 128–130, 155–156
corrupt financial practices of, 29–30
Cox and, 208–209
lawsuits against, 249–250, 285, 286–287
mansion purchase and, 202–204
The New Yorker article and, 251
North and, 231–233, 235, 241, 242–243
NRA-ILA and, 34–35
NRA's hiring of, 45–46
NRA's relationship with, 40–41
NRATV and, 278
Obama daughters and ad from, 69
Phillips and, 106, 219
power of, 30, 149–161
pushback from, 227–228
S. LaPierre and, 20, 22, 126–127
split from, 285–286
Stanford and, 109
W. LaPierre and, 3, 48–49, 249
wealth displays of, 41–42
whistleblower complaints and, 218
work environment of, 152–154
Allen, Megan, 130–131
American Conservative Union (ACU), 102, 116–117
Anderson, Robert, Jr., 140
Aquilino, John, 12, 13, 14, 17
Arnett, Ray, 45–46
Arulanandam, Andrew, 198
assault weapons ban, 52, 69–70
Attlee, Tracey, 46

Baker, James, 51, 53, 69, 76
Baker, Jennifer, 198, 283
Barnes, Fred, 187
Begich, Mark, 89
Belke, Abra, 54–57, 58–61, 65–66, 68–69, 76, 78–79
Bickel, John, 221
Biden, Joe, 69
Bloomberg, Michael, 74, 77, 84–87, 90, 91
Bobbit, John Wayne, 121–122

Bolton, John, 121
Bongino, Dan, 205
Boren, Dan, 255–257, 258, 273, 280
Brewer, Bill
  Ackerman McQueen and, 227–229,
    244–248, 249–250, 252
  background of, 221–223
  bankruptcy filing and, 295
  compliance attempts and, 208, 228
  Cox and, 210
  culling of NRA board by, 262
  hiring of, 193–194, 223–224
  influence/power of, 226–227, 254,
    284–285
  lack of gun experience of, 220
  McQueen and, 224–225, 286–287
  North and, 238–244, 263
  NY AG investigation and, 269
  prioritized payments to, 204, 226
  whistleblower complaints and, 219
Brown, Dudley, 76
Brownell, Pete
  Butina and, 169–170, 174, 177
  Congressional investigations
    and, 213
  investigation of NRA and, 194
  LaPierre's "post-employment
    contract" and, 206
  NRA delegation to Moscow and,
    163, 164–165, 167, 168
  resignation of, 113, 214, 230, 273
"burn books," 226
Bush, George H. W., 51, 52, 150
Bush, George W., 52
Butina, Maria
  arrest and detention of, 31, 195
  background of, 118–119
  birthday party for, 190
  Byrne and, 147–148
  DNC emails and, 178–179
  downfall of, 190–199
  entering United States, 122
  Erickson and, 121–122
  first tips about, 112–113
  Kislyak and, 144

  in Moscow, 119–121, 162, 163–173
  at NRA annual convention, 174–175
  redacted intelligence report
    involving, 146
  reporting on, 192
  "The Second Pozner" and, 138–142
  sentencing of, 196–197
  testimony from, 193
  Torshin and, 114
  Trump and, 146–147
  unraveling of operation of, 137
Butz, Dave, 37
Byrne, Patrick, 147–148

Carr, Diana, 116–117
Carter, Harlon, 45
Cassidy, J. Warren, 43, 46
Childress, Richard, 244, 254–255, 256,
  263, 266
Christman, Scott, 198, 283
Clancy, Tom, 49
Clark, Laurel, 21
Clarke, David, 164, 168
Clay, Rick, 176
Clinton, Bill, 85
Clinton, Hillary, 4, 180, 181, 183,
  186, 187
Coburn, Tom, 70–71
Columbine High School shooting, 50,
  61–62
Conservative Political Action
  Conference (CPAC), 228, 247
Cooper, Chuck, 9, 262
Cors, Allan, 118, 143, 164
Cotton, Charles, 217, 249, 255
Cotton, Tom, 78
Cox, Chris
  accusations against, 281–282, 284
  Ackerman McQueen and, 34
  after Sandy Hook, 61, 64–65
  Butina and, 177–178
  Democratic background of, 50
  firing of, 262
  investigation of NRA and, 194

Landini Brothers and, 29
LaPierre and, 14, 258–259
Manchin-Toomey bill and, 72, 74, 78
NRA annual meeting and, 267
NRA-ILA and, 32–33
ouster of, 269, 280–283
potential departure of, 208–210
presidential election of 2016 and,
    180–181, 183, 185, 187
succession plans and, 210–211
Trump, Jr., and, 176–178, 182
Trump and, 265
Cummins, Emily, 217–218, 219, 226

Davis, Aaron, 94
Davis, Wit, 284–285
Dearborn, Rick, 175–176
Dell'Aquila, David, 276
Demers, John, 140
Democratic National Committee
    emails, 178–179
Dillon, Susan, 248
Driscoll, Robert, 196

Emanuel, Rahm, 52
Erickson, Paul
    background of, 121–122
    Brownell and, 165, 194
    Butina and, 122, 138, 140, 141, 173,
        190, 196
    Byrne and, 147–148
    charges against, 197
    DNC emails and, 178–179
    first tips about, 112
    in Moscow, 120, 139
    NRA delegation to Moscow and, 163
    O'Neill and, 172
    pardoning of, 197
    in prison, 113
    reporting on, 192
    self-reflection by, 199
    Trump campaign and, 175–176
Everytown for Gun Safety, 90–91, 200

FBI investigations, 143, 144, 148,
    192–193, 194–195, 197
Federal Assault Weapons Ban, 85
Feinblatt, John, 74, 84–87, 89–90
Feldman, Richard, 24, 46, 91
Flynn, Michael, 143, 162
Foss, Joe, 234
Frazer, John
    Ackerman McQueen lawsuit and,
        250, 285
    background of, 215–216
    bankruptcy filing and, 292
    Brewer and, 224, 227, 239
    Cox and, 281
    on Hallow, 100
    Hart dismissal and, 253
    lack of vetting of, 216
    LaPierre/North conflict and,
        240–241, 249
    NRA annual meeting and, 267
    NY AG lawsuit against, 288–289
Fritz, Mike, 21

Goldschlager, Arnold, 164, 168
Goldschlager, Hilary, 164
Gore, Al, 85
Gottlieb, Alan, 74, 77
Gray, Cameron, 205
Gregory, David, 87
Gregory, Joseph, 164, 166, 167, 171–172
Grinnell College, 212, 213
Gun Control Act (1968), 44
gun legislation/regulation. *See also*
    Manchin-Toomey bill
    failure of, 4
    NRA's early support for, 44
    opposition to, 3, 45

Hallow, Millie
    background of, 99–101
    Boren's call to, 255–256
    Brewer and, 226
    Brownell's trip to Moscow and, 165

Hallow, Millie (*cont.*)
  Butina and, 138, 169–170
  Cox and, 280
  Erickson and, 121
  LaPierre and, 9, 48, 259–260
  McQueen's death and, 286
  North and, 230, 232, 233, 263
  NRA role of, 101–104
  Russia and, 177
Hallow, Ralph, 99
Hammer, Marion, 37–38, 159, 268
Hart, Bobby, 176
Hart, Steve, 223, 230, 244, 249,
    252–254, 262, 284–285
Heller decision, 183
Heston, Charleton, 28, 48, 107
Hoback, Steve, 93–94, 275–276
Holder, Eric, 52
Huckabee, Mike, 284
Hughes, Mary, 105
Hutchinson, Asa, 63

"I Am the NRA" ad campaign, 45
Internet Research Agency,
    144–145, 146
Iran-Contra Affair, 234

James, Letitia, 4, 207–208, 268–269,
    273, 288–290, 291
Journey, Phillip, 292–293, 297

Kalashnikov, Mikhail, 115
Keene, David
  background of, 115–117
  Butina and, 120–121, 122, 138, 142,
    146, 177
  Kislyak and, 143
  in Moscow, 120, 139, 162–163, 164,
    166, 168
  NRA-ILA and, 198
  reporting on, 192
  Sandy Hook and, 61
Keene, David M. (son), 116

Keene, Donna, 138, 143, 146, 162–163,
    169, 177, 192
Kislyak, Sergey, 142–144
Knight, Timothy, 272–273
Knox, Jeff, 276
Knox, Neal, 16, 35, 47–48, 50, 264

Lammert, Elaine, 198
Lander, Andy, 275–276
Landini Brothers, 27–30
Landrieu, Mary, 69
LaPierre, Susan
  Allen and, 131
  background of, 21–22
  Belke and, 55–56
  burn book on, 226
  Butina and, 178
  corrupt financial practices of, 4, 20,
    22–23, 29, 125–129
  faked 911 call and, 67–68
  hunting by, 18–19
  importance of social standing to,
    8–9, 24
  influence of, 17, 24–25
  loyalty concerns of, 271–272
  mansion purchase and, 202–204
  at Memberdrive, 105
  North and, 230
  personality of, 18, 22
  Schneider and, 273–274
  staff treatment and, 23–24
  Wayne and, 7–9, 19–20
  Women's Leadership Forum and,
    123, 124–126
LaPierre, Wayne
  Ackerman McQueen and, 3, 48–49,
    247, 249, 252
  after Columbine, 61–62
  Allen and, 130–131
  anxiety of, 9, 17, 49–50, 63, 151, 204,
    247, 284, 294, 296
  attempt to oust, 267–268
  attempts of to depart, 284
  background of, 10–12
  bankruptcy filing and, 291–294

Belke on, 79
on Board of Directors, 36
Brewer and, 223–224, 228, 229,
 240–244, 248
Brownell and, 214
calls for accountability and, 267
claims of ignorance from, 1–2,
 129–130, 248, 249, 255
class action lawsuit against, 276
corrupt financial practices of, 2–3,
 25–26, 29, 128–133, 136,
 155–156, 216
Cox and, 280–283
culling of NRA board by, 262
current status of, 297
Democratic background of, 12, 50
diminished standing of, 277
doctor visits of, 156–157
drop in revenue and, 188–189
early NRA work of, 12
as EVP, 46–47
faked 911 call and, 67–68
fear/paranoia of, 50, 136, 202
financial crisis and, 274–275
Hallow and, 99–100, 102–104
Hammer and, 37–38
Hart dismissal and, 253–254
hiding behavior of, 50
indifference of to guns, 15–16
lobbying and, 12–13, 154
Makris and, 28
management style of, 96–97
Manchin-Toomey bill and,
 80–81
mansion purchase and, 202–204
mass shootings and, 50, 61–63,
 64–66, 68, 201
McConnell and, 51–52
McQueen and, 38–39, 41, 154,
 244–245, 286
medical deferment for, 10
nominations and, 254–255
North and, 5, 230–233, 235,
 236–237, 238, 239, 263–265
note-taking habit of, 14–15, 287
NRA deficit and, 47

NRA delegation to Moscow and,
 170–171
NRA departures and, 97–99
NRATV and, 159–160, 278–279
NY AG lawsuit against, 288–290
Old Town and, 30–31
personal gain and, 4
personality of, 8, 10–11, 13–14, 24,
 49–50, 149
"post-employment contract" for,
 206–207
public allegations against, 256
reelection of, 269–270
salary increase for, 25, 206
Sterner and, 131–132
succession plans and, 210
Susan and, 7–10, 19–20
tax fraud investigation of, 297
threats of public allegations against,
 256–258
travel arrangements for, 107–110
Trump/Trump administration and,
 18, 265
on universal background checks, 73
at WLF event, 274
Lavrov, Sergei, 167
Lehman, David, 283, 284
Lesko, Debbie, 272
Lewandowski, Corey, 182
Liberatore, Jim, 164, 166, 168
Loesch, Dana, 159, 279

MacNair, 108
Maisch, Patricia, 89
Makris, Tony, 9, 27–29, 30–31, 48,
 96–97, 156–157, 189, 246,
 247–248
Maloney, Sean, 272–273
Manafort, Paul, 115, 122
Manchin, Joe, 70–71, 73, 76, 78
Manchin-Toomey bill, 3, 5, 89–90
March for Our Lives, 200
Marjory Stoneman Douglas High
 School shooting, 200–201, 209
Marshall, Hal, 223

Mayors Against Illegal Guns, 74, 86,
    89, 90
McCain, John, 52, 184, 185
McCain-Feingold campaign finance
    reforms, 51, 158, 184
McConnell, Mitch, 51–52
McKenzie, David, 132–133, 245
McMains, Kristi, 187
McQueen, Angus
    background of, 151–152
    Brewer and, 224–225, 244–245,
        246, 285
    death of, 286
    declining health of, 227, 228
    influence of, 150, 154
    LaPierre and, 9, 38–39, 41, 203,
        256, 257
    lifestyle of, 42, 160
    NRATV and, 160
    personality of, 38, 40, 150–151
    Phillips's departure and, 219
    zero-sum mentality and, 31
McQueen, Marvin, 152
McQueen, Revan, 225, 228–229,
    286, 287
Meadows, Carolyn, 274, 293
Memberdrive, 105
Menino, Tom, 86
Mercury Group, 30, 48, 61, 156, 242
Metaksa, Tanya, 98–99
Milius, John, 48
Miller, Stephen, 49
Mills, Owen, 292
Moms Demand Action for Gun Sense
    in America, 83–84, 88–90
Mueller, Robert, 143
Muñoz, Cecilia, 87

National Association for Gun Rights
    (NAGR), 75–76
National Rifle Association (NRA).
    See also LaPierre, Wayne
    Ackerman McQueen and, 38–42,
        149–161
    annual meetings of, 45, 265–268

audit committee of, 35–36, 216–217,
    218–219, 235, 249
bankruptcy filing of, 290
Bloomberg on, 87
Board of Directors of, 35–38,
    272–273
Butina and, 137, 141–142, 172, 198
class action lawsuit against, 276
committees of, 35–36
compliance attempts by, 208
cost-cutting measures and, 204–205
decline in revenue for, 188, 204
decline of, 3–4
deficit of, 47
Democrats and, 50–51, 52–53
founding of, 43–44
fundraising and, 133–135
General Operations of, 31–35
headquarters of, 27
InfoCision and, 133–135
Institute for Legislative Action
    (NRA-ILA), 31–35, 54–56, 76–77,
    182–183, 186, 198
internal conflict and, 33–34
investigations into, 91–92,
    193–199, 213
Landini Brothers and, 27–30
layoffs at, 289
legislative strategy of, 90–91
Manchin-Toomey bill and, 72–73,
    74–76
members of, 5
Mercury Group and, 40–42
Moscow delegation from, 162–173
nominating committee, 36, 254–255
NY AG and, 268–269, 288–290
Parkland, Florida, shooting and,
    200–201
presidential election of 2016 and,
    180–189
pushback from members of,
    275–276, 278
religious imagery for, 43
reporting on corruption of, 277
revenue decreases and, 275, 289–290
Russia and, 111–122, 137–148

Russian troll farm and, 144–145
before Sandy Hook, 43–53
Sandy Hook and, 3, 58–60, 66,
   68–69
success and endurance of, 295–297
two tiers within, 93–95
women working at, 95–96
zero-sum mentality of, 31
Nice, Janet, 273–274
Nikolaev, Konstantin, 119–120, 167
Noem, Kristi, 272
North, Betsy, 231, 243, 259
North, Oliver
   Ackerman McQueen lawsuit and,
      249–250, 252
   background of, 233–235
   Brewer and, 194, 220, 238–243, 246
   Brownell and, 214
   Butina investigation and, 198
   Cox and, 210–211, 280–281
   Hart dismissal and, 253
   LaPierre's corruption and, 257–258,
      259–261
   at LaPierre's wedding, 9
   legal action against, 285
   NRA deal with, 230–233
   as NRA president, 5–6, 235–240
   ouster of, 254–255, 263–264,
      266–267
   reelection of, 248–249
   special committee formed by,
      262–263
NRA Foundation, 127
NRATV (NRA News), 40, 157–160, 188,
   204–205, 231, 233, 278–279, 285
Nugent, Ted, 36–37, 272

Obama, Barack/Obama administra-
   tion, 4, 52, 62, 69, 87, 122, 128,
   134–135, 136
Office of Advancement, 20
Officers Compensation Committee
   (OCC), 36, 202, 205–206
O'Leary, Brad, 24, 149–150
O'Neill, George, 172–173

O'Neill, Tip, 12
CXIIIREX (One-Thirteen Rex),
   28–29
open carry, laws banning, 44
Out of Pocket project, 155–156,
   229, 248
Owens, Marcus, 91–92, 289

Palin, Sarah, 115
Parkland, Florida, shooting,
   200–201, 209
Paul, Rand, 147
Payne, Tammy, 158
Pence, Mike, 251, 282
Perrine, Nick, 141
Perry, Rick, 183
Phillips, Woody, 9, 29, 104–107, 172,
   202, 219, 228, 284, 288–289
Pincus, Rob, 159
Pisarsky, Igor, 167
PM Consulting, 47, 51, 149–150
Porter, Jim, 80–81
Powell, Josh
   Ackerman McQueen and, 252
   after Sandy Hook, 68
   on Board of Directors, 36
   Brewer and, 224, 246
   Butina and, 178
   corrupt financial practices of,
      106, 128
   cost-cutting measures and, 204
   Landini Brothers and, 28–29
   LaPierre and, 97, 202, 260
   McQueen and, 39, 42, 286
   NRA-ILA and, 33
   on NRA's attempted move to
      Texas, 291
   NRATV and, 160, 278
   NY AG lawsuit against, 288–289
   ouster of, 283–284
   on Phillips, 105–106
   zero-sum mentality and, 31
Pozner, Vladimir, 138
Preston, Kline, 115
Pryor, Mark, 78, 89

public education division, firing of,
45–46
Putin, Vladimir, 114, 119, 138, 147,
162, 166–167, 175–176

Quayle, Dan, 13

Ramos, Rigoberto, 27
Rascal Flatts, 126
Reagan, Ronald, 44
red flag laws, 209
Redmond, Helen, 212–214
Regnery, 49
Reid, Harry, 52
Republican Party. *See also individual
Republicans*
Butina and, 138–140, 142, 147,
173, 175
NRA support for, 183–184
Putin and, 176
Richards, Nancy, 106
Right to Bear Arms, 119, 162
Rockefeller family, 172–173
Rogozin, Dmitry, 120, 167–168
Romney, Mitt, 184, 185
Ross, Vanessa, 94, 96
Ross, Wayne Anthony, 11
Royce, Ed, 122
Rubio, Marco, 69, 183
Russia, infiltration of NRA by,
111–122, 137–148. *See also* Butina,
Maria

Sandy Hook Elementary School
shooting, 3, 34, 57–66, 82–84, 213
Save the Second, 276
Scalia, Antonin, 181, 183
Schertler, David, 3
Schertler & Onorato, 2
Schneider, Esther, 272–274
Schneiderman, Eric, 92
Schropp, Tyler, 29
Schumer, Chuck, 75

Scott, Rick, 201
Second Amendment enhancements, 74
Second Amendment Foundation,
74, 77
"Second Pozner, The," 138–139
Selleck, Tom, 36–37
Sessions, Jeff, 143
Shchyogolev, Igor, 167
Sheets, Wayne, 98
Shirley, Craig, 100, 116, 122
Simes, Dimitri, 141
Sochivko, Elena, 119
social media, Russian manipulation of,
144–145
Spray, Craig, 293
Stanford, Gayle, 107–110, 241, 253, 293
Stanford, Peter, 108
Sterner, Colleen, 131–132, 133
Stone, Roger, 115, 122
SVR (Russian intelligence agency), 141

Tabard Inn, 111
Taganskaya crime syndicate, 114, 197
Tait, Frank, 267
Tanner, John, 33
Taylor family, 134
Toomey, Pat, 71, 73, 76, 77, 78
Torshin, Alexander
background of, 114–115
Butina and, 112–113, 118, 119–120,
138–139, 140, 141–142, 147,
171–173, 190, 192
Internet Research Agency and, 145
Keene and, 117
at NRA annual convention, 174–175
NRA delegation to Moscow and,
163, 166, 167, 168
reporting on, 192
sanctioning of, 197
Trump campaign and, 176, 179
troll farm, Russian, 144–145
Trump, Donald, Jr., 176–178, 182
Trump, Donald/Trump administration
Butina and, 146–147, 175–176,
178–179, 191

Cox and, 282
election of, 3–4, 18, 181–189
Erickson and, 197
Kislyak and, 143
NRA annual meeting and, 251,
    265–266
NRA support for, 185, 290
Trump Foundation, 182
"26 Days of Action Against Gun
    Violence," 213

United Russia party, 114
universal background checks, 70.
    See also Manchin-Toomey bill

Volkov, Michael, 262

waiting periods, 44
Walker, Scott, 142, 183
Wall Street Journal, The, 252
Walters, Carin, 102
Walters, Ian, 102

Wardlaw, Brady, 22
Watts, Shannon, 82–84, 88–90, 91
Wayne LaPierre Show, The, 48, 99–100
WBB Investments, 202–203
Weaver, Kyle, 97, 98
West, Allen, 269
whistleblower complaints,
    217–219, 251
Winkler, Bill, 202, 203, 246
women
    at Ackerman McQueen, 153–154
    at National Rifle Association
        (NRA), 95–96
Women's Leadership Forum (WLF),
    20, 22–24, 123–126, 128, 131,
    271–272, 273–274
Wyatt Company, 104–105
Wyden, Ron, 170, 193

Youth for Tomorrow, 127

Zaytsev, Igor, 119
Zegna, 2–3, 129–130

About the Author

Tim Mak is the Washington Investigative Correspondent for NPR, where he can often be heard on *Morning Edition* and *All Things Considered*. Over more than twelve years in journalism, he has focused on national security, political campaigns, and nonprofit accountability. He has previously worked at *The Daily Beast* and *Politico*. He is also a nationally certified emergency medical technican who enjoys surfing, hill sprints, and playing the guitar.